Hard Questions

Hard Questions

Learning to Teach Controversial Issues

Judith L. Pace

ROWMAN & LITTLEFIELD
Lanham • Boulder • New York • London

Published by Rowman & Littlefield
An imprint of The Rowman & Littlefield Publishing Group, Inc.
4501 Forbes Boulevard, Suite 200, Lanham, Maryland 20706
www.rowman.com

6 Tinworth Street, London SE11 5AL, United Kingdom

British Library Cataloguing in Publication Information Available

Library of Congress Cataloging-in-Publication Data

Names: Pace, Judith L., author.
Title: Hard questions : learning to teach controversial issues / Judith L. Pace.
Description: Lanham, Maryland : Rowman & Littlefield, 2021. | Includes
    bibliographical references and index.
Identifiers: LCCN 2020044153 (print) | LCCN 2020044154 (ebook) | ISBN
    9781475851960 (cloth) | ISBN 9781475851977 (paperback) | ISBN
    9781475851984 (epub)
Subjects: LCSH: Social science teachers—Training of. | Social sciences—Study and
    teaching.
Classification: LCC H62 .P2185 2021 (print) | LCC H62 (ebook) | DDC 300.71—dc23
LC record available at https://lccn.loc.gov/2020044153
LC ebook record available at https://lccn.loc.gov/2020044154

♾️™ The paper used in this publication meets the minimum requirements of American National Standard for Information Sciences—Permanence of Paper for Printed Library Materials, ANSI/NISO Z39.48-1992.

This book is dedicated to my parents, Evelyn and Oscar Pace, and to my life partner, Sam Zuckerman.

Contents

Preface   ix

Acknowledgments   xiii

Introduction: Preparing Preservice Teachers for Controversial Issues   xv

1   Mark Drummond: Controversial Issues as a Path toward
Reconciliation in Northern Ireland   1

2   What Mark's Students Learned   19

3   Paula Barstow: A Pragmatic and Safe Approach to Controversy
in Northern Ireland   41

4   What Paula's Students Learned   61

5   Ian Shepherd: Teaching Sensitive and Controversial Issues
through Historical Inquiry in England   79

6   What Ian's Students Learned   97

7   Liz Simmons: Teaching Controversial Issues through
Democratic Discussion in the U.S. Midwest   119

8   What Liz's Students Learned   139

Conclusions, Hard Questions, and Recommendations   157

References   181

Index   189

About the Author   195

Preface

The world is in turmoil. Communities, nations, and regions around the globe are rocked by conflict—clashes steeped in historical hatreds, social and economic inequality, and political power struggles, forcing us to question how to sustain life on this vulnerable planet. These political, socioeconomic, and racial/ethnic antagonisms often turn public discourse into perilous disagreements, liable to explode into recriminations and name-calling, and generating more heat than light. How are teachers to deal with these controversies in the classroom? Is it possible to do so in ways that promote inquiry, thoughtful analysis, and dialogue, and ultimately strengthen democracy, human rights, and peace?

This book is predicated on the idea that taking up controversial issues in schools is hard, but also a golden opportunity to cultivate ideals and practices that open minds, teach civil discourse, and encourage engagement with the wider world. Moreover, a thoughtful and positive approach to controversy—one rooted in critical thinking and respect for others—is desperately needed in schools around the world. As this book shows, in a United States riven by a president who has stoked violence, in an England convulsed by Brexit, and in a Northern Ireland where centuries of conflict have yielded to a fragile truce amid persistent divisions, examining issues of politics, history, and human and civil rights with students is urgent and difficult.

How can we prepare teachers to undertake this essential, but difficult, work? How can we educate them to dodge the multiple pitfalls and teach controversial issues successfully? In an era when teacher education programs around the world are subjected to political and economic forces that increase accountability, bureaucracy, and competition, how can we ensure that new teachers are ready to work for democracy?

The search for answers to these questions raises questions of its own. Under what conditions do new teachers take up the teaching of controversial issues? Which factors support their efforts and which hold them back?

This book, based on a cross-national research project, answers these questions by looking at what actually occurs in teacher education courses and secondary school classrooms when controversies are considered. We see a fundamental tension throughout: How do the ideals of the university square with the realities of schools? What actually happens when teacher candidates and new teachers try to apply in real-world classrooms what they've learned about teaching controversial issues? Such an examination offers crucial lessons for teaching at all levels of schooling.

The book shows how university-based teacher education courses provided conceptual and practical tools along with encouragement for teaching controversial issues. We meet four teacher educators—two in Northern Ireland, one in England, and one in the United States—and sit in as they prepare their preservice teachers to teach controversial issues in history, citizenship, and social studies. We listen to preservice and first-year teachers who studied with these teacher educators attempt to put into practice what they have been taught.

In the face of many other demands, the teacher educators I studied devoted time in their courses not only to prepare preservice teachers for teaching controversy, but also to keep the risks involved in this practice contained. And despite myriad obstacles, most of the preservice and novice teachers I interviewed courageously experimented in exploring controversies with their students. Their practice exhibited thoughtful and creative teaching, and, at the same time, threw into relief the tensions inherent in this process.

There is now a robust international literature on teaching controversial issues, its benefits for students and society, contextual factors that shape it, and its challenges for teachers (see Ho et al., 2017). But there is very little written about how teacher educators prepare preservice teachers for this work, and even less about how preservice teachers learn to enact it.

This book is the first to examine teacher educators' efforts to prepare their graduate students for teaching controversial issues *and* the graduate students' responses to these efforts. The knowledge it provides addresses a major gap in both social studies education and teacher education research. Additionally, the international sample and settings offer important comparisons and yield rich data. My goal is to inspire teachers and teacher educators to pursue teaching controversial issues in principled and feasible ways, and to encourage more scholarship on this vital endeavor. Hopefully, this work will push school leaders and policymakers to create better conditions in schools for undertaking this work.

The cases in this book tell a multifaceted story. We begin with the experiences, principles, and contextual influences that animate teacher educators' commitments and practice. We follow them into their class sessions with preservice teachers and look at some interesting and richly described lessons. We see from the preservice teachers' perspectives the impact the teacher educators had on conceptual learning and initial teaching practice. From there, we explore the challenges new teachers confronted as they navigated between educational ideals and the realities of classrooms, schools, universities, and societies. In the process, we identify the conditions under which teaching controversy either diminished or flourished.

This book is written for a wide audience that includes classroom teachers at all levels, school leaders, teacher educators, students of education, policymakers, and scholars interested in the teaching of controversy. Readers will see how teachers are prepared to take up this ambitious and risky practice in divided societies, how novices experiment with it, and how these experiments are supported or undermined by school leadership and policy.

Carole Hahn (2006) explained that cross-national research opens up new possibilities for practice and policy. It builds bridges between cultures and furthers international understanding. Investigating the teaching of controversial issues internationally sheds light on cultural norms and sociopolitical conflicts.

This book fosters transatlantic comparisons and provides a detailed vision of varied approaches that shed light on the familiar and allow us to imagine new possibilities. For example, given Northern Ireland educators' experience with teaching controversy in a sharply divided society, we in the United States now facing unprecedented polarization can learn vital lessons from them about how to contain the risks to students and teachers. Likewise, U.S. teachers who have given great attention to cultivating civic discourse in the classroom have much to teach their counterparts in the U.K.

The world is in a precarious political, environmental, and moral space. The coronavirus pandemic, U.S. Presidential election, and the uproar over police violence against Black people have only intensified the need for meaningful educational responses to controversial issues. I hope this book provides powerful tools for preparing knowledgeable, thoughtful, skilled teachers committed to engaging with their students in the hard questions we confront as communities, nations, and a species.

Acknowledgments

I want to thank the many people who supported this project. First and foremost, I am deeply grateful to the four teacher educators whose courses I studied for welcoming me into their worlds and being such wonderful hosts. They, and the preservice teachers who participated in the study, were amazingly generous and taught me so much. My thanks also go to faculty, administrators, and staff at the four research sites who provided logistical support, contextual knowledge, and hospitality.

Numerous colleagues were helpful at various stages of the project. I especially thank Diana Hess, Keith Barton, Joe Kahne, Carole Hahn, Walter Parker, and Johan Wasserman for their support during the research design process and recruitment of participants. I also thank Wayne Journell, Jeremy Stoddard, Jane Bolgatz, and LaGarrett King who participated in pilot interviews.

Educators in Northern Ireland, Ireland, and England informed my understanding of teaching controversial issues in different contexts. I thank Sean Pettis, Tom Shaw, Fionnuala Waldron, Brian Ruane, Anne Marie Kavanagh, Ben Mallon, Hugh Starkey, Robin Whitburn, Abdul Mohamed, Terry Haydn, Lee Jerome, and Jeremy Hayward for our conversations, helpful resources, and/or visits to their classes. I'm grateful to Margaret Crocco and her colleagues for a visit at Michigan State University at an early stage in the project.

Sincere thanks go to Lisa Sibbett, Dave Donahue, and Jeremy Glazer for reading parts of the book and making smart suggestions. Lisa generously gave me extensive feedback. Wayne Journell, editor of *Theory & Research in Social Education*, and four anonymous reviewers of my 2019 article "Contained Risk-taking: Preparing Preservice Teachers to Teach Controversial Issues in Three Countries," offered insightful suggestions that pushed my thinking in important directions. Thanks also go to Raphael

Heller, who edited and published my December 2017 article in *Phi Delta Kappan*, "Preparing Preservice Teachers in a Divided Society: Lessons from Northern Ireland."

Wendy Ledger's transcription services were high quality and reliable, notwithstanding the challenge of voices with a variety of accents! Four graduate students at the University of San Francisco provided vital assistance at various stages of the project. I thank Grace Wakefield, David Bromfeld, Joani Gillam, and Ann Marie MacVey for their help with data analysis and bibliographic references. Colleagues at the University of San Francisco who supported me in various ways include Shabnam Koirala-Azad, Ramona Valencia, Kim Nguy, Chris Witte, Helen Maniates, Sarah Capitelli, Candice Harrison, Monisha Bajaj, and Willie Melaugh.

As always, my work was supported by the love of family and friends. My siblings, Lynne and Dave, and nieces and nephews were sources of strength, comfort, and joy. In particular I want to thank my sister and brother-in-law, Lynne and Scott Currier, for carrying tremendous responsibility for our family. Our mother, Evelyn Pace, who died in May 2019, was my ardent cheerleader. Our father, Oscar Pace, continues to amaze me with his indomitable spirit. I thank my friends, and especially Rosemary Brosnan, for being there through sad and happy times; listening to my stories and asking great questions; recommending books, articles, and films; and inspiring me with their strength, wide-ranging interests, and political activism.

Sam Zuckerman deserves massive credit for his boundless love and support throughout the process. He is the most enthusiastic travel partner, astute thought partner, and terrific editor I could ask for. His devotion, wisdom, humor, and delicious meals pulled me through. I am incredibly fortunate to share my life with him and I thank him with all my heart.

I am grateful to the Spencer Foundation and its helpful staff. The Spencer Foundation's funding allowed me to conduct the cross-national research project that generated this book. And finally, I thank Tom Koerner and Carlie Wall at Rowman & Littlefield, for their interest in this book and for shepherding me through the publishing process.

Introduction

Preparing Preservice Teachers for Controversial Issues

In many parts of the world, as social and political conflict intensifies and democracies are threatened, educators are raising their voices about the need to teach controversial issues in the classroom. Critical and open dialogue on issues related to violence against marginalized groups, policies to advance human rights, and histories that continue to divide society is considered an essential vehicle to promote the toleration, recognition of differences, and civic equality that underpin democracy (Gutmann, 2004). Recent events surrounding the U.S. election, coronavirus pandemic, and police violence against Black Americans underscore the crucial importance of this endeavor.

Teaching controversial issues is a key to answering what Walter Parker (2003) poses as "the central citizenship question of our time": *"How can we live together justly, in ways that are mutually satisfying, and which leaves our differences, both individual and group, intact, and our multiple identities recognized?"* (p. 20). It contributes to the cultivation of independent thinkers who support democratic values and ask hard questions to make responsible and well-informed decisions (Engle & Ochoa, 1988).

But what do we know about how the teachers of the future are being prepared to take up this demanding pedagogical practice? What is taking place in university teacher education programs to ensure that new teachers have the tools to handle explosive issues concerning racism, sectarianism, and immigration? A huge void exists in the educational research literature about what is happening in teacher education classes and in the classrooms where newly minted teachers work to put what they have learned about teaching controversy into practice (Hess, 2008).

This book attempts to fill part of that gap through a detailed examination of four teacher educators in three countries as they show their graduate students deeply thought-out ways of teaching controversy. And it follows a number of those students as they take what they have learned to their first teaching experiences. In that way, *Hard Questions: Learning to Teach Controversial Issues* breaks new ground by exploring areas of teacher education that have rarely been examined before.

We do know that some teacher educators are preparing their students to teach controversy. But we understand very little about what they do and why they do it. In particular, we know next to nothing about the connection between that preparation and new teachers' learning to teach controversial issues in their own practice. Additionally, educators know very little about what their counterparts in other parts of the world are up to. These gaps in understanding keep us stuck in the status quo, isolated from different ways of thinking and teaching that can broaden our vision, practice, and policies.

This book is based on observations of university teacher education courses in three countries—Northern Ireland, England, and the United States—and interviews with both teacher educators and their graduate students from these institutions. It follows preservice teachers into their school placements and, in a few cases, first-year positions, to find out how they approached controversial issues in real classrooms and what they learned from adopting tools, taken from the university, in their practice.

On the conceptual side, *Hard Questions* seeks to understand how the teaching of controversial issues is interpreted in different national and educational contexts and by practitioners with varied expertise. It shows how teaching controversy is sometimes bolstered and sometimes undermined by individual, institutional, and societal factors. Such an examination can help improve practice of both university and classroom teachers. In particular, this deep dive into learning how to teach controversy offers insights into how we can face the challenges of teaching in divided societies and what we can do to create the school conditions that support this vital work.

My development of a grounded theory is especially important for helping educators handle the risk-taking that is part and parcel of teaching controversy in polarized contexts.

This book shows that teacher educators taught their graduate students, and enacted in their own courses, a set of strategies I call *contained risk-taking* to make teaching controversial issues safer (Pace, 2019). Their graduate students also practiced contained risk-taking as they experimented with teaching issues in student teaching placements and first-year teaching positions. Risk-taking was not only contained by teachers but also *constrained* by contextual factors, such as insufficient timetabling for classes. On the other hand, it was *supported*, at least in some cases, by other factors, such as supportive mentor teachers. The book demonstrates how risk-taking can be contained, constrained, and supported in a wide variety of classroom and school settings.

This book is not an evaluation of teaching. It does not analyze the practices it describes using intricate theoretical frameworks, and it does not determine causal relationships between what teacher educators taught and what their graduate students learned. It documents people's intentions, their actions, and how these intentions and actions were mediated by cultural, sociopolitical, and institutional forces. It uses descriptive narration to highlight the voices of research participants and tell their stories with nuance, complexity, and empathy. The book explores the efforts of educators undertaking difficult and noble work.

This introductory chapter provides conceptual and contextual grounding for the book. It presents international scholarship on what teaching controversial issues entails, what it demands of teachers, and what factors influence how it is enacted, particularly in sociopolitically divided societies. The focus here is on national contexts with political systems less restrictive than highly centralized and authoritarian systems, for example, those in Singapore or China (Ho et al., 2017).

The chapter includes an overview of pertinent scholarship related to teacher education. It then describes the research project that generated this book and lays out the questions that drove my inquiry. It also describes the research participants and settings, and the sociopolitical climates in which learning to teach controversy took place. The introduction concludes with an outline of the chapters that follow.

RELEVANT SCHOLARSHIP ON TEACHING CONTROVERSIAL ISSUES

There is now a robust and growing body of international scholarship on teaching controversial issues. Within that literature, and in the minds of educators, conceptions of controversial issues vary (Hess, 2008).

Conceptions of Controversial Issues

Robert Stradling et al. (1984) defined controversial issues as "those problems and disputes that divide society and for which significant groups within society offer conflicting explanations and solutions based on alternative values" (p. 2). Diana Hess (2009) defined controversial political issues as "questions of public policy that spark significant disagreement" (p. 37). She explained that issues considered controversial vary by context and can change from open (currently debated) to settled (resolved)—and vice versa—across time and place. For example, in the United States, a woman's right to abort a young fetus is protected at the federal level, but is contested in many states.

Slavery, an open issue for the nation less than 200 years ago, is settled, and now, reparations for enslavement and its legacy are debated.

Controversial questions may be embedded in history, for example: "Why did the United States use atomic bombs to end the war with Japan?" (Ho et al., 2017). They may include sensitive questions related to contested histories (Foster, 2014; Kello, 2016), and are often connected to sociopolitical oppression and/or ethnic conflict (Wasserman, 2011). In divided societies such as Northern Ireland and Cyprus, many educators associate controversial issues with historical events, political questions, and cultural expressions that evoke emotional reactions tied to community allegiance and identity (Zembylas & Kambani, 2012).

In their review of research, Li-Ching Ho et al. (2017) made the point that controversial topics, which certain stakeholders deem problematic to teach, are often confused with controversial issues, which involve questions that merit exploration through multiple perspectives. Racism is a topic, while police violence against Black people is an issue (Journell, 2016). The Man a Course of Study curriculum developed by Jerome Bruner and colleagues in the 1960s included controversial topics, such as natural selection and Netsilik culture, which generated hostile reactions from the religious right (Dow, 1991).

Although some people may dispute the theory of natural selection, it does not meet Robert Dearden's (1981) "epistemic criterion" for an issue that should be taught as controversial, because arguments against the theory's empirical validity are not rationally defensible (Hand, 2008). Giving a fair hearing to perspectives on empirical questions that are not backed by evidence defeats the educational aim of developing rational thought. Hand and Levinson (2012) argued that the controversial issues we teach should truly be "unsettled," rather than questions to which teachers have the answers (p. 618). Otherwise, the whole point of exploring and discussing the issues is lost.

Analysis of different types of controversial issues is important for teaching, and we will return to this claim in the final chapter. Theoretical distinctions on defining controversial issues were not given much attention in the courses I studied and can be blurry in real life. Many of my research participants used the term "controversial issues" to mean topics that provoked highly charged reactions due to their sensitive nature or their association with violent conflict.

Pedagogical Approaches and Capabilities

Controversial issues can be taught in a variety of ways. Much of the scholarship focuses on deliberative pedagogies that engage students in exploring different perspectives through activities that include inquiry, critical analysis of sources, formulation of arguments, position-taking, and/ or decision-making (Simon, 2005). Examples of deliberative pedagogies are

Structured Academic Controversies, Socratic Seminars, Town Hall Meetings, Legislative Simulations, and Moot Courts (Hess & McAvoy, 2015).

Importantly, Ho et al. (2017) include discussion-based approaches emphasizing rational discourse as well as approaches called "conflict dialogue pedagogies" that address the emotions of teaching controversial issues in divided societies. The latter include dramatic role-play and peacemaking circles (Bickmore & Parker, 2014) along with relationship-building and autobiographical sharing (McCully, 2006). Teaching of controversial issues also may involve simulations of historical events and international negotiations (Wright-Maley, 2015) as well as political elections and Supreme Court cases (Parker & Lo, 2016).

According to research, the key activity with significant benefits is discussion of issues in an open classroom climate, in which the class examines diverse perspectives, the teacher encourages students to express their opinions, and students feel free to disagree with their teacher and peers (Hahn, 2011). Benefits include development of political tolerance as well as political knowledge and engagement (Hess & McAvoy, 2015).

Facilitation of dialogue in which students participate equitably to critically explore hard questions places great demands on teachers (Parker & Hess, 2001). In fact, studies find that discussion through which students exchange robust ideas about significant issues is a rarity in social studies classrooms (Barton & Avery, 2016). It occurs less often in lower-track classrooms and with students from lower-income, immigrant, Black, or Latinx backgrounds (Kahne & Middaugh, 2008), which is a major impediment to civic equality (Levinson, 2012).

In addition to discussion facilitation, skillful teaching of controversy requires a diverse and aspirational set of capabilities (Foster, 2014; Hess & McAvoy, 2015; Kerr & Huddleston, 2015):

1. Self-awareness of beliefs and values, and thoughtful decision-making about disclosing views to students.
2. Understanding the role of teaching controversial issues in educating for democracy and human rights, including its purposes, methods, and challenges.
3. Creating an open and respectful classroom climate.
4. Identifying meaningful issues and designing inquiry-based curriculum with rich curricular-instructional resources and supports for student learning.
5. Employing different teacher roles and pedagogical methods appropriately.
6. Using strategies such as creating norms, gradually working up to hot-button issues, and employing structured discussion formats to manage classroom dynamics.

7. Turning challenging questions and comments into learning opportunities.
8. Exercising professional judgments about ethical dilemmas.

These capabilities were addressed through different methods in the teacher education courses described in this book. Reports from novice teachers showed evidence of their thinking about these elements and in many cases learning to practice them.

Realities of the Charged Classroom

The requirements of skillful teaching beg the question of how preservice teachers can be educated to take on this ambitious endeavor, particularly given challenging classroom realities that range from classes with heterogeneous academic abilities to insufficient time. My book *The Charged Classroom: Predicaments and Possibilities for Democratic Teaching* showed that classrooms are charged spaces—full of powerful opportunities for democracy education, yet, at the same time, rife with tensions inherent to teaching that have been intensified under current conditions such as school testing policies and political polarization in the wider society (Pace, 2015).

For example, the perennial tension between student engagement and classroom control (Metz, 1978) is magnified when politically charged content is explored and deliberative pedagogies are used. Many teachers avoid practices such as teaching controversial issues because, along with lack of confidence, they fear it threatens classroom order and curriculum coverage, which are paramount (Barton & Levstik, 2004; McNeil, 1986).

The concept of the charged classroom is especially relevant in "divided societies" with legacies of violent conflict and subjugation. Here, exploration of controversy can arouse volatile emotions and aggravate intergroup tensions (Barton & McCully, 2007; Zembylas & Kambani, 2012). Students may bring to school entrenched perspectives, identification as blameless victims rather than perpetrators, and prejudices toward specific groups they learn at home and in their communities (Gallagher, 2004; Barton & McCully, 2010). Beliefs and attitudes born out of violent conflict amplify motivated reasoning—wherein the way people select, process, and remember information is shaped by social identity, emotion, and other affective factors (Clark & Avery, 2016).

The democratic possibilities and tensions of the charged classroom are heightened by conditions in schools and society. Even in societies not divided by recent war, political polarization produces extreme views and contentious media discourse. Regional and local politics can either support or challenge teachers' efforts (Hess & McAvoy, 2015; Washington & Humphries, 2011). Larger sociopolitical discourses, which reflect and recreate problems such as homophobia and racism, get reproduced by students in school (Beck, 2013). Referring to the U.S. context, Journell (2016) acknowledged that teaching controversial issues may be a "frightening proposition." Teachers fear that "[d]iscussions of certain issues also have the potential to generate intolerant discourse that can offend, alienate, or intimidate students" (p. 2).

School culture, politics, demographics, and tracking of classes all influence teaching as well (Lightfoot, 1983). Support from colleagues, department chairs, parents, and students can encourage teaching controversial issues (Hess & McAvoy, 2015). Progressive school cultures are more conducive than school cultures that suppress conflict (Cornbleth, 2001; Pace, 2008). The implementation of accountability policies such as high-stakes testing may constrain teaching (Pace, 2011).

However, teachers' aims and political beliefs also shape their teaching of controversial issues, and may even counteract institutional conditions (Hess, 2005). Pedagogical motivations include preparing students for democratic life and the real world, understanding multiple perspectives and the people behind them, developing critical thinking and decision-making, engaging students in learning, and instilling particular values (Ho et al., 2017).

Many individual, institutional, and sociopolitical influences shape the teaching of controversial issues. Ho et al. (2017) state that "teachers and students navigate a complex terrain of institutional and curricular constraints; societal discourse and expectations; national, group, and individual histories; local, state, and national politics; personal beliefs; and multiple and overlapping identities involving ethnicity and religion" (p. 323). As this book vividly shows, these factors not only mediate teaching, but are used by teachers to explain why they avoid, contain, or approach controversy.

TEACHER EDUCATION

Scholars and policymakers have called for university-based teacher education to prepare preservice teachers to teach controversial issues (Andrews et al., 2018). Very little research informs us about how such preparation is done. A few studies document reports of preservice teachers that, despite the importance of teaching controversial issues, their teacher education programs did not prepare them sufficiently (Ersoy, 2010; Woolley, 2011).

Prior research indicates that teacher educators are stymied by the fact that their efforts "leave so little imprint on classroom practice" (Barton & Levstik, 2004, p. 244). The development of pedagogical content knowledge may be necessary but is not sufficient to overcome the apprenticeship of observation—what we learn about teaching from having been taught for so many years (Lortie, 1975).

A study by Robert Dahlgren et al. (2014) found that a sample of eight student teachers, from two U.S. universities assigned to teach a controversial issues lesson, demonstrated "a strong disposition" (p. 218) toward doing so despite external obstacles in field placements. At the same time, their lessons tended to be teacher-centered with limited discussion among students.

Dahlgren et al. (2014) identified different stances that characterized the student teachers' approaches to teaching controversy and the range of historical and contemporary issues they taught. But neither the lessons nor the university coursework that prepared them was described, which leaves a major gap in our understanding of how preservice teachers learned to teach controversial issues.

While research on teacher education for teaching controversial issues is scant, Parker's (2003) and Hess's (2001, 2004) essays on their own preparation of preservice teachers are important contributions. In Diana Hess's social studies methods course, teachers identified and assessed individual goals for discussion participation. They participated in several contemporary public issues (CPI)[1] discussions, led by Hess, that utilized different structures. They built conceptual understandings of high-quality discussion through examination of videos and of CPI through discussion of criteria. They discussed pedagogical controversies such as teachers' roles and whether students' verbal participation should be assessed. The novice teachers each developed a CPI discussion lesson plan, received feedback, and taught it at their school placement. They reflected on the lesson using specified standards and revised accordingly.

Walter Parker described how he prepared teachers to conduct discussion by using demonstrations, rehearsals for leading seminars, and lesson planning for controversial issues deliberations. Parker modeled the facilitation of Socratic Seminars and Structured Academic Controversies (SACs) and elicited critique from his students. The students then planned and conducted short seminars and developed SAC lesson plans. Class debriefings included problem solving on teaching challenges that accompany these practices.

Both cases represent versions of practice-based teacher preparation, in which a core practice is represented by the teacher educator, decomposed by the group, and approximated by individual students with coaching and feedback (Grossman et al., 2009). This model addresses a recurrent problem in teacher education: The disjuncture between idealistic, theoretical university-based courses and the constraining realities of classrooms and schools limits the impact of coursework on teaching (Wideen et al., 1998). Providing conceptual and practical tools that teachers can adopt in the classroom (Grossman et al., 1999), modeling the use of these tools (Lunenberg et al., 2007), and creating opportunities to rehearse them (Lampert & Graziani, 2009) are key to preparing teachers for ambitious practice.

The essays do not reveal how the teacher educators handled knotty dilemmas such as balancing an open classroom climate and safe space. We do not learn how specific classes taught by Parker and Hess played out and how their preservice teachers took up the conceptual and practical tools they were taught. We need more research on what preservice teachers do with the preparation they receive for teaching controversial issues.

Learning to teach in schools involves the development of knowledge and skills related to subject matter, pedagogy, students' learning, the teacher's roles, managing student behavior, and working with colleagues (Grossman et al., 1999). It stretches beyond individual cognition because learning to teach is socially situated within institutional settings (Barton & Levstik, 2004). It involves solving problems, such as how to navigate competing curricular demands (Pace, 2015). Learning to teach controversial issues adds a complex layer to the typical predicaments novices face.

Crucially, learning to teach controversial issues involves a paradox: A central task in constructing teacher identity is figuring out how classroom authority works (Pace & Hemmings, 2006, 2007). But teaching controversial issues involves bringing conflict into the classroom, which may threaten the very authority novices are trying to build (Britzman, 2003). How are preservice and first-year teachers to manage this paradox? This book, with its detailed observations of teacher education class sessions and extensive interviews with novices about their initial teaching experiences, contributes new knowledge that helps us address these and other hard questions.

A CROSS-NATIONAL STUDY

In 2016-2017, I conducted a cross-national research project to discover how teacher educators prepare their preservice teachers to teach controversial issues (Pace, 2017, 2019). My book *The Charged Classroom* generated provocative questions about how teacher education could advance democratic aims (Pace, 2015). This pushed me to study experts in teaching controversial issues in diverse contexts where the practice was particularly relevant. With help from my professional network, I recruited two teacher educators at different universities in Northern Ireland, one in England, and one in the Midwestern United States. All four were highly respected by their students and colleagues.

As we know, political, social, and cultural contexts matter greatly for teaching controversial issues. As it turned out, the locations I selected were on the cusp of a dramatic escalation of political turmoil that unfolded in unimaginable ways. Conflict over political leadership and overturning of long-standing policies in these countries have toppled governments and shaken the world. At the time of this writing, the president of the United States has just been impeached and acquitted. The United Kingdom is about to leave the European Union. The power-sharing government of Northern Ireland, which fell apart almost three years ago, has just reopened.

All three countries purport to be liberal democracies and share many cultural commonalities and interconnected histories. All are currently struggling with sociocultural divisions and political polarization that make teaching controversial issues all the more urgent and even riskier. The U.K.'s agonizing difficulty reaching a Brexit deal with the European Union was largely due to the question of the border between Ireland (part of the E.U.) and Northern Ireland (part of the U.K.) and the long, difficult history that border represents. The antipathy toward immigration that fueled the Brexit leave vote is paralleled by the rise of xenophobia in the United States under Trump.

Despite these similarities, there are also important demographic, political, and educational differences. The United States is much more racially and ethnically diverse than Northern Ireland, where the vast majority of people are of Irish, Scottish, or English descent. England has a very diverse multicultural population, mostly from its former colonies, but is less diverse than the United States. The U.S. Constitution legislates separation of church and state, which is not the case in the other two countries. Although de facto school segregation exists in all three countries, segregation by religion is the norm in Northern Ireland.

Three Sociopolitical Contexts

Northern Ireland is an especially fertile setting for teaching controversial issues because of its history of conflict and educational initiatives aimed at addressing it. Division is rooted in centuries of conflict between the native Irish on one side and British rulers and the Protestant settlers they brought from England and Scotland on the other side. The 1998 Good Friday peace agreement created a power-sharing government, dramatically decreasing sectarian violence. But the legacy of "The Troubles," a 30-year period of violent conflict in which more than 3600 people were killed and 30,000 injured, and the lack of a formal reconciliation and transitional justice process, continue to divide society (Worden & Smith, 2017). Generally speaking, the Protestant community is Unionist and identifies as British while the Catholic community is Nationalist and identifies as Irish— though there are exceptions as well as factions within these groups.

Many people want a peaceful and more cohesive society, but unresolved trauma, injustice, and mistrust persist. Some 93% of students still attend religiously segregated schools, reinforcing division. Educators and scholars have developed powerful models for teaching controversial issues, such as

"Speak Your Piece" and "Prison to Peace" (McCully & Emerson, 2014). The curriculum in history (Kitson, 2007) and citizenship (Worden & Smith, 2017) holds enormous potential for it. But a culture of conflict avoidance in schools and the broader society hinder these efforts (King, 2009). More recent issues, such as equal marriage and abortion, also divide a country where religious feelings are often strong.

In England, political divisions over immigration and British identity erupted with the 2016 Brexit vote to leave the European Union. The border between the Irish Republic and Northern Ireland, open since 1998, has been perhaps the most contentious question raised by Brexit. And, following the Brexit vote, the specter of a breakup of the United Kingdom has arisen as pro-independence sentiment grows in Scotland and Wales. The recent parliamentary election, which solidified Boris Johnson's grip on power, raised the specter of antisemitism and simmering social class tensions between elites in London and the working class.

Debates over the "Prevent Duty"—part of a counterterrorism policy that obligates teachers to take measures deemed to protect students from extremism and mandates teaching of British values (Jerome & Elwick, 2019)— reveal Islamophobia and cultural conflict. At the same time, traditional patriotism, power, and privilege coexist with critical examination of Britain's past in relation to war, empire, and class division. As in Northern Ireland, a culture of politeness constrains open dialogue about contentious sociopolitical questions. And, as in both the United States and Northern Ireland, religious beliefs clash with scientific theories and progressive values.

The United States too has become increasingly polarized over the past thirty years (Hess & McAvoy, 2015). But Donald Trump's presidency has created a particularly fraught political landscape by fueling racial, cultural, and religious divisions and promoting a radical agenda. That agenda has threatened democratic values once widely accepted, such as respect for the press, political equality, and civil rights. A plethora of controversies divide citizens over immigration, race, gun violence, policing, abortion, and more. The Midwest, where my U.S. research site was located, is a complex mixture of conservative areas where most citizens vote for candidates from the Republican Party and liberal areas where most vote for Democrats. Progressive social causes such as LGBTQ rights and support for activist groups such as Black Lives Matter are highly contested in schools depending on their location.

These were the settings where I conducted my research. The preservice teachers I studied realized they would be serving sociopolitically and culturally diverse student populations and communities. In England the student teaching placements were located in both economically depressed former mining towns and affluent villages. In Northern Ireland, they took place in Loyalist and Nationalist enclaves, in religiously segregated and integrated schools, and in cities, suburbs, and small towns. And in the Midwestern United States, student teachers were placed in either a politically diverse and conflict-averse suburban school district or the multicultural progressive schools in the state's biggest city.

Teacher Education Contexts

I recruited the four teacher educators I observed based on several factors: (1) recommendations by colleagues who understood the study's purpose; (2) informal interviews by phone or Skype determining that these teacher educators had experience and were continuing to prepare preservice teachers to teach controversial issues; (3) course schedules and locations conducive to visiting each location twice during the academic year to conduct observations and interviews; and (4) locations in English-speaking liberal democracies wrestling with divisive political controversies.

In Northern Ireland I studied two teacher educators' (called "tutors") methods courses at different universities, which allowed me to enlarge and diversify my sample with minimal travel. The courses were Paula Barstow's[2] Citizenship course and Mark Drummond's Citizenship and History courses. In England I studied Ian Shepherd's History course. In the Midwestern United States I studied Liz Simmons's "advanced" Discussion in Social Studies course. The courses in the U.K. ran through the academic year. The course in the United States ran from March to June.

All courses served graduate-level preservice teachers preparing to teach students at the post-primary level (ages 11–18). The four teacher educators had rich experiences as school teachers, curriculum designers, professional developers, and scholars. They all had taught methods courses at the university for at least ten years.

The fifteen preservice teachers I interviewed volunteered to participate in the study. I attempted to select individuals who represented the cultural and gender diversity of the graduate student population in these courses.

Data Collection and Analysis

I was a participant observer during the 2016–2017 academic year, visiting each course for a minimum of twelve hours spread over four to six class sessions, except for Mark's citizenship course, which I visited for nine hours spread over three class sessions. Data collection entailed writing detailed field notes and making audio recordings of lessons focused on teaching controversial issues. I resided in England and Northern Ireland in the fall for eight weeks and in winter for four more weeks. I stayed in the Midwestern United States in late winter/early spring for a month and late spring for another week.

I conducted a series of three audio-recorded, semi-structured individual interviews with each teacher educator and with fifteen preservice teachers total. Final interviews were conducted through Zoom conferencing. The U.K. interviews occurred in fall, winter, and summer. The U.S. interviews occurred in early spring, late spring, and the following winter. I gathered curricular-instructional and policy documents related to the courses and their institutional contexts. The preservice teachers were asked to send me lessons they created and taught on controversial issues and pertinent course assignments they completed.

Additionally, I was a participant observer at the four universities. During my stays in the different locations, I followed the news, watched films, read books, attended museum exhibits, theater performances, and local events, and talked with many people to build my understanding of historical, social, cultural, educational, and political contexts.

ORGANIZATION OF THE BOOK

The core of the book consists of pairs of chapters that revolve around each teacher educator, the university courses observed, and the graduate students interviewed. Chapters on the teacher educators and their courses tell us about the tutor's identity, professional background, and teaching context. They uncover teacher educators' core beliefs about teaching controversial issues and their goals for preservice teachers' learning. The chapters describe class sessions on teaching controversial issues to illustrate what they taught, the methods that were used, and preservice teachers' responses. Each chapter closes with a set of key lessons learned from the teacher educator and their course(s).

Chapters on the preservice teachers interviewed from each research site begin with profiles that tell us aspects of their identities that are relevant to teaching controversial issues. These include their educational background, teaching experiences, and sociopolitical leanings. We also learn about their conceptions of controversial issues. The preservice teachers relay the most important lessons they took away from their courses about teaching controversial issues.

Then the chapters focus on teaching experiences described by each of the preservice or first-year teachers, highlighting lessons they taught that we agreed revolved around a controversial issue. They report the supports, challenges, and constraints they experienced. And they give advice to teacher educators and identify questions about teaching controversial issues that remain. The chapters close with key takeaways from what preservice teachers reported about learning to teach controversial issues.

The first four chapters are located in Northern Ireland. Chapter 1 focuses on Mark Drummond and his preparation for teaching controversial issues in citizenship and history courses. Chapter 2 documents the student teaching experiences of four of his students. Chapter 3 focuses on Paula Barstow and her preparation for teaching controversial issues in her citizenship course. Chapter 4 examines the experiences of four of her students.

Chapter 5 moves to the history course taught by Ian Shepherd in England. Chapter 6 focuses on four of Ian's students. Chapter 7 looks at Liz Simmons and her advanced social studies course in the U.S. Midwest. Chapter 8 examines three of her students who began their first year of teaching after her course.

The book's final chapter synthesizes what the research presented in this book tells us about preparing novice teachers to teach controversy and connects these findings to prior scholarship. It identifies important cross-case themes and comparisons, contributions to the field, and critical questions raised. The conclusion offers recommendations for teaching controversial issues, preparing preservice teachers to do so, supporting these efforts in schools, and conducting new research.

DEVELOPMENT OF A GROUNDED THEORY

Through an iterative process of collecting and analyzing data, writing, and then analyzing data further, I developed a grounded theory (Corbin & Strauss, 1990) about *contained, constrained, and supported risk-taking* in the teaching of controversial issues. This theory emerged from the classification of Northern Irish history teachers in a study conducted by Kitson and McCully (2005) and the application of activity theory to the study of learning to teach (Grossman et al., 1999).

Kitson and McCully (2005) interviewed history teachers and categorized them on a continuum ranging from avoiders and containers to risk-takers. At one end were teachers who avoided all controversy and were not concerned with the social aims of history teaching. At the other end were teachers who embraced social aims of history and took risks to encourage students to empathize across differences and explore contemporary interpretations of history. Risk-takers used immersive approaches such as role-playing and provocative resources such as political wall murals. Containers taught historical events that were potentially controversial, but only used historical sources and thereby minimized chances of emotional volatility. Some taught controversies analogous to ones in Northern Ireland but situated in distant locations.

The teacher educators in my study, working in citizenship and social studies as well as history, both taught and practiced what I call *contained risk-taking* (Pace, 2019). This means they encouraged tackling hard questions with dialogic and deliberative pedagogies and provocative resources. But they also addressed the risks of teaching controversial issues, such as difficult reactions from students, parents, and school leaders, by instructing preservice teachers to use several strategies. We will learn what these strategies were and how they were taught throughout the rest of the book, and revisit them in the final chapter.

The four teacher educators modeled contained risk-taking in their own class sessions. They employed the strategies they taught as they led their graduate students in exploring controversial issues, which kept sessions from getting heated. Likewise, most of the preservice and novice teachers I interviewed practiced contained risk-taking in their student teaching and first-year classrooms. They proactively limited undesirable risks as they attempted to engage students in controversy. A few avoided and contained controversy, but many made valiant efforts under palpable constraints.

My grounded theory also draws on Pamela Grossman et al.'s (1999) use of activity theory for examining the process of learning to teach and the variable influence of university-based teacher education. They explained that according to sociocultural theorists (e.g., Cole, 1996; Wertsch, 1981), learning occurs through problem solving and is mediated by social interactions, tools, and practices located in distinct, yet related, settings.

Conceptual tools include principles, theories, and frameworks that guide teaching. Practical tools are methods, strategies, and resources that teachers use. Learning occurs through a process of adopting tools and making sense of what they do and how they should be used. As novices utilize new tools in the classroom, their actions are mediated by myriad influences from university courses; school placements; and their own sociopolitical, cultural, and educational backgrounds. These influences can either support or constrain efforts to appropriate these tools.

This book shows how contained, constrained, and supported risk-taking played out in a variety of classroom and school settings. It illustrates the various tools preservice and first-year teachers used to teach controversy. And it explores how both constraints and supports, located in different settings, mediated their learning. This new knowledge has the potential to strengthen challenging, yet crucial, practices at all levels of schooling. And it points to a fertile area for social studies and teacher education research as well as new directions in school policy and leadership.

NOTES

1. Hess has since used the term "controversial political issues."
2. Pseudonyms are used for all identifying information.

Chapter 1

Mark Drummond

Controversial Issues as a Path toward Reconciliation in Northern Ireland

Mark Drummond is a fount of wisdom on teaching controversial issues in a divided society. In this chapter, we sit in on Mark's Citizenship and History courses at a university in Northern Ireland. As an educator who works with many groups at home and abroad, he draws upon profound lived experiences as well as original scholarship on education in his own divided post-conflict country. Living in a society torn by violent conflict animates Mark's work, philosophy, and approach to controversial issues, and shapes his views on preparing preservice teachers to engage with the fundamental questions that divide Northern Ireland. His pedagogical methods encourage students to explore new perspectives and examine deeply held beliefs.

Mark was a social studies and history teacher, and has worked with practitioners and scholars on cutting-edge projects at home and in other post-conflict areas. The driving force behind his work is his commitment to using education as a means of reconciliation, peacemaking, and social cohesion. For Mark, controversial issues include sensitive and contentious histories as well as current conflicts that spark strong emotive responses tied to identity, community, culture, and history.

BIOGRAPHICAL INFLUENCES

Mark was raised in a Protestant family, but had childhood friendships across the religious divide, until attending a Protestant grammar (selective) school separated him from Catholic friends. Then, while studying at university, a pivotal event occurred.

That event was Bloody Sunday. On January 30, 1972, British soldiers opened fire on peaceful civil rights protesters in Derry, killing thirteen (a fourteenth civilian died four months later) and injuring many more. Mark recalled that all lectures at the university were suspended for a few days and a "constant stream of people who had been on the march . . . gave testimonies." It seemed to him that "something fairly catastrophic had happened." Until that time, he had supported civil rights reform, but what came to be known as the Bogside Massacre made him think that "more radical nationalism may have had a case" and that there was a "need for social reform at a much deeper level."

Later as a young social studies teacher, Mark became involved in a pathbreaking project that brought together diverse teachers, including civil rights activists from Derry, to address conflict in Northern Ireland. It also brought together Catholic and Protestant schools for residential workshops and field trips. Mark noted that the Schools Cultural Studies Project was "very much about getting controversial and sensitive issues into the school system at a time when it was probably least likely to happen" and was therefore "a very radical project." The group of teachers had to work through their own emotionally and politically charged differences and mistrust. Mark said that "those conversations . . . had a huge impact on all of us."

Mark became a field officer for the project, based at the university. He returned to teaching social studies and history for several years and then became history tutor for the university's Post Graduate Certification in Education (PGCE) program.

Soon Mark was recruited to help lead a new project that used television programs with newscasts on conflicts in other countries that had parallels in Northern Ireland, each followed by a studio debate among a large group of seventeen- to twenty-five-year-olds. "Speak Your Piece" convened teachers and youth workers for a series of residential and daylong workshops on using the TV programs.

The projects Mark worked on were shaped by the "community relations paradigm," which aims to "foster social cohesion by building mutual understanding between individuals and groups" (McCully & Emerson, 2014, p. 143). They put social psychology theories about intergroup contact and prejudice reduction into practice by breaking through the boundaries of a segregated society and bringing together young people from different communities.

At the university, Mark earned his doctorate and grew into his role as teacher educator, first in history and then also in citizenship. Over the years, he collaborated on research and development projects at home and abroad on an array of topics, including history education, education and peacebuilding in post-conflict societies, and citizenship education.

UNIVERSITY PROGRAM

When I conducted my study, Mark's primary role at the university was "tutor" for the PGCE History course, which included selecting and advising graduate students, teaching history methods, and supervising all the student teaching placements. The course was highly selective because teaching is a high-status profession in Northern Ireland. While many young university graduates would like to teach history, jobs are scarce. Mark's history students commuted from as far as two hours away.

The program recruited people with an Honors undergraduate degree in history and entailed 36 weeks of full-time study. The program awarded candidates a teaching certificate with credits toward a master's degree in education, and prepared them to teach in post-primary (secondary) schools. It aimed to develop knowledge and skills specific to teaching history as well as more generic teaching capabilities. The program included a nine-month history methods class, general lectures, tutorials, and two blocks of student teaching at two different schools. The history methods class, which generally met for six- to seven-week blocks three times a week for half-day sessions, alternated with ten- and twelve-week student teaching blocks.

The connection between teaching history and teaching controversial issues was stated on a web page providing an overview of the program and the extrinsic, social aims of the subject:

> In Northern Ireland history teaching has an important role in helping young people understand past conflict so that they can better contribute to a more just and peaceful society. The PGCE programme is committed to education contributing to the vision of Northern Irish society as embraced within the Shared Future agenda. Those enrolling can expect to be challenged to reflect on the impact education can have on a society emerging from conflict.

Alison Kitson conducted research on history teaching in Northern Ireland in the early 2000s. In an important book chapter she explained that while history itself is "often regarded as . . . the cause of an enduring conflict," the "history curriculum in Northern Ireland is often lauded as a model . . . for other societies in, or recently emerging from, conflict" (2007, p. 123).

However, as in England, history is a compulsory subject only until age fourteen. And although the curriculum at Key Stage Three (Years 8, 9, 10; ages 11–14) addresses contested issues related to the roots of conflict, it ends with the Partition of Northern Ireland in 1922, never getting to the more recent conflict. It is up to teachers to proactively make connections between the past and present that disrupt stereotyped understandings and an "Us versus Them" mindset.

Within the PGCE, Mark also taught the "elective specialist course" in Local and Global Citizenship. The thirty-hour course aimed to prepare teachers with the competencies needed to teach Northern Ireland's Local and Global Citizen Curriculum, which includes exploration of controversial and sensitive issues. Mark also taught in the undergraduate and master's programs, and worked with doctoral students. He spent five days a week at the university from morning until evening unless making visits to schools elsewhere in Northern Ireland to supervise student teachers.

ELEMENTS OF PREPARING FOR TEACHING CONTROVERSIAL ISSUES

What do preservice teachers need to learn to be ready to teach controversial issues? That question was the entry point to Mark's views on his approach to this preparation. Mark's response was an argument that teachers must have prerequisites to succeed in this endeavor.

Agents of Change

Mark stressed the importance of teachers' "aptitude," which involved "personality" and interpersonal skills. He stipulated that "this type of work isn't for everyone, and there might be those who have a sympathy for it, but not an empathy." He added that some teachers can be "positively dangerous in this type of work."

For Mark, teachers of controversial issues had to be committed to social change and had to have direct experience with difficult dialogue. They must be aware of their own positionality on controversial issues and be willing to risk discomfort. Mark clarified, "I'm not saying that teachers of controversial sensitive issues are born, but I think they have to have engaged beyond their professional lives in some form. It's a very grand work, [and] I think there has to be some sort of transformative process." In recruiting students for the Citizenship course, a subsidiary to their primary subject, he was transparent about "looking for people who want to be agents of social change."

Mark explained that people learning to teach controversial issues must build trust with one another, understand learning as a constructivist process, and gain curricular tools and pedagogical skills. The first part was "critical," yet challenging. Referring to the citizenship course, Mark acknowledged the time constraint that impeded preparation: "The type of work I'm talking about is difficult in a one-year student program, where you have five three-hour sessions followed by five three-hour sessions months later, because you don't engage in those sorts of discussions off the bat. You have to sit down and build trust."

Developing trust was easier in the History course. Because History is a major subject, the group spent much more time together, meeting a few times a week. Referring to the history cohort, Mark said, "Often the trust manifests itself in humor and comments across that have sectarian humor that crosses that line."

Strategies for Contained Risk-taking

Mark noted several essential curricular-pedagogical elements for teaching controversial issues. He taught them to his students, through modeling, providing conceptual and practical tools, and discussing what it meant to teach controversial and sensitive issues. These elements constituted strategies that helped teachers engage students in controversy, while also addressing the risks faced by classroom teachers in Northern Ireland and other divided societies. They contributed to an approach that embodied what I have called "contained risk-taking" (Pace, 2019), a major theme of this book.

The first was *using rich resources as entry points* into difficult territory. Mark said, "I think that one of the hardest aspects of teaching CI is how do you get into the issue, and I think you often get in through a good resource that shortcuts it and often it's a piece of footage, a piece of drama, a piece of documentary film, an interview."

Mark gave an important explanation: "A good resource helps to legitimize . . . the right to discuss difficult issues because this society has been dominated by an avoidance culture. Students will tell you that they sit in classes where a kid raises a potentially sensitive issue, and the teacher closes it down immediately." In a divided society, resources not only provided a gateway into controversy but also showed how multiple viewpoints could co-exist and be validated.

The second element was *creating an open and trusting classroom ethos*, in which the expression of different views was supported and the class worked its way toward increasingly controversial material. Mark talked about counteracting the avoidance culture in Northern Ireland by communicating both explicitly and implicitly to students, "We discuss controversial issues in here." Mark talked about building trust by establishing his affinity with the local community. One could liken this to the school counselor approach that Erickson and Shultz (1982) called "co-membership." Mark said he then uses that trust to support minority voices.

Speaking about his classroom work, Mark warned that, during the conflict, teachers "had to give voice to the more hardline voices and make sure that they felt able to express their views because if they didn't, they would just go underground." This might feel untenable to teachers with a social justice mindset sensitized to protecting vulnerable students, raising a hard question about how to strike a balance between an open classroom climate and safe space (Pace, 2019). We will return to this question in subsequent chapters.

Mark emphasized the necessity of working toward teaching controversy over time. The third element was the "gradient of controversy"—building up to increasingly controversial topics by starting with analogous issues from abroad like apartheid in South Africa, and then moving to local issues. To dive into the most contentious material before developing trust could be too threatening and cause students to withdraw.

The fourth element was *organizing discussion* of controversial issues by starting with small groups and culminating with whole group synthesis. Teachers needed to learn to hold back, ask questions to help clarify students' points, and encourage exchanges among students. These could be brief, yet significant. I asked Mark probing questions about classroom discussion, coming from a U.S. perspective and influenced by the work of Walter Parker, Diana Hess, and other scholars who advocate sustained classroom discussion (Hess, 2002, 2009; Hess & McAvoy, 2015; Parker, 2003).

He acknowledged that full-blown Socratic dialogue was rare in Northern Ireland. "I think discussion is much more spontaneous, and student expectations are probably quite low in terms of how much they will contribute." Cross talk tended to happen in "short bursts." Mark said, as a facilitator, he preferred an organic flow and was not comfortable with highly structured discussion formats such as Structured Academic Controversies. "Also that's not the tradition. What you feel has worked is what you follow." He questioned whether discussion approaches developed in the United States were "appropriate for dealing with cultural and political sensitivities in this part of the world."

Mark's perspective on classroom discussion was also underpinned by respect for privacy: "I have reservations about kids talking for talking's sake or talking for credit. . . . they're entitled to hold those views, and to express those views when they feel it's appropriate to express them. So my role as a teacher is to encourage them but not to demand or to create an expectation where they feel obliged." Mark's comments underscore his conception of controversial issues discussion as strongly linked with exchange of personal perspectives on sensitive topics that arouse emotion for students rather than a rational deliberation of public issues removed from students' lives.

The fifth element was *teaching students to use evidence to support or challenge viewpoints*. New teachers needed to ask themselves: "Can they (students) substantiate what they're saying from evidence? And if they can't, can I then provide the evidence to challenge or to corroborate?" This was important for teaching in general, but also for preventing discussions from becoming circular and uninformed.

The sixth element was *integrating emotional and intellectual responses* to the material. Mark said teachers had to constantly balance these and get students to see how they were connected: "You're getting people to acknowledge that emotions influence the way that they express views, the positions that they take."

However, affective responses needed to be channeled, and too much emotional arousal would be threatening and shut down discussion. In addition to the gradient-of-controversy approach, Mark showed how to use fictional characters to engage students with opposing views representative of communities in conflict and help them learn to think about how people's backgrounds and identities shaped those views.

Mark told me he focused explicitly on teaching controversial issues during a week in the winter block, within each course. His first goal was for the students to clarify their own thinking about particular issues by exchanging views and reflecting on them. Second, he wanted them to gain greater confidence in handling controversial issues by seeing him model different methods they could apply in their classrooms.

MODELING THE TEACHING OF
CONTROVERSIAL ISSUES IN CITIZENSHIP

On several occasions during the fall of 2016 and winter of 2017, I observed Mark's Citizenship course, composed of nine preservice history, geography, and art and design teachers, and his history course, discussed later in this chapter.

The development of a citizenship curricular area in Northern Ireland was considered critical to peace and reconciliation efforts (Worden & Smith, 2017). Local and Global Citizenship (LGC) has been required at Key Stage 3 since 2007. The inquiry-based curriculum revolves around exploration through local and global lenses of four themes: diversity and inclusion; human rights and social responsibilities; equality and social justice; and democracy and active participation. Mark had been involved in its development.

Worden and Smith (2017) explained that, although the pilot citizenship curriculum stipulated that schools designate time for teaching LGC, the subject was incorporated into a curriculum area called Learning for Life and Work, which also included employability, personal development, and home economics. Schools are free to make time for LGC classes or infuse it in other subjects and/or school activities. A website with curricular-instructional resources, which include teaching controversial issues, provides teachers with support. But LGC is a very-low-status subject in the schools.

Walking Debate on Northern Ireland's School System

Despite time constraints, Mark considered citizenship the best course for demonstrating pedagogical methods for teaching controversial issues. Every week he modeled activities teachers could use with their students, generating wide-ranging discussion. Two observed activities were particularly interesting for addressing controversial issues that continue to divide society. One was on how to deal with Northern Ireland's segregated school system. The other was on the inflammatory annual Loyalist parades that commemorate the Battle of the Boyne, which cemented British rule over Ireland.

The first vignette, based on my October 4th field notes, illustrates Mark's modeling of a Four Corners Walking Debate that explored different perspectives on how to address school segregation. The class had been assigned to read articles representing opposing views held by education scholars. Before the activity, Mark gave a brief historical overview of three approaches that addressed conflict in the religiously segregated school system of Northern Ireland and spoke about his involvement with all three as a father and an educator. The first, called "shared education," created links, including joint courses and extracurricular activities, across Catholic and Protestant schools within a segregated system. The second created religiously integrated schools. And the third mandated a common curriculum, Education for Mutual Understanding, across schools.

Importantly, the integrated schools movement reached less than 7 percent of students, due to a shrinking school population that apparently made it economically unfeasible to build new schools. Integrating existing schools was perceived as too difficult, partly because integrated schools were not academically selective, whereas the current system was divided between non-selective high schools and selective grammar schools.

The vignette shows how the activity gave students the opportunity to take positions on key questions, learn about each other's personal connections to the issue, and change their minds. Preservice teachers learned about a practical tool that encourages students' thinking and participation.

Mark segued into the activity, inviting students to position themselves in one of the four corners of the classroom, designated as Strongly Agree, Somewhat Agree, Don't Know, and Strongly Disagree, in response to the following questions:

1. Segregated education has been at the heart of Northern Ireland's difficulties.

2. There will never be huge support for integrated education while academic selection exists.
3. Shared education is the answer to greater social cohesion, because it allows mixing but retains cultural identities.

Almost everyone agreed with Question #1. They were split among Agree, Don't Know, and Disagree on #2. Most aligned with Don't Know on #3, with a smattering at Agree and Strongly Agree.

On Question #2, Mark disclosed his own view about the role of selective schools in worsening social class division, adding that the worst violence during the conflict occurred in the lowest socioeconomic areas. For #3, Mark put himself in the Disagree corner, explaining that he was taking education scholar Alan Smith's position. He argued that Shared Education reinforced the status quo, ate up massive resources, and was unsustainable.

Mark then stepped out of that position, and skillfully queried students about their positions, drawing out their prior knowledge. Will asserted that shared education had generated changes in rugby, a major sport. It had evolved from its identification as a wholly Protestant sport to one in which Catholics participated. He had been coached by a Roman Catholic, and the one rugby pub in his town was fully integrated. Another student then moved his position to Agree, and Mark commented on it: "You moved! I meant to say you could move. Younger pupils move, adults tend not to. Good that you moved!"

Other individuals gave reasons for being uncertain about shared education as the answer to social cohesion. They raised important points about ethnic minorities such as Chinese families having to choose between the two types of schools and the limits of tolerance versus deep understanding between the two communities.

Mark asked students what they thought about the four corners method, praising them for the long discussion. He made points and raised questions about teacher facilitation, playing devil's advocate, and whether/when the teacher should disclose their own views. He let the class know they would further discuss these important questions about teacher roles and disclosure in February.

Walking debates allow students to take positions and change their minds on the basis of arguments they have heard. A preferred alternative to polarizing debates, they reveal an issue's complexity and participants' common ground if skillfully facilitated (Simon, 2005).

Throughout the walking debate, Mark modeled not only how to run the activity, but also how to take up different stances to push students' thinking, diversify the perspectives represented, and enliven the discussion. His careful questioning and engaging talk about his personal and professional experiences encouraged students to share their own. He demonstrated knowledge of the students by inviting individuals he knew were from pertinent school communities to contribute. The discussion activity created a natural opportunity for students to talk about their past schooling with the class, which in some cases revealed their religious backgrounds and home communities. This personal sharing contributed to the group's trust building.

Simulation on July 12th Marching

In February, Mark explicitly devoted a Citizenship session to teaching controversial issues, which revolved around a simulation of a fictional marching (also known as parading) dispute. In this session, he wanted to make preservice teachers aware of their own reactions to the contentious issue of July 12th marching and the regulations governing it, influences that shaped their reactions, and how community conflict escalates. He also wanted them to learn about the elements of teaching controversial issues that he discussed in our interviews.

Parades are held throughout Northern Ireland on various occasions, but the most highly charged one commemorate "the Twelfth"—the July 12th, 1690, victory of William of Orange, a Protestant, over James II, a Catholic, at the Battle of the Boyne. The commemoration starts the night before with burning of bonfires. Then, on July 12th, marching bands from traditional Loyalist organizations such as the Orange Order lead tens of thousands of people in an expression of pride in their cultural heritage and their commitment to British rule and identity.

Many Catholics experience the parades as triumphalist provocations, particularly when marching routes go through Catholic neighborhoods. Even in recent years, protests, riots, and police interventions have occurred. Disputes over marching routes and other logistics are supposed to be settled by the local Parades Commission, but negotiations can be extremely difficult and produce unsatisfactory results.

An article in *The Atlantic* dated July 11, 2017, explained, "Fundamentally, conflicts over parades are conflicts over the national character of the state and public space. Should this state, this city, this town, this neighborhood, even this street reflect the culture, values, interests, and desires of Protestants or Catholics?" (Blake, 2017).

The following vignette describes the parading simulation activity, which reveals how this controversy manifests itself and the challenge of resolving it:

On February 14th, Mark gave a brief lecture on the six elements of teaching controversial issues he outlined in our interview. He segued into an overview of the history of parading disputes, which escalated during the Troubles and persist today.

Mark set up the simulation by telling the class that "Ballymillis," a fictitious village, had experienced increasing religious segregation and conflict over marching. Three years ago, the Orange Lodge marchers left the Orange Hall playing sectarian songs. Violence erupted. The following year, the Orange Lodge's application to the Parades Commission for permission to march was met with a protest and application for a counter-march.

The Parades Commission determined that the Orange Lodge would leave the night before, not march through the village, and congregate on the main road outside Ballymillis. But the Orange Lodge attempted to march from the Orange Hall and were met with police and a peaceful protest. The Orange Lodge proceeded to the congregation point, but eventually tried to enter the village and was blocked by the police. A Residents' Committee offered to negotiate, but the Orange Lodge refused to talk.

Now the dispute was in Year Three and a determination had to be made. Mark told the group: "Your task: Can you find a way through this that satisfies both parties, the Orange and residents?" If a compromise was not reached at least five working days before the parade, the Parades Commission would make decisions and the police would be responsible for enforcing them. Referring back to a class session on the United Nations Declaration of Human Rights, Mark said that the Parades Commission would operate within a human rights framework, and indicated which rights were in play.

Mark assigned roles to the class. Three students were assigned to be the Residents' Committee. Two were members of the Orange Order. Two represented the media—RTE News (from the Republic of Ireland) and the BBC. A student and I were mediators. Another visitor, with Mark's input, acted out separate roles, first as the Parades Commission and then as the police who had responsibility to oversee the Commission's decision. Students' giggling turned into laughter as they read their role cards, which they were not to disclose. The simulation would devote five minutes to each of five days.

The groups dispersed to separate rooms to discuss their demands. The mediators tried without success to bring groups together to talk, even though a compromise seemed within reach. The media disrupted the negotiations process by broadcasting incidents that were reported during the course of the five days of discussions. For example, at a crucial stage of the negotiations, news was broadcast that Loyalist paramilitaries from Belfast were seen in the village and that representatives from the Residents' group, including Sinn Fein politicians, met to discuss a coordinated strategy with members of other committees engaged in similar disputes.

Mark conducted a debrief of the simulation by calling on each group to present their perspective on what had occurred. Students commented on the role of

the media. One said that the news broadcasts "fueled each fire as we tried to extinguish it." Another said the media plays on emotions by reporting on "things like children being stoned in a bus."

Students were asked to share reactions from the various groups. The Orange Order felt stuck, particularly because one of their members was quite rigid. Someone commented that "the Residents' Committee . . . spoke better at what they wanted and were clear in their objective and their willingness to talk probably served them better." Mark made a specific point: "Which I think says something about the outlook of both sides—one more confident in its rights, and the other feeling under pressure, turning inward, feeling misunderstood, yeah."

Mark followed the activity with a video clip on the marching controversy that teachers could use either before or after the simulation, and another video clip representing opposing perspectives. He asked what the class thought of this exercise. Their responses were pragmatic. One graduate student said that showing the video beforehand would work well with a younger group with less background knowledge, but with older students, it would be interesting to see how the exercise played out without being influenced by the video.

Another person asked how to scale up to a class of thirty students. Mark said the roles could be duplicated and supplemented with "ordinary members," and shared that the largest group he had done it with was twenty-four at an all-girls school in the Republic (of Ireland). He talked about the challenge of "how you would portray 'the other'" when working with segregated groups: "I would deliberately pick some representatives of the class who I knew might be more open to alternative opinions and then mix them with others who might be influenced by them in that group."

Mark asked if the exercise deepened their understanding. Students voiced their perspectives and Mark, in his characteristic way, chimed in:

Student: I think maybe it becomes more of a personal battle competition rather than actually trying to solve the issue. You're trying to win the argument . . .
Student: Yeah, because both sides said, "We won." They were like, "I think we won" sort of thing.
Mark: Isn't there realism to that though? . . . People get trapped in positions especially when it's been played out in public and there's the danger of loss of face or the perception of loss of face.
Student: I think it helps how passionate people can get about it. Some people are maybe like, "Why do some people get so hot about it?" But once you get in a classroom environment and you really want to win, you can see why people get so invested into it, and in real life, in Ireland . . . as well.

Student: Especially like the candidates as well having a community who elected you. You feel under pressure to deliver. If you don't fulfill your role, then you have a couple of hundred dissatisfied residents.

Mark: The other thing that struck me listening to both groups, there was dissension within those groups or differences of opinion, but that didn't get conveyed. Presumably the mediators were trying to convey that, but what reached the other group tended to be a brick wall of intransigence or a refusal to budge, whereas listening to the groups talk, there were people taking different lines, and there was tension within those groups.

Mark's simulation and the short lecture that preceded it offered knowledge as well as conceptual and practical teaching tools. His students learned more about the politics of marching disputes and factors that made conflict resolution in their divided society so challenging. They debriefed a lesson they could hopefully use with their own students, given sufficient time and space.

Mark acknowledged that other controversial issues might be more relevant for young people today, such as same-sex marriage, which then was illegal in Northern Ireland. But during the debrief, the graduate students had much to say about the prevalence of bonfires and marching, and, in some communities, young people's involvement. In our final interview that summer, Mark said that commemorations of July 12th, particularly the bonfires, were extremely contentious that year, which underscored the persistence of this conflict in Northern Ireland.

PREPARING TO TEACH IRISH HISTORY

Mark's History course was composed of fourteen graduate students—twelve from Northern Ireland and two from the Republic—from a mix of Catholic and Protestant backgrounds, the latter being the majority. During the fall term, I accompanied the class on a field trip and observed once at the university. In the winter I observed three class sessions.

Mark devoted February 13th and 14th, after people came back from their first student teaching placements, to teaching the sensitive and controversial history of Ireland. He had already built the foundation for a disciplinary and inquiry-based approach to teaching history, following Britain's Schools Council History Project of the 1970s. We will learn more about this project in chapter 5.

Mark co-constructed conceptual understanding of teaching controversial history with his students, offered practical tools for teaching in a divided society, and utilized student teachers' experiences in their teaching placements. His sessions were a combination of planned and improvised as he stimulated people's thinking with questions and materials, lectured on history and education, and responded to the graduate students' ideas.

History in Northern Ireland Is Controversial

Mark began the two days on Irish history by providing an opportunity for students to express their preconceptions and anxieties about teaching this controversial subject. Their responses electrified the classroom, as seen in the following vignette:

On February 13th, Mark provoked the class with the claim that we should not designate some history as controversial, rather, everything should be taught as "history." Individuals immediately refuted the claim, arguing that history in Northern Ireland was inherently contentious and teaching it must be responsive to community context. Siobhan said, "We don't teach the Troubles in depth because it's too close to home . . . Another school may embrace the whole thing." Will said in his community, where people were involved in a massacre, "fresh wounds can be opened." Emma shared that her mentor teacher said she could not teach the conflict "because it's still so raw."

The class talked about teaching more distant history, such as the Easter Rising of 1916, which still can trigger people's experience of the Troubles. A few shared that even during their undergraduate education, certain classes, for example, about the British role in the Irish famine, devolved into "ferocious" disputes. Class participants noted that history remains charged because of how it's used by politicians and communities to support contemporary causes.

Dan said, "Kids aren't coming into your classroom without other influences," such as family. "They have preconceptions." Seamus added they may come with misinformation. Mark emphasized this fundamental concept: "Kids do not come in with blank slates . . . history is tied to community and personal identity." Victoria noted the importance of what she called "historical memory"—"We choose what we want to remember and forget . . . Are you going to go into the heart of east Belfast and say the British [were responsible for] the famine?" She shared that her "upper class" students resisted examining historical evidence about the Troubles, making "derogatory remarks about Bobby Sands, Republicans," and so on.

Mark's provocative assertion elicited the most animated responses I observed in any course. This was in part due to group cohesion developed by February, but also spoke to preservice teachers' charged reactions to the claim that history is not controversial. Their comments made four vital points about how much context matters for teaching history in their country.

First, the ongoing impact of the conflict's legacy, even for young people born years after the Good Friday Peace Agreement of 1998, is powerful.

Second, community history and politics shape teaching controversial issues. Third, young people bring to school views of history formed by family, community, and identity, as well as politics and the media. Fourth, history is so contentious that students can become uncivil and resistant even in "upper class" and university settings considered more distant from the conflict. Through these responses, preservice teachers cathartically communicated challenges they anticipated and had already faced in their classrooms.

Instead of shying away from these challenges, Mark told a story from the early 1990s about a skilled history teacher whose students suddenly clammed up when asked to make connections between the execution of Irish rebels after the 1916 Easter Rising and the deaths of imprisoned Hunger Strikers in 1981. Mark then asked the class to brainstorm ways to challenge prior beliefs and open up, rather than shut down, students' thinking. He conveyed the importance of questioning students about their beliefs without making them feel threatened.

In a free-flowing conversation about myth busting in the history classroom, Mark conveyed vital points about the mistake of teaching Unionist versus Nationalist perspectives as a pigeon-holing binary instead of a complex continuum, as well as contextual influences, changing identities, and the challenge of helping students understand history in context.

Strategies for Exploring Contested History

Later in the session, the class addressed an essential question Mark posed: "How can history teachers question views, disrupt historical myths, and channel emotion without threatening identity?" They explored different historical events, curricular resources, and pedagogical methods, which included clips from popular films that depict the Easter Rising executions, evoking conflicting perspectives and surprisingly strong emotions even today.

The following vignette describes how Mark followed up with more resources and strategies for tackling students' interpretations of the past:

> The next day Mark projected a Power Point slide that said, "Metacognition. What in my background might influence how I interpret the 1641 rebellion?" He asked, "How do we get students to think about the influence of background, family, and community on how they see the past?" He showed how fictional characters who represent stereotyped perspectives (Loyalist vs. Republican) were used by teachers to develop students' understanding of what makes people interpret historical events in radically different ways.
>
> Then Mark distributed to each pair of students a teacher-made packet on the 1641 Irish rebellion. It contained two copies of a violent image representing the alleged massacre of thousands of Protestants at Portadown for students to

annotate from the views of "Native Irish" and "Protestant Settlers'" (who were English and Scottish), thereby making them take up the perspectives of both sides. The next two pages bore the heading "1641—What happened?" and presented excerpts from primary and secondary sources with a table and questions to help students analyze the sources.

Serendipitously, two people in the class had taught the rebellion during their school placements and shared with the class how their lessons played out. James, having student taught in a predominantly Protestant school, asked his students to think about why Catholics would commit violence against the settlers. And then he asked what they thought Protestants would want to do in the aftermath of that violence. He wanted students to see the rebellion as the first explosion of sectarianism eventually leading to the Troubles.

Tony, having student taught in a Catholic school,[1] also used different sources to get students to think about both the native Irish and settler perspectives. First he put up an Orange Order banner with an image of the Portadown massacre. He got his students to think about how other images on the banner, like the Union Jack, revealed that the banner was a "more recent representation of the event." His class "did the source work from multiple perspectives," and he then got them to write about "their interpretation of the image." The students "were able to actually understand what this image means . . . and how it's used to remember what happened from the settler (Protestant) perspective."

Mark joked that he had been looking for one of those banners. He teased Tony, "You've obviously got connections with the Orange Order," and the class erupted in laughter, given the irony that Tony was Catholic. Tony kept the laughter going by saying that when he put up the banner, students found it funny because it said "LOL" for Loyal Orange Lodge.

Mark validated preservice teachers' concerns about the challenges of teaching controversial history and gave them concrete tools to meet these challenges. For two sessions in a row, he posed questions to home in on a central problem of practice—how to productively disrupt entrenched views of history divided along community lines.

Mark provided practical tools in the form of a packet created by a former student that makes students confront an emotionally charged, pivotal event in history from both native Irish and settler perspectives. Two students spontaneously shared their experiences with teaching this event, and Mark probed the methods and resources they used to drive home lessons about using the discipline of history to address controversy. Their exchanges and the packet illustrated how to engage students in robust historical inquiry that develops empathy and critical understandings about how history is used to justify current positions. The injection of humor contributed to a supportive atmosphere for exploring teaching across the divide.

Tony's story about teaching the rebellion beautifully showed how a teacher can use an artifact charged with symbolism and associations in the classroom to examine opposing perspectives with empathy rather than hostility. We will see in the next chapter that preservice teachers found this part of class especially helpful.

To complement these sessions, Mark brought cutting-edge resources through a guest speaker from the Nerve Centre, known as Northern Ireland's leading arts media organization. The speaker presented an innovative project called *Teaching Divided Histories* that uses film, digital imagery, animation, comic books, and webcasting to explore the history of conflict. A set of short videos showcasing the project's resources, implementation in classrooms, and testimonials from researchers, curriculum developers, school staff, and students can be found at https://www.nervecentre.org/teachingdividedhistories. Mark's preservice teachers were excited to see the abundance of primary resources and try out digital media activities to engage with controversial history.

COMMITMENT AND CONTAINED RISK-TAKING

From this chapter, we see vividly that controversial issues are deeply intertwined with identity, community, history, and politics. Teaching these issues involves disrupting myths, misconceptions, and stereotypes by developing students' capacity to inquire, reason with evidence, and understand different perspectives. To genuinely make a difference, it also means addressing emotional reactions and helping students develop metacognitive awareness of where these reactions come from. But teachers must take these risks in ways that are sensitive and do not threaten students' group identity. They must use strategies to create a conductive ethos built on trust and humor, gradually working up to conflict. And they must employ creative resources and dialogic pedagogies to guide student engagement with the issues.

Mark shows us how teacher educators can prepare their preservice teachers for a difficult practice, validating their knowledge and addressing their anxieties. He modeled both simple and complex dialogic activities. During the debriefs, preservice teachers had an opportunity to reflect on their learning and ask questions. Mark also modeled how to create a cohesive classroom ethos, listen to students, and respond in ways that sparked thoughtful exchanges.

Mark offered conceptual and practical tools for one of the most difficult educational aims—creating long-lasting change in the hearts and minds of young people. But while he encouraged his students to teach controversy and deal with the emotions it evoked, he did not push them to do so. He understood that teachers cannot be forced to embrace such challenging work.

Mark believed his preservice teachers had the pedagogical skills needed for teaching controversial issues, but lacked confidence. He hoped that modeling pedagogical methods, providing curricular resources, and imparting principles of practice would build that confidence and encourage preservice teachers to take risks and creatively adapt the tools he provided. But he understood that his brief time with them limited preparation for taking these risks.

As we will see in the next chapter, during student teaching placements, the preservice teachers interviewed from Mark's History and Citizenship courses ranged in the extent to which they embraced teaching controversy. Mark said that opportunities and support for teaching controversial issues during student teaching and beyond varied greatly. Their individual proclivities and the school contexts in which they taught shaped their readiness to take risks and experiment with the tools he provided. Their experiences give us fascinating, informative food for thought about supports and constraints for teaching controversy at schools in a divided society.

KEY TAKEAWAYS

1. Successful teachers of controversial issues have an aptitude for it, a commitment to be agents of social change, and experience with difficult dialogue.
2. To prepare preservice teachers to teach controversial issues, teacher educators cultivate trust, a constructivist orientation toward learning, and the adoption of curricular resources and dialogic pedagogical tools.
3. Teaching controversial issues is fostered by rich resources, a trusting and open classroom ethos, thoughtful selection and sequencing of controversial issues, discussion that moves from small groups to large groups, use of evidence to support and challenge views, and integration of emotional and intellectual dimensions.
4. Rich resources include digital media, primary sources, popular movies, photographs, fictional characters, and historic images.
5. Pedagogical tools for teaching controversial issues include digital technologies, walking debate, simulation, metacognition, and critical analysis of primary, secondary, and popular sources.

NOTE

1. In a previous publication (Pace, 2017), an error was made regarding the religious identity of Tony's school.

Chapter 2

What Mark's Students Learned

What did Mark's preservice teachers report about what they learned from him about teaching controversial issues? Based on a series of interviews, this chapter looks at their conceptions of controversial issues and key takeaways from Mark's courses. It documents their descriptions of efforts to tackle controversial questions in history and citizenship during student teaching placements, and how these efforts were encouraged or impeded by various factors. It examines their struggles to navigate the disjuncture between educational ideals and the realities of classroom teaching (Pace, 2015). And it concludes with their advice to teacher educators.

The four preservice teachers from Mark's History and Citizenship courses, all of whom volunteered to be interviewed for my project, represented a fascinating mix of identities, school experiences, and interests. Will was in both the History and Citizenship courses, Emma in History, Aoife in History, and Alex in Citizenship. Interviews were conducted with each of them in the fall, winter, and early summer, except for Emma, who was interviewed twice, but was not available for the third interview.

These preservice teachers had enrolled in the Post Graduate Certificate in Education (PGCE) program either immediately or a year or two after earning their undergraduate degree. They valued being in class with Mark and what they reported learning about teaching controversial issues aligned with his principles of practice. However, their adoption of pedagogical tools provided in Mark's courses and their experiences with teaching controversy varied widely, and were shaped by identity, student teaching circumstances, and school contexts (Grossman et al., 1999).

The following profiles provide key information about elements that contribute to novices' emerging teacher identity, such as educational background and personal orientations to subject matter. In the case of teaching controversial issues, sociopolitical identities also come into play (Hess, 2005).

PROFILES OF PRESERVICE TEACHERS

The teacher candidates were open-minded people with exposure to diverse perspectives. Emma, a preservice history teacher, identified as British, Northern Irish, Unionist, Protestant/Christian, and rural. She grew up in the Free Presbyterian Church, founded by Ian Paisley, the infamous evangelical Protestant minister and Loyalist politician. But as an adolescent, Emma attended a Friends (Quaker) grammar (selective) school where about one third of the students were Catholic.

Emma said she was influenced by her A-level (advanced) politics teacher who spoke matter-of-factly about the Troubles, ascribing fault to both sides. His approach enabled students to have open discussions in a religiously mixed class. By contrast, she said the situation in Northern Ireland was still precarious and, although "open conflict" was over, she felt an undercurrent of continuing resentment: "I think I'm always just scared of saying something. . . . people in general are just far too easily offended . . . if it has to do with politics, religion, any number of things." Emma dreamed of teaching history and religious education at her old school.

Aoife grew up in the countryside in a Catholic family and identified culturally as Irish. She was very involved with the traditional Irish music scene and lived close to the border, but was proud to be Northern Irish. Her parents were devout, but were not political. The area where they lived was majority Protestant. She said her sisters were dating Protestant and Jewish men, which was not a problem for her family.

Aoife said that in high school she was exposed to the politics of Ireland and Northern Ireland, but learned more from documentaries about the Troubles and her sister's dissertation on promoting residential integration of Catholics and Protestants. Her Catholic grammar school teachers were very good, but she found it problematic that they taught from a Nationalist perspective and did not take seriously the Unionist point of view. Her experience made her resolve to not teach from a particular political stance. At university, Aoife studied history and politics. She worked and traveled abroad with the British Council. Given the scarcity of teaching positions, she was open to teaching English abroad for a year before settling in Dublin or Belfast.

Will, enrolled in both the History and Citizenship courses, was from a major town in a rural area. He grew up in a Protestant family and attended a state-controlled (de facto Protestant) school. The surrounding area was majority Catholic, and he had friends from both communities through his involvement with sports. Will identified as British but said he had a growing sense of "Northern Irishness," which reflects a trend among younger people (McCully & Reilly, 2017).

After university, Will coached rugby and helped teach history at his old school, mentored by the history teacher who inspired him to be a teacher. He was interested in teaching Irish and Northern Irish history, focusing on political conflict, as well as citizenship and politics courses. Will said he had vague memories of encountering controversial issues in Irish history at school, but they were treated superficially. He remembered the subject Learning for Life and Work, which was mostly "from the book," but did not remember studying citizenship.

Alex was also enrolled in Citizenship but his PGCE focus was geography, He was from a major city and identified as "Northern Irish." Secondarily, he considered himself more British than Irish. He grew up in a Protestant family, but was not religious. Alex enjoyed his years at a predominantly Protestant grammar school and loved his teachers. But he remembered that citizenship as a subject was not taken seriously and controversial issues were avoided.

Alex thought that his study of post-colonialism as a geography major at university in England sensitized him to racial inequality. He acknowledged his white male privilege. He said he was gay and that this influenced his stance on particular issues. Alex noted he would love to teach in an integrated school.

CONCEPTIONS OF CONTROVERSIAL ISSUES

The preservice teachers' understanding of controversial issues included contested history, controversial topics, and controversial political issues. Their Northern Irish identity, the subjects they were learning to teach, and Mark's attention to emotions influenced their conceptions.

Will initially identified controversial issues in history as pertaining to the Unionist versus Nationalist struggle, dating from the Ulster Plantation to the Troubles. He expanded his definition to include both contested histories and current issues, such as "Trump and Brexit." He said controversial issues involved emotion if they related to students' lives and identities. When students acquired viewpoints from family, media, and other influences outside of school, it made issues more controversial in the classroom.

Alex defined controversial issues as major disagreements in which people were unable to understand different views due to the emotions attached to one's own opinions. In geography, the main issues involved migration, ethnic diversity, and development. In citizenship they included sectarianism in

Northern Ireland and issues related to diversity, equality, and inclusion. Alex said he would include equal marriage and abortion under the latter category.

Aoife defined controversial issues in contextual terms—those that provoke an emotional reaction from a particular group. She gave an example: "I could teach the hunger strikes in a Nationalist school, and it probably wouldn't be particularly controversial, and I could go and teach it in a Unionist school, and it would be." When asked to expand she said, "What makes it controversial is the people in the room might not agree with what you're saying based on the history that they have heard, or it's challenging their perceptions or accounts."

Emma defined controversial issues as any subject that is "emotive" about which people on different sides have strong feelings. She said it was important to teach Home Rule and the events leading up to the Partition of Ireland, the Troubles, and even post–Good Friday Agreement violence.

KEY LEARNING FROM THE HISTORY AND CITIZENSHIP COURSES

Mark's preservice teachers highlighted several conceptual and practical tools for teaching controversies they learned from the History and Citizenship courses. These tools fell into three categories: (1) purposes and principles of practice, (2) curricular-instructional resources, and (3) dialogic pedagogies. They aligned with the elements Mark talked about in our interviews and what he taught in class sessions.

Purposes and Principles of Practice

The four preservice teachers learned about the extrinsic purposes, or *social aims*, of teaching controversial issues and, more generally, of teaching history and citizenship in a post-conflict society. Teaching these subjects could be a vehicle for working through deep divisions into a more peaceful and cohesive future. Aoife said that she learned that teaching controversial issues in history was "one of the only ways to move society forward."

Will gained awareness of "the importance of teaching in a society emerging from conflict." He noted that "you can't change kids' identities or the communities they're coming from or the outside perceptions they have of history, but you can maybe, I think, change their mindset in that they look at other perspectives and, you know, through a critical lens, they become aware of their own lens then that they're looking at history from." Will's aspiration included Mark's notion of teaching students to be metacognitive about their beliefs.

Mark's preservice teachers learned that good teachers make history relevant and connect the past with the present. They educate young people to be critical readers and thinkers who use evidence to interpret the media and other sources of information. The preservice teachers learned that ideally they should be risk-takers prepared to embrace controversy instead of shying away from it.

All four preservice teachers talked about dealing with controversy sensitively and thoughtfully, which required *thorough preparation*. Teachers must research the issues, and have facts and evidence at the ready to support or challenge opinions and address student questions. They need to know what activities engage students and motivate them to express their thoughts. They also must know their students well, understand the communities they come from, and anticipate their reactions. If controversy came up unexpectedly, it is fine to recognize it with students and hold off on further discussion to allow time for planning next steps.

Mark's graduate students learned that teachers must *expose students to different perspectives* on an event or issue in order to broaden their knowledge, challenge their stereotypes and preconceptions, and disrupt myths. The teacher's job is not to change students' minds, but to allow them to examine thoughtfully their own and those of others. All four were adamant about not imposing particular ideas on students, revealing a perennial anxiety about accusations of indoctrination, but also an understanding that doing so would not be effective and perhaps spark resistance.

Alex noted the importance, and challenge, of never devaluing students' opinions, even when they are hard line and seem uneducated: "It's so easy to say like, 'No, you can't think like that,' like 'You need to think like this.' Maybe, in an ideal world, you would obviously love them to think like that, but you don't want to force anyone to think a certain way. . . . You need to be the facilitator to give them this information and give them the resources, allow them to see the bigger picture." Alex's comments show the dilemma between correcting student biases and respecting their right to think for themselves.

Relatedly, all four said that teachers needed to create an *open and respectful atmosphere* to promote discussion of issues. Teachers' personal sharing, knowing students well, and taking up different positions facilitated the community building needed for a healthy exchange of views. They appreciated that Mark was exemplary in creating a space in which diverse voices could be heard. Will thought teachers could disclose their views when appropriate while the others seemed focused on remaining impartial and unbiased.

Another important principle evident in preservice teacher learning was *caution*. Aoife implicitly referred to the gradient of controversy concept: "Maybe it's important to not go in all guns blazing. You know, don't start with a topic that you know is going to really rise up tensions." From Mark she learned that teachers could use analogous events to lead up to more emotionally charged, close-to-home events.

Resources

The preservice teachers remarked on the creative and powerful *curricular-instructional resources* Mark showed them to represent different perspectives and get students to wrestle with open-ended questions. Photos and digital technology provided compelling visual images that unsettled students' thinking and emotions. Historical sources, both primary and secondary, could be analyzed from opposing viewpoints. Fictional characters representing extreme views could facilitate reflection on the perspectives students learned from family and community.

The history teachers were excited by the Nerve Center guest speaker's use of film clips and digital resources that depicted contested historical events of Ireland's Decade of Centenaries, such as the executions that followed the 1916 Easter Uprising. Emma enthused about the teacher-made packet Mark used in class: "Today I loved the sheet where again the '41 Rebellion . . . a challenge to pupils to annotate the picture from an Irish native point of view and from an English settler point of view. I thought that was fantastic, how the same source can be held in two different perspectives."

Emma also commented on the exchange, described in the previous chapter, in which her peers Tony and James talked about getting their students to take on different perspectives in their teaching of the 1641 Rebellion by showing images and using primary sources:

> Did you notice [James] and [Tony] both said that they had done the 1641 Rebellion, but [James] had taught it to bring out a sympathy . . . for the Irish natives, but because he was in a predominantly Unionist school, but [Tony] had taught it to bring out sympathy for the planters because he . . . was in a predominantly Nationalist school. . . . You know, it lets them form opinions and their views on a more rounded basis of information.

Emma said that examples like this helped her see how to teach differing sides of an issue.

Aoife also commented on the effectiveness of Tony's move to put up the Orange Order banner and ask students to tell what they saw in the images of the 1641 massacre that it represented. She thought it was a potent way to get young Catholics, living in a very Nationalist area, to learn a different perspective on history. We will see later that Aoife struggled with this challenge.

Dialogic Pedagogies

The preservice teachers deeply appreciated Mark's modeling of *dialogic ped-agogies* (Mark's term for democratic inquiry and discourse) they could use in their own classrooms. Importantly, he involved them in activities that made them experience the teaching of controversial issues from the standpoint of learners (Grossman et al., 1999). Immersing them in these pedagogies was particularly significant because exploring controversy through dialogue was not what they learned about teaching through their "apprenticeship of obser-vation" as students (Lortie, 1975).

Will valued modeling how to facilitate active learning: "I think that a lot of the stuff that Mark's done with us around different perspectives, different interpretations, and the use of evidence in teaching, allowing kids to—obvi-ously you still have an important role, but allowing kids to come to their own views about things and guiding them in that way."

He said these active learning approaches, which many teachers did not use, broadened his repertoire beyond his own school experience: "That's the sort of ideas that I wanted to learn as a teacher, but maybe when I was in school, I didn't necessarily learn that way, but those are what I imagined, and I think . . . there's massive potential." He also commented on the way Mark set up and worked with small groups to facilitate peer teaching and learning.

In Citizenship, dialogic pedagogies included walking debate, simulation with role-playing, and a card sort with symbols affiliated with different groups. Alex explained the effectiveness of Mark's modeling of these activi-ties, which included questioning students:

> I think the fact that he gets us to . . . have a go at them—he doesn't just tell us like, "Oh, it would work really well to do a role play" or "It would work really well to try to sort these cards." He like lets us do it and lets us argue it out between ourselves, which makes you far more aware of how people will deal with the activities and deal with the disagreements maybe, and then Mark's way of getting feedback is a really good way to learn, I think, from him in terms of after activities, how he questions. So you put that there. So why did you put that there?

Preservice teachers benefited from taking part in the activities and reflecting on them as students and teachers.

From the parading simulation in Citizenship, Will learned that putting students in the shoes of different characters made them more empathetic: "I think this week we've definitely seen a potential to open minds and think of different perspectives in that way, which was quite interesting." Alex commented on the simulation's relevance and picked up on Mark's idea about assigning roles and the role of the media:

> It's an issue that comes up every year honestly around parading. . . . if you know your class quite well. . . maybe you give a role to someone that you know will like challenge them a little bit . . . probably the most important bit was the influence of the media. That is just more and more and more important nowadays, like right through the election that you guys had and right through our election that we just had. . . . that simulation really demonstrates how the media can just stir the pot and has so much influence over the situation and the progress that can be made.

The simulation's lessons for the preservice teachers included the importance of teaching students to be critical consumers of media, the potential of simulation for opening student's minds, and the nuances of using pedagogical tools to greatest advantage.

The preservice teachers' readiness to use the tools Mark provided varied considerably. Risk-taking was mediated by their individual identities; school curriculum, culture, and community; and the students and mentors they worked with at the school sites (Grossman et al., 1999).

STUDENT TEACHING EXPERIENCES

Kitson and McCully's (2005) interview study of Northern Irish history teachers identified three kinds of teacher orientation toward controversial issues. *Avoiders* did not teach controversial issues and were not concerned with the social aims of history education. *Containers* taught potentially controversial historical events, but limited students' attention to historical sources, minimized chances of emotional volatility, or taught analogous controversies in distant locations. *Risk-takers* embraced social aims of history, eagerly tackled controversial issues, used immersive approaches, critically analyzed resources, encouraged empathy across differences, and addressed contemporary interpretations of history. These characterizations can be applied to teaching citizenship and other subjects.

The teacher candidates' responses to teaching of controversial issues ranged, understandably, from avoidance to contained risk-taking. All four said they had wonderful experiences, albeit with some tough challenges. Although school timetables varied, typically history and geography were scheduled for two 35- to 50-minute periods per week and citizenship for only one period. Student teachers participated in a wider range of classes than their counterparts in the United States, but they shared responsibility for teaching them with inservice teachers.

Table 2.1   Student Teachers' Main Experience Teaching Controversial Issues

	Course	*Focus*	*Curricular and Pedagogical Tools*
Will	Year 9 Citizenship	Human Rights: What rights should all people have? How should human rights abuses be resolved?	Walking debate, privilege exercise, role-playing
Emma	Year 10 History	Home Rule Crisis: What was the Home Rule Crisis? What did propaganda posters communicate?	Small groups interpret posters
Alex	Year 10 Citizenship	Democracy: Free speech? Mandatory voting? Lowering the voting age?	Walking debate
Aoife	Year 10 History	Early history of Northern Irish state: Why did Unionists discriminate against Catholics?	Unionist catchphrases and perspectives, paired discussion on reading and feedback back to class, written conclusions for homework

All four taught content regarded as controversial during student teaching placements. The Year 10 history curriculum, parts of which three of them taught, includes events in Irish history that occurred one or more centuries ago, but are still contentious. However, the extent to which the teachers engaged students in active exploration of controversies from multiple perspectives varied.

Table 2.1 shows what each student teacher reported about their main experience with teaching controversy. It identifies the school subject, focus of the lesson on controversial questions, and the pedagogical tools used.

Supported Risk-taking

Will was able to take more risks than the others, but this evolved over time. The history curriculum he taught in his first placement, a non-selective high school with mostly Protestant students, provoked controversy that he did not anticipate. When teaching about the Ulster Plantation, a policy that brought primarily Scottish and English Protestants to settle in the northern province of Ireland, a few students remarked, "So that means we're Scottish or English."

Will said he told the class to "park" the issue of identity. Mark had observed that lesson and commented on the "interesting" response to students. Will returned to it, and linked past to present in a lesson on how the plantation of Ulster can impact identity today. It was challenging to get the students to understand that Ulster at that time was part of Ireland—even when they saw maps, they insisted it was Northern Ireland. They also struggled with the fact that three of the counties in Ulster are part of the Republic. And they did not empathize with the native Irish who lost their land. It made him think more about outside influences on his students' education and the "baggage" that they brought to the classroom.

Will intentionally delved into controversial issues during his second placement at an urban state-controlled grammar school with a significant Catholic minority. Will appreciated that the school's tolerant culture and range of political views supported discussing issues from multiple perspectives. Also, although periods lasted for only thirty-five minutes, each week history met three or four times (depending on the grade level), citizenship met three times, and politics met for three double periods. Although short periods did not allow for immersive experiences, Will took risks in connecting the past to the present, using provocative resources, and employing dialogic pedagogies.

Will said that in his Year 10 Irish history class, the topics he taught included the famine, Unionism, Nationalism, the Easter Rising, the Ulster Covenant, and "an awful lot of more recent history that would be seen as controversial." He linked political wall murals to history, which worked well because the students were familiar with the murals from their daily lives. He had attended a workshop on teaching with murals at the Citizenship PGCE event that Mark organized at the university.

In his Politics class, Will had students in small groups discuss political parties. He said the students were passionate when expressing their views. Over time he structured the discussion more, by assigning students to argue strengths versus weaknesses. The students still were able to include their own opinions. At times it was challenging to manage, but he developed confidence:

> There were times where you just had to rein it back in, and you yourself take control or summarize yourself in a way that wasn't too subjective, one way or the other, and very much from letting them go to you just pulling them back in, and that was the best way to cool tensions as they would arise.

Will remarked upon the fact that students were used to open discussion at their school. He thought the mix of students and the school culture moderated the impact of potentially controversial content. Teaching the same issues at his first school placement, with "much more Unionist views, was much more challenging.

Will said that lessons on human rights in Year 9 citizenship generated the most controversy among students. The pedagogical tools he learned in

Mark's Citizenship class were very helpful for framing human rights issues. After providing background on human rights law, the class had discussions about what rights all people should have, what rights were necessary in classrooms and schools, and the rights of the child.

Will described the walking debate, a pedagogical tool he learned in Mark's Citizenship course. He would call out a potential right, and the students would move along a spectrum from Agree to Disagree. Will told me, "There were quite stark differences. Things like 'Everyone has the right to have a parent make decisions on their behalf,' I had so many rush in, 'Yeah, they know better,' and yet some were like, 'No, no, I'm my own person. I get to make my own choice.' Points like that that I thought wouldn't be so heated . . . and were quite debated."

Will also used Mark's privilege exercise, in which students were given different identities and they had to decide if, under certain conditions, they could move forward. Will said it was "quite good in making them think about exclusion possibly and inclusion and making them take on other people's perspectives and views." It helped them think about "why we have a list of human rights."

After that, Will had students imagine themselves as government officials trying to resolve difficult human rights situations: "I gave them scenarios where human rights have potentially been abused . . . and asked them how as a government representative would you resolve this situation for who is to blame in this situation and how would you change it?" His class also compared human rights abuses in other countries, such as North Korea, the experiences of minority communities within Northern Ireland, and their own lives. He wanted students to appreciate how fortunate they were.

Surprisingly, Will said that the lessons on human rights generated more controversy than those on contentious Irish history in Year 10. It is possible that the pedagogical tools he used in Citizenship stimulated more student reactions than those he used in history or that students at this school did not hold strong emotions about the past.

Our final interview reflected the confidence Will had gained. He said the mixed abilities of students and a very busy schedule teaching several different subjects were challenging, but he really enjoyed trying out new approaches at a highly regarded, liberal institution. Will transcended his apprenticeship of observation. He likely benefited from taking two of Mark's courses, teaching in a supportive school context, and having a year of prior teaching experience.

Containing Conflict

Emma said she loved her first student teaching placement, yet was anxious about dealing with controversy there. She started our second interview with a predicament she faced with her Year 9 students when selecting a topic for their local history class project. Small groups were exploring various options. One group "latched on to the Troubles," and wanted to focus on the bombing of their town. Emma felt "they weren't mature enough," but she "didn't want to be seen as just shutting them down." She knew "they were coming from a very Loyalist and Protestant viewpoint on it." She explained, "One of the wee boys, like the ringleader especially because he lived in a very contentious area . . . was like, 'Such and such were shot at the bottom of our fields.' Clearly this was a big thing in his household."

She told the group they would have to address both sides, thinking that would discourage them, but it didn't. After letting them "run with it for a week," she managed to steer them toward a historical ruin right on the school grounds that another group was already researching and would make a perfect local study.

Emma acknowledged that some might criticize her judgment that the students were too immature, but justified her avoidance of risk. She thought the students did not have the necessary context, which was not part of the history curriculum until Year 10. She also felt it was not appropriate because the project involved many different schools with students from different backgrounds and from North and South of the border, so that sensitivity was paramount.

Emma also was assigned to three Year 10 history classes. She recounted how she set a firm tone before launching into contentious content:

> I sat for a good ten or fifteen minutes and just talked: "This is what we have to do. Northern Ireland, #1, is on the curriculum. #2, you are old enough now and mature enough I hope." I kind of challenged them in that way. . . . and basically told them, "This is an emotive topic. There are going to be strong feelings on either side. We do not want any derogatory remarks or anything that is offensive. We want to discuss these things like adults and rationally, and I'm trusting you to do that, and I'm warning you now that that's what we're going to be doing. So please just be grown up about it."

Emma's discourse indicated a complex mix of messages to construct authority and win students' cooperation before launching into conflictual content (Pace, 2006, 2015). In this retelling, she invoked the authority of the official curriculum and appealed to students' desire to be treated as adults. She softened the imposition of her demands with the polite "We." And she mixed her rhetoric of good will with a "warning," ending an imperative framed as a polite request with "Please." Focused on maintaining a peaceful classroom, she did not explain the benefits to student learning or to society that underlie teaching contested history. Her talk indicated anxiety about the potential for inflammatory student responses.

Emma described how she taught the Home Rule Crisis and events leading to the partition of Ireland into North and South. She followed the booklet used by her mentor teacher, which provided her with a scheme of work that served as a helpful guide. Her mentor granted her autonomy, and she added "just a bit of source work." Emma used Nationalist and Unionist propaganda posters for and against Home Rule for the sources.

In a higher-ability class, she organized small group discussions for students to interpret the posters. For her "bottom Year 10 class" of ten students, she led a whole class lesson on the posters, believing those students needed teacher facilitation to maintain their focus. Emma was surprised and pleased that "they really got into it" and said she was determined to let them figure out the posters' meanings rather than telling them.

From Emma's report it seemed that much of her teaching involved lecture with PowerPoint slides, students' individual research, and creating a timeline of events. She focused on understanding objective facts and correcting misconceptions, for example: "The fact that Home Rule was not an independent Ireland, Home Rule was an Irish Parliament but still under the British Crown. . . . Getting through to them as well that it was Ireland and not Northern Ireland and Southern Ireland."

Based on our interview, Emma both avoided and contained controversial issues during her first student teaching placement. She did have students interpret potentially provocative resources, the propaganda posters. But she did not connect the posters to conflicts throughout Irish history and into the present. When asked what she learned from student teaching that related to teaching controversial issues, Emma said she learned to trust her students. She added, "Maybe I labored the point too much because they were very good, and I don't attribute that completely to me giving them that lecture and kind of like trying to make them feel more mature. I do think it was in them as well."

Emma's orientation to controversy seemed heightened by her school placement. She told me that parents, presumably Catholic, had previously challenged another history teacher who, when teaching about the Protestant Reformation, assigned her students to write a letter to the Pope "summarizing the problems of the Catholic Church at that time." So when Emma planned to assign her students to write a letter from Henry VIII to the Pope about "wanting a divorce or something like that," her mentor teacher suggested she drop the idea.

Emma said that teaching controversial issues was essential. But she worried about "fresh wounds" in families that had experienced trauma. She said that she and other teachers needed to learn to teach with sensitivity. Emma admitted, "This is going to sound awful, but I do see myself a wee bit as like a mother hen. Do you know what I mean? I just worry about wee ones." Emma's identity and student teaching context impeded her risk-taking during her first placement.

Adjusting to Students

Alex said the integrated school where he had his first placement was "really lovely." He appreciated the students, the geography department, and the staff's readiness to deal with controversy and sectarianism. However, his opportunity to teach citizenship was limited to teaching the theme of democracy to a low-track Year 10 class. Struggling with a difficult class was a constraining influence on adopting the tools he learned in Mark's Citizenship course.

He explained that Year 8s and Year 9s did not take citizenship at this school, and only the two "bottom" classes of Year 10, which was streamed (tracked) from "top to bottom," took citizenship, instead of a second language. Alex was told that "citizenship is kind of brought into personal development within the Year 8 and 9 program and then also special assemblies." The situation underscored the subject's low status and crowded school schedule.

Citizenship met for forty minutes once a week. Alex struggled with a very challenging class: "It was the toughest class that I taught. . . . which I think made it difficult to really get into the citizenship aspects. I tried a walking debate and stuff with them, but they would very quickly just start talking to each other . . . they would just have run riot in the class if you didn't keep on top of them."

In the walking debate, Alex posed controversial questions about democracy, such as whether everyone should be able to say whatever they want, voting should be mandatory, and only people eighteen or older should have the right to vote, and so on. Alex said it was hard to engage the whole class in active learning because of the mix of engaged, disinterested, and academically struggling students. Alex thought that maybe he tried the walking debate too early in his placement, as he had not yet developed relationships in part because he only saw his citizenship students once a week.

He tried another scenario in which students called out who should have the right to make decisions in school. It became chaotic and unpleasant:

[You] then just had the class saying like, "Just pupils, just pupils, just pupils," and then there was maybe like the odd kid who would be like, "I think the teachers and the pupils," and you would get the nasty ones in the class, "Why would you think that?" like shouting across the room, like it wasn't a nice environment.

Alex said that much more successful were "wee games" in which students competed to answer factual questions about democracy. A colleague commented on the effectiveness of this competitive approach with this group of students. While trying to see the bright side, Alex knew this was not what teaching controversial issues should ideally entail:

But the actual knowledge that they were gaining from that task maybe wasn't that great. They weren't getting that chance to critique their own opinions, but at least it was getting them to think about what a democracy is, what factors contribute to democracy, that kind of way. . . . but it was just hard to get them to even articulate their opinions sometimes. . . . That makes it difficult then to get to the real heart of controversial issues.

Alex also tried to talk with the class after the "collapse of Stormont" (power-sharing government in Northern Ireland) was reported on the news, but they were not informed: "They were like, 'I have no idea.' I was like, 'Didn't anybody see the news last night?' Didn't they see a paper, like what's happening?" Students simply replied, "'I don't know, Sir.'" So he then tried to make them think about various ways "we could get involved," such as reading the paper and putting on BBC News online. He hoped they would follow up, but said he felt sad that students were unaware of important events affecting them.

Alex's story represents a series of attempts to engage students in vital subject matter. It is emblematic of concerns felt by teachers no matter their level of experience or national context. Establishing classroom control, promoting harmonious interactions, and engaging students are fundamental expectations of teachers. Yet teachers are dependent on students to feel successful and adjust their teaching to the academic status of their classes (Metz, 1978; Page, 1991). Alex's story helps us understand why teachers tend to avoid controversy with classes designated as low ability (Kitson, 2007), which feeds the critical problem of unequal civic learning opportunities (Kahne & Middaugh, 2008). It raises the hard and necessary question of how to prepare novices for the challenges he described.

In his second placement at an elite state-controlled school, Alex was pleased to find himself in a surprisingly multicultural student body with a significant number of Catholic students. Alex did not get assigned any citizenship classes. He spoke enthusiastically about teaching geography and described a two-day Year 8 lesson on the history of Belfast, from the volcanic period to current developments—a stunning example of curriculum that is a mile wide and an inch deep. Toward the end of the lesson, he used provocative photographs of security gates, car bombings, and so on that showed the impact of the Troubles on the city center.

The photos elicited strong responses, and students spontaneously brought up many interesting family stories about that period: "'Sir, my uncle was taken by the paramilitaries and told to drive a bomb to the police station.'" Alex said there were "so many hands in the air," but time constraints forced him to cut them off: "Really unfortunately it became a rush to get it done . . . because they wanted it on the exam. So you were trying to go right from like

the volcanic history of Belfast right through to present day developments."
He thought giving students space to tell personal stories was important, but
wondered how, given sufficient time, he could harness these stories to bring
about meaningful learning for the class.

Alex's stories demonstrated a desire to take risks in teaching controversial
issues. He tried the walking debate method, asked controversial questions,
and used provocative images that sparked students' participation. At the same
time, challenging student behavior, lack of opportunity to teach citizenship,
ability group tracking, and curricular demands constrained his ability to do so.
His experience exemplifies the tensions of teaching in the charged classroom.

Wrestling with Identity

Aoife told me student teaching at an ethnically diverse, working-class
Catholic secondary school in a "deprived" area was the most challenging
thing she'd ever done. The students struggled academically, many were just
learning English, and some brought serious problems from home. But ultimately it was a very rewarding experience that served as a "wake-up call" and
made her recognize her own sheltered upbringing.

Aoife said the most controversial topic she taught at this placement was the
Ulster Plantation—King James's settlement of Ulster with Protestants back in
the early 1600s. She said it was actually a "dry" and difficult subject, though
essential to understanding conflict in Northern Ireland. Aoife said her approach
made it "slightly controversial," but students' responses unsettled her.

She had divided the class in half; one half was assigned the native Irish
side and the other half the settler side. Students were asked to think about
questions such as the following: "Imagine you're a Protestant settler moving
over to Ireland. What are your hopes? What are your fears?" During class it
seemed to work well and she wanted to follow up with a debate the following
day. But Aoife said it didn't work as a take-home assignment because, while
the students taking the Protestant settler side did fine, the students taking the
native Irish perspective projected their community's "grievances" toward
Protestants on events of 400 years ago.

Regarding controversial issues in general, she concluded, "I think you have
to be so careful about how you approach it" because "no matter what you
teach here, people will tie their own feelings to it." Aoife said she was concerned about inflaming students through issues that would "rise their anger."
At the same time, she thought that emotive issues were also the most exciting
for students. The dilemma between disrupting students' biases and playing it
safe followed into her second placement.

Aoife was happy with her second student teaching placement at a prestigious Catholic grammar school with high-achieving students. For Year

10 history, she taught about Northern Ireland after Partition, including discrimination against Catholics. Aoife said she had thought she would love
teaching this material, but discovered she did not, precisely because it was
so controversial.

Aoife had decided that before launching into various forms of discrimination against Catholics, she would start with "Why did Unionists discriminate
in the Northern Ireland state?" Aoife wanted students to see why Catholics
were "seen as such a threat to Unionists." She wanted the class to understand how the rise of the IRA fed the Unionist "mentality" of feeling "under
siege."

But teaching this content made her feel very removed from her own identity. She felt a sense of bitterness and guilt about betraying her family when
teaching a perspective that justified discrimination. Aoife thought about the
stories she had been told as a child. Her parents had been denied access to
a university education. But she felt she had to teach the content in a balanced way. She worried that diving immediately into the injustices suffered
by Catholics, including grandparents and great-grandparents of many of her
students, would "leave a mark" on them and make them bitter.

Aoife took risks in presenting the Unionist perspective at a Catholic school
and connecting the past to the present. She started the two-day lesson (70
minutes total) by asking students to interpret "Unionist catchphrases like
'We have what we hold,' 'police under siege,' 'no surrender,'" written on
walls all over Belfast. She presented historians' arguments on their meanings
and helped students connect them to prior learning about IRA campaigns in
border areas and earlier events such as the Wexford massacre of 1798 and the
Easter Rising of 1916. She had them read independently, then discuss in pairs
that shared what they had learned with the whole class.

For homework students were asked to write their conclusions, which
contained the risk of emotionally charged reactions. In contrast with her first
placement, she felt that most students, with one notable exception, wrote
what she wanted to hear, not their honest opinions. But she sensed that they
had "blocked out" what she was trying to teach. Her teaching of Year 10
history concluded before the subject became even more intense with a focus
on the 1960s Northern Irish Civil Rights Movement and the Troubles. She
expressed ambivalence, saying she did not enjoy teaching history that was so
contentious, but then noting she was disappointed missing the chance to teach
the even more emotionally charged recent past.

Aoife said her lesson was motivated by learning from Mark: "So even just
the idea of actually posing the question . . . as well to trying to . . . frame
another perspective and that sort of open dialogue, making sure that I would
have always said . . . You can have whatever viewpoint you want." While
she felt guilty about almost teaching "an overtly Unionist perspective," she

also worried about teaching a Nationalist perspective: "I would never want them to think that, 'Well, she said it was okay for me not to like Protestants or Unionists.'" Concerning the Civil Rights Movement, she said, "I would be afraid that somehow you would rile up, you know, this sense of injustice. You don't want that either. It's so difficult to know how to handle it."

Aoife openly expressed ambivalence about teaching contentious history. By our second interview, she had learned that history should not be taught as one side versus the other. But she had not figured out how to transcend a binary perspective when teaching about Northern Ireland's divided past. Aoife said her school granted significant autonomy, but the teachers she worked with were too busy to discuss her dilemma. Therefore, while the school did not constrain her risk-taking, it did not support it either. It is interesting to speculate how a religiously mixed student population would influence her teaching.

SUPPORTS AND CONSTRAINTS

The reports of student teaching experiences by Mark's preservice teachers yield important findings about supports and constraints located in various categories such as teacher identity, school structures, and community history (Grossman et al., 1999). These factors either encouraged or discouraged risk-taking in adopting tools learned from Mark to teach controversial issues.

In her study of history teaching in Northern Ireland Alison Kitson (2007) analyzed particular factors. One was the local community. In "hot spots" where people had experienced violent conflict, teachers were more reluctant to address more recent Northern Irish history than teachers in "cooler spots" (p. 141). Another was students' academic ability. Those in non-selective high schools felt wary about how far they could go with "challenging and complex issues" (p. 143), while those teaching high achievers had more confidence in their students. A third factor was religious composition. Teachers in schools with a balanced representation of Catholics and Protestants said that this influenced their teaching positively. These teachers used an inquiry approach with plenty of discussion and debate, and past-present connections (p. 144).

Mark's preservice teachers' experiences lend further evidence to Kitson's findings. For example, Emma and Aoife's avoidance and containment of risk-taking were influenced by teaching in religiously segregated schools located in communities attached to powerful collective memories of the violent past. School and community contexts seemed to intensify these student teachers' fears of stirring up difficult student emotions.

Like the teachers in Kitson's study, Alex, Aoife, and Emma spoke about having to adjust their teaching to students labeled as low ability. Alex stopped using dialogic pedagogies after confronting rambunctious behavior. Aoife said low literacy levels and students' lack of self-confidence at a school in a socio-economically struggling area limited what she could teach. Likewise, Emma said her class of Year 10 lower-ability students needed teacher-led lessons instead of group work.

The low status of history, geography, and citizenship and the insufficient time devoted to these subjects significantly limited opportunities for delving into complex and controversial issues. Aoife and Emma referred to the multiple demands on class time. For example, students' memories needed to be refreshed, informal chatting was important for building rapport, and it took time for students to settle in. Classes with 35- to- 50-minute sessions that met once or twice a week allowed little time to cover broad subject matter and explore issues in depth.

Preservice teachers also identified supports for teaching controversy. One was the official curriculum. Despite their limitations, Northern Ireland's history curriculum and textbooks are models for teaching students balanced perspectives on a contentious past (Kitson, 2007; Terra, 2014). Will said that the tolerant culture and mix of students at his second placement supported his teaching controversial issues. Student teachers also benefited from autonomy. Although typically mentor teachers sat in the back of the classroom, the student teachers said they were free to teach as they wished.

An overarching, crucial finding is that Will, Alex, and Aoife all experimented with approaches they had never experienced as students before studying with Mark. Will employed dialogic pedagogies and resources such as political murals to engage students in questions about history, human rights, and politics. Alex tried to engage students in questions about democracy through a walking debate and used photographic images from the Troubles that sparked students' sharing of family stories. Aoife got her students to consider opposing perspectives on history and used provocative resources such as Unionist catchphrases.

Emma, although not a risk-taker, allowed her students to discuss a potential class project on the Troubles and queried them about it rather than cutting them off at the outset. She had students discuss propaganda posters in small groups. These actions reflected Mark's influence and stretched the teachers beyond their own secondary school experiences.

ADVICE TO TEACHER EDUCATORS
AND REMAINING QUESTIONS

When asked for their advice about preparing preservice teachers to teach controversial issues, these informants suggested that teacher educators follow Mark's example and have their preservice teachers try a variety of organized activities that engage students and spark discussion. Seeing these activities

modeled and participating in them were key to taking up curricular and pedagogical tools. While they deeply respected Mark's expertise and were grateful to be his students, they identified helpful additions to his courses.

They wished there had been more time for group work in Mark's class to
develop lessons together. Aoife would have liked opportunities to practice
teaching lessons on contentious history and get feedback from classmates.
Relatedly, they strongly advised having people share their stories about
their teaching of controversial issues and how it went during school placements—perhaps in groups of people teaching the same content. Then they
could grapple with challenges, such as how to get students to constructively
participate in discussion.

For the Citizenship course, Alex would have liked more time spent discussing a range of controversial issues (e.g., sexuality, gender, disability
discrimination, and ageism) and getting his peers' perspectives on them. He
thought that sectarianism was not the most pressing issue for many students
at this point in Northern Ireland's history. He worried that focusing on sectarianism might amplify social divisions and make prejudice a bigger part of
students' lives.

Notwithstanding Mark's explicit attention to emotion and identity, Emma
and Aoife were left with burning questions about these dimensions of teaching controversial issues. For Emma, a big question was how to balance open
discussion with sensitivity to students' family histories and communities:
"You could have someone whose father or grandfather, grandmother, whatever was killed in an atrocity or . . . committed an atrocity."

Aoife wanted to know how to teach history in a divided society when
the teacher has a personal stake in it. She tried to separate herself from her
identity in order to feel confident bringing in challenging perspectives, but
this created tension and turbulent emotions. Even with exposure to Mark's
conceptual and practical tools, she said she did not know how to respond to
student emotions and resistance to perspectives that challenged their identity.

Intercultural education scholars Zembylas and Bekerman (2008) examined the idea of *dangerous memories*. In societies divided by a legacy of
violent conflict, dangerous memories are those held by "the Other" about
their suffering as a result of that violence. The authors present two examples
from research in their own countries: In the first case, an Israeli educator
cannot let go of fixed collective memories to open himself to the suffering
of Palestinians who do not condemn terrorism. In the second case, a Greek
preservice teacher allows new experiences with Turkish Cypriots to disrupt
the historical narrative she learned from her family.

Zembylas and Bekerman asserted that teachers and students must "try very
hard to escape from being prisoners of collective memories" (p. 143). What
they call a "pedagogy of dangerous memories" involves not forgetting but

making room for both communities' memories of suffering. It goes beyond merely tolerating the Other to bearing witness, transforming one's emotional relationship with the past, and acting differently as a result, with the aim of developing solidarity. Teaching dangerous memories is exceptionally challenging, both emotionally and pedagogically.

Aoife's report of teaching in a Catholic school about why Unionists felt so threatened that they discriminated against Catholics suggests that she was taking seriously Mark's lessons about attending to different perspectives and developing empathy across communities. She taught memories that were particularly dangerous, given that Unionists were seen at her school and in her community as the oppressor. Teaching dangerous memories is profoundly challenging, especially for a young student teacher.

The remaining questions voiced by preservice teachers—how to teach struggling students in lower-track classes and how to deal with identity and emotion when teaching contentious history—resonate with educators everywhere. They underscore the paradoxical relationship between establishing authority and bringing conflict into the classroom (Britzman, 2003).

The profound challenges described by my interviewees made me question the U.K. teacher education policy of leaning on school sites to provide the lion's share of student teacher mentoring. During their two school placements, student teachers were visited by university faculty only four times and did not attend a weekly seminar. The active process of learning to teach controversy begs for reflective debriefs with peers and expert guidance. We will revisit the question of university involvement during student teaching in subsequent chapters.

KEY TAKEAWAYS

1. In Mark's courses, preservice teachers valued learning about principles of practice and were especially enthusiastic about engaging with curricular-instructional resources and dialogic pedagogies for teaching controversial issues.
2. Student teachers' ability to take risks varied and was mediated by individual identity, teaching assignments, student academic levels, and school and community contexts.
3. Student teachers encouraged their students to consider different perspectives through tools such as walking debate and role-play, political murals and catchphrases, primary and secondary sources, propaganda posters, and human rights scenarios.
4. Student teachers faced challenges such as struggling students in lower-track classes, students' reactions to controversy in hot spot communities,

their own emotions about teaching controversial issues, and limited time. These challenges constrained risk-taking.

5. Risk-taking was supported in a liberal and relatively diverse school with high-achieving students and classes that met a few times a week.

6. Advice for teacher educators included following Mark's lead, particularly with modeling, and having preservice teachers develop lessons on controversial issues together, practice teaching controversial issues in class, debrief their student teaching experiences, and discuss a wide range of controversial issues.

Chapter 3

Paula Barstow

A Pragmatic and Safe Approach to Controversy in Northern Ireland

Paula Barstow is an experienced social sciences and citizenship teacher educator as well as a human rights scholar and activist with very strong convictions. In this chapter, we see how she prepares preservice teachers to teach controversial issues in citizenship. As someone who has worked with young people in a variety of school and communities, Paula is passionate about children's rights and especially interested in developing young peoples' critical understanding of politics. These passions permeated the Citizenship methods course she taught for a mixed group of politics, sociology, and religious education preservice teachers.

Paula's conception of teaching controversial issues grew out of her experiences as a political activist, teacher, and teacher educator. In contrast with Mark Drummond, Paula is not interested in addressing students' emotional responses to conflict or building relationships across differences. In fact, she believes teachers do not have the resources and time to do so. She advocates a pragmatic approach that fits within school constraints and ensures safety for students and teachers.

At the same time, Paula advocates critical pedagogy that elevates the voices of young people and aims to create a more just society. Paula comes from what she called a "human rights and social justice" perspective rather than a "community relations" perspective. She explained that the latter is concerned with changing individual attitudes, whereas the former emphasizes "collective responsibility" for social justice at all levels of society, including government.

Paula defines controversial issues as distinct from sensitive issues. Sensitive issues often relate to the personal development curriculum, including such topics as sexual relations and healthy eating. Controversial issues are "broader, big sociopolitical issues that deeply divide opinion." She offers a

41

range of practical tools with conceptual underpinnings that allow teachers to explore these public issues with students.

BIOGRAPHICAL INFLUENCES

Paula's approach to preparing preservice teachers to teach controversial issues grew out of her political and professional background. Although younger than Mark, she too was formed by coming of age in a divided society. She grew up in a religiously and politically conservative Protestant family. But Paula became involved in human rights activism and left-wing politics as a young adult and came to support the fight for a united Ireland. Like others who want unification with the Irish Republic, she referred to Northern Ireland as "the North of Ireland."

Paula was the first Protestant in all of Ireland to teach in a (Catholic) Christian Brothers school, which she told me was "controversial in and of itself." She originally taught science and math, but began exploring political issues with students during extracurricular activities and "form classes" (advising), as well as in youth work and political organizing outside of school.

In the early 2000s, because of her human rights education background, Paula was asked to join the initiative that produced Northern Ireland's Local and Global Citizenship (LGC) curriculum. Controversial issues were embedded in the curriculum, posing a special challenge for teachers. Paula critiqued the initial approach: "I was also very involved in youth work and lobbying and human rights activism. So I was dealing with controversy quite a bit, and I became quite frustrated with the fact that teachers were not being, as I felt, adequately supported in developing their skills to teach controversial issues."

Paula participated in workshops on teaching controversial issues and how to bring along other teachers in this effort. But she felt people talked more about why some issues were so controversial, why teachers avoided them, and how important relationships and a conducive climate were for tackling them. She noted that little was said about how to actually dive into political issues themselves.

Paula left her school to become an "advisory officer" for citizenship education and trained teachers to implement the new curriculum. She noted, "So then I had to put into practice what I had been critical of in the past." This made her reflect on the principles underlying the practices she employed. She developed a model, featured in a manual for teachers, that she created in collaboration with colleagues. Paula used this model with her graduate students.

UNIVERSITY AND SCHOOL
CONTEXTS FOR CITIZENSHIP

To understand the preparation of citizenship teachers in Northern Ireland requires looking at institutional structures and policies. Both Paula and Mark had to contend with the weak status of citizenship as a school subject, but their programs differed. For example, Mark's university did not offer a Post Graduate Certificate of Education (PGCE) in Social Sciences. His Citizenship course was an elective for which he recruited preservice teachers who wanted to be agents of change. As a result, his students were a highly motivated group dedicated to the subject. By contrast, Paula's course was a requirement for the Social Sciences PGCE, which meant she worked with a larger, more politically diverse group.

University Program

In the mid-2000s, Paula became a university faculty member and took over the Social Sciences and Citizenship courses in the PGCE program. Local and Global Citizenship (LGC) was a subsidiary credential that could be added to a student's major subject. The methods course was scheduled for three hours each Monday afternoon. Because Paula taught the Monday morning course on generic learning and teaching methods to the same group of students, she was able to occasionally take time from the morning to address citizenship.

Paula's program required that social sciences teacher candidates take the citizenship course. In fact, because politics and sociology are offered only to students sixteen and older, they needed the citizenship subsidiary to get a job. Religious education candidates also took the course. As a result, Paula had twenty-four students in her course in contrast with Mark's nine.

The PGCE structure and admissions requirements at Paula's university were similar to those at Mark's. Program content included three parts: (1) Professional School-based Experience, which was the equivalent of student teaching placements; (2) Subject Studies, which were methods courses focused on major subjects such as English, mathematics, religious education, and social sciences; (3) Educational Studies, which included lectures and workshops on the role of the teacher, the Northern Ireland curriculum, assessment, learning theories, pastoral care and child protection, classroom management, and diversity and inclusion. Course schedules differed somewhat between the two universities, but the time devoted to the Citizenship course was comparable.

Paula's Social Sciences course met for a full day once a week. On other days, she held tutorials, taught other courses in the PGCE and master's programs, supervised student teachers majoring in Social Sciences, and advised doctoral students. She also had administrative duties, such as coordination of the Social Sciences PGCE. And she was involved in a center on human rights, research projects, and collaboration with other citizenship educators in different countries.

School Policy for Citizenship

Paula bemoaned the status of the citizenship curriculum in Northern Ireland. She said, "I mean it has incredibly low status within schools . . . even lower status than it has in England." At least in England there was an exam-based elective in citizenship at the high school level. Primarily, she blamed its low status on its incorporation into the Learning for Life and Work (LLW) curriculum area, which she considered "utter nonsense." Paula's explanation of the status of LGC shed light on the limitations that constrained the teacher learning opportunities of Alex (in the previous chapter) and other preservice teachers (in the next chapter) during student teaching.

Paula's account fleshes out an article by Elizabeth Worden and Alan Smith (2017) about how LGC education plays a critical role, but occupies a precarious place in the Northern Irish curriculum. She explained that initially citizenship had been promoted through its pilot project with "a huge amount" of funding from the Department of Education. Paula and others involved in developing the curriculum, training teachers, and rolling it out in schools envisioned it as a stand-alone subject in the Revised Northern Ireland Curriculum of 2007, part of a curriculum area, along with history and geography, called Environment in Society.

After three years of development work, "nearly every school in the North was delivering citizenship education in some capacity." Then, pressure from employers led to the creation of the new LLW curriculum area by the Council for the Curriculum, Examinations and Assessment (CCEA), which promoted employability and personal development. Paula said that "citizenship was plunked into it, and none of us were particularly happy about that."

In fact, she argued it was the "biggest downfall" of citizenship education. To add insult to injury, home economics was added to LLW. Because LLW was required by law, but not its components, many schools that had previously devoted time to citizenship as a separate subject were able to "just timetable for Learning for Life and Work." Instructional time was reduced, in some cases to one 35-minute period a week for all of LLW. Moreover, many teachers assigned to citizenship were not trained to teach it. Paula concluded, "So there's 101 reasons why it has low status."

Paula said that her students, because of their major subjects—also considered low status compared with mathematics or English—would be more inclined to see the value of citizenship. But they were "tainted" by their own experience in secondary schools, where it was devalued and often taught by teachers with no subject expertise. She tried to make her students understand the intellectual challenge of teaching citizenship concepts, and that they should not view it as "some kind of Mickey Mouse subject." She emphasized that not only was the subject "really substantial," but it was also "very political, very sensitive, very controversial, and they should be nervous as hell going to teach it."

As noted previously, individual schools had the autonomy to decide how much time to devote to LGC and whether to teach it through classes, integration with other subjects, and/or whole school activities. Quality of citizenship education varied tremendously across schools. Paula had worked for years with colleagues in an international network to "push policy" on citizenship education, without success. The Department of Education was not interested. School leaders were preoccupied with tracking achievement in literacy and numeracy, among other concerns. The network had decided to focus on supporting citizenship education practice by building a network of teachers committed to the subject.

Despite its low status, the LGC curriculum had ambitious aims for student learning. Teaching controversial issues was central. In fact, an entire CCEA web page was devoted to a training program on teaching controversial issues in LGC at Key Stages 3 and 4. Despite the efforts of a dedicated cadre of educators, the paradox between the undermining of citizenship education and its critical role in a post-conflict society struggling with democratic participation was stark (Worden & Smith, 2017).

A PRINCIPLED AND PRACTICAL APPROACH TO TEACHING CONTROVERSIAL ISSUES

While training teachers in Northern Ireland's citizenship curriculum, Paula developed a model for teaching controversial issues that consisted of an iterative sequence of reflection and planning activities. The model formed the basis for an intensive session with the graduate students that resembled workshops she had conducted with teachers.

A Model for Teaching Controversial Issues

According to the model, first, teachers reflect on their *stance* toward the issue, taking account of their own biases. Like Mark, Paula encouraged her students to think about their own viewpoints. Second, teachers need to set *realistic goals,* such as raising awareness and changing behaviors, not changing attitudes. She commented, "I'm at heart a human rights activist, and to my mind, there's something about rights and equality that's about changing behaviors even if attitudes don't change . . . it's like the Martin Luther King quote, 'Law cannot make my brother love me, but it can stop him from lynching me.'"

Developing young people's critical political understanding was key. Paula believed that teaching about the structural and historical roots of contemporary conflicts was crucial for deeper understanding and critical thinking. Paula talked about "layering in" this part during the upcoming session with preservice teachers: "If they're teaching about global injustice and inequalities, then they need to understand colonization . . . and debt, and they need to let the children know that these controversial issues are controversial because of the historical roots to them. If you're looking at the rise of Islamic State, then you have to think about the war in Iraq."

Third, teachers work out how they will *frame the issue*. Framing included what kinds of questions teachers pose to ground student thinking about the issue, and what content and resources would promote deeper understanding. Paula spoke at length about the importance of framing controversial questions in public, rather than personal, terms. For example, instead of asking students how they felt about ethnic minority communities, teachers should pose questions such as, "How can we evaluate Northern Ireland's response to the increase in people from ethnic minority communities?"

In addition, issues should be framed in ways that call for more viewpoints than those represented in particular school communities. She gave an example to explain how teachers could do so:

So instead of the hands up, who believes in gay marriage? Instead of that type of approach, which is, "What do *you* think? What do *you* believe?," what I tend to do is "Let's look at the issue of gay marriage, and let's look at the arguments around it, and let's look at multiple perspectives around it," and that allows people to self-position, but you're not expecting them to expose their position unless they want to.

Paula's emphasis on a pragmatic, safe, and structural approach was influenced by her critical and human rights worldview, and the legacy of conflict in the North. Framing issues as public versus personal protected both teachers and students from stigma, marginalization, and hostility in a persistently troubled political climate. In contrast with many teachers, one of her goals was to help teachers choose a framework for exploring controversy "without going to the individual level." She explained how she would teach this approach:

So, in a very practical way, how I would explain that to teachers is, "Instead of saying things like, 'How would you feel if an Orange Order Parade went through your community?' and instead of going to the feelings and the emotions of the individual, I am more inclined to go to 'Let's look at parading as an issue, and let's choose a framework that works for that.'" . . . So I say, "Let's use human rights as a frame to explore this, and let's look at this issue as a tension between competing rights. How do we work within that framework to understand the issue?"

Human rights was the framework Paula most often used. She appreciated that these principles provided "a language to look at the tensions to negotiate . . . the balancing in the name of rights in order to find a solution to a particular issue." They helped students understand the need to take on different perspectives: "I have a right to this, but I have to acknowledge that you have a right, too." She noted that "some of the more moral/sensitive issues perhaps need a slightly different framing," and said she "always work[ed] with teachers to help them choose a framework that will help them explore the issue and its controversy without going to the individual level."

After framing the issue, teachers think about the range of *pedagogical strategies* they might use, for example, jigsaw or deliberation. She would provide them with a toolkit of strategies from which to choose.

Then they do a *pedagogical risk assessment* in which they ask themselves questions to ensure that they're providing opportunities for exploring multiple perspectives, expression of everyone's ideas, debriefing, and closure. Paula used the term "risk assessment" for important reasons:

Because when I'm working with teachers, it's coming from this idea that they are scared of teaching controversial issues. . . . [A]nd it's not just risk to them. It's risks to the young people. . . . So, yes, a walking debate . . . passes the test in terms of everyone can position themselves, so everyone can feel that they've contributed. But will they feel exposed in it, if it's a particular issue?

Paula's use of the term "risks" referred to potential threats, both to good teaching and to classroom participants. She wanted preservice teachers to draw on their disciplinary knowledge in teaching controversial issues and veer away from students' personal and community attitudes. She felt strongly about preparing teachers to be pragmatic and ensure safety given the institutional conditions of schools. She distinguished her approach from others that aimed for social cohesion:

I think a lot of the strategies that were developed to deal with controversial issues here in the North came out of youth sector, kind of residential work, identity exploration work, and pragmatically speaking, in a classroom situation, you've got half an hour, forty minutes. . . . I personally think it's irresponsible to rip the heart out of a child and to expose their prejudice or racism, sectarianism, and then twenty minutes later, send them off to French.

Paula drew a clear line between the roles of youth worker and classroom teacher, and critiqued approaches that did not fit the constraints of schools and protect young people.

Containing the Risks of Teaching Controversial Issues

Paula's considered approach exemplifies the theory of *contained risk-taking* (Pace, 2019). The model she taught emphasized containing potential threats, both real and perceived, that teaching controversial issues poses to teachers. The pedagogical risk assessment explicitly addressed concerns she felt teachers should face proactively.

Paula criticized whole group discussion as the centerpiece of a lesson because she saw it as too risky—difficult-to-manage tensions could arise quickly (Barton & McCully, 2007) and some students inevitably felt their voices weren't heard. Like Mark, she used plenaries to "pull ideas together" that emerged from small group discussions.

Paula advocated a variety of more contained discussion methods, such as jigsaw, deliberation (Structured Academic Controversy), carousel conversation, circular brainstorm, speed debate, walking debate, and silent conversation (written instead of verbal). As the course progressed, she modeled all of them, endorsing them as scaffolds for discussion: "You don't put kids into a group and ask them to discuss something. You give them stimulus, and you give them structure, and you support them. . . . even if it's just going from a Think-Pair-Share, that's it, just having little simple strategies to support them and develop in their discussions."

What do preservice teachers need to teach controversial issues? Paula answered this by addressing the unique conditions of student teaching in someone else's classroom:

> I think what's different about student teachers is they're dropped . . . into another teacher's class . . . I'm kind of saying, "What do we have immediate control over?" They have immediate control over their stance. They have immediate control over their goal. They have immediate control over the methods that they use. They have immediate control over the resources and the perspectives that they pull on. They don't have immediate control over their climate, their classroom climate. They don't have time to take the children away on a two-week residential to build trust. They just have to get on with it.

She emphasized with her preservice teachers the importance of thinking through their stance, goals, framing, and methods to be prepared to work realistically within constraints, yet not shy away from exploring challenging issues.

PREPARING PRESERVICE TEACHERS FOR CONTROVERSIAL ISSUES IN CITIZENSHIP

In fall 2016 and winter 2017, I observed Paula and her citizenship class, composed of 24 preservice politics, sociology, and religious education (RE) teachers, for five class sessions. Each lasted three hours, except for a double session on October 10th. In a class of 24, a handful of students were Catholic and the rest were Protestant. One student was from the Republic of Ireland; the rest from the North.

Workshop on Teaching Controversial Issues

On October 10, 2016, Paula conducted an intensive workshop on teaching controversial issues in which she put into practice the various principles and methods she had discussed with me (Pace, 2017, 2019). In the session, Paula involved all twenty-four participants in working with conceptual and practical tools. She blended the presentation of her model for teaching controversial issues with modeling of classroom activities that utilized resources she and others developed, and involved students in planning exercises and reflective conversations. She offered extensive guidance based on her teaching experience and principles of practice. Importantly, she encouraged students to talk about their experiences, anxieties, and opinions.

Paula introduced the workshop by stressing her commitment to teaching controversial issues and her earlier frustration at the lack of practical training. She gave a quick preview of the session and said the day would emphasize practical methods after she laid groundwork. By the end of the session, she told students, they should be able to:

1. Describe the key features of a controversial issue.
2. Justify your own perspective in relation to teacher "goal" and "stance" when teaching controversial issues.
3. Identify practical strategies for creating conducive climate.
4. Frame controversial issues in a "safer" manner.
5. Select appropriate classroom methods for the "safe" teaching of controversial issues.
6. Apply the "toolkit" of concepts and methods to other teaching contexts.

Paula said she would provide a variety of methods for them to try in their student teaching placements. The class would reflect on how they had worked when they reconvened in February and would write essays on the teacher's role in handling sensitive and controversial issues at the end of the school year. The following vignette illustrates Paula's skillful approach in engaging preservice teachers in this venture.

Paula facilitated the class's dive into the workshop with a spectrum activity in which each person wrote down controversial issues related to their major subject on Post-its. They expressed their level of comfort or anxiety in teaching them by placing the Post-its on a spectrum, laid out on the floor, with "happy to teach" at one end and "wouldn't touch with a barge pole" at the other end. Paula encouraged them to be honest, saying, "You should be anxious about teaching some issues, so don't think it's a failure." Issues were placed all over the spectrum and ranged from personal topics such as sexuality, suicide, and abortion to societal topics such as refugees, immigration, and the Troubles. The room was buzzing as preservice teachers chatted informally about what they observed and why issues were placed in particular locations.

With everyone back in their seats, Paula facilitated discussion, first in pairs or trios, and then with the whole group, to "crystallize" the informal conversations. She asked the class to identify factors that might influence whether an issue is controversial or not, and how people felt about teaching them. Individuals raised questions, told stories, and shared knowledge that pointed to the influence of religion, student ages, parental attitudes, school location, school ethos, and political climate.

Paula followed with an interactive PowerPoint presentation. The slides defined controversial issues as questions that "deeply divide society, challenge personally held values and beliefs, generate conflicting explanations, evoke emotional responses, [and] cause students to feel threatened and confused." As contextual factors, they cited school location, school ethos, and sociopolitical climate. The presentation offered a rationale for teaching controversial issues that included their relevance, enduring significance, preparation for democratic citizenship, and development of interpersonal skills and critical thinking.

During the presentation, Paula drew out the preservice teachers' prior knowledge and shared her own experiences, keeping up an amusing commentary throughout. Paula expressed her concern for her students as "beginning teachers . . . being plopped into this." She said they needed a practical approach to "deliver these issues in thirty-five, forty-minute slots . . . that builds your confidence" and allowed them to "try something and see if it works and evaluate it and then become more and more of a skilled professional."

Paula concluded with her priority: "So unashamedly, I am going to write there: 'Safety' is the word of the day . . . we need safety for the teachers and we need safety for the pupils." Paula juxtaposed the risks of teaching controversial issues with what she would be teaching them about taking control of their goals, stance, framework, and, most importantly, the methods they would use. All of this would go into their "toolkit" for teaching controversial issues.

Paula's introduction, opening discussion activities, and PowerPoint presentation set the workshop's tone. Her brief remarks about her personal experience set up the session as an antidote to frustration about the lack of practical approaches in teacher education. Goals were clearly spelled out and were built on aims that spoke to teacher concerns. The spectrum activity gave people a chance to express enthusiasm or trepidation about teaching controversial issues. The discussion deepened their understanding of contextual influences that affect teaching.

Further on, the PowerPoint provided scholarly definitions, research findings, and reasons behind this ambitious and risky practice. The conclusion to the first part of the workshop assured preservice teachers that, despite challenges, there were key elements of teaching controversy that remained under their control, which would be the focus of the rest of the session. By explicitly acknowledging preservice teachers' anxieties, Paula empathized with her students, while promising them they would gain tools they needed to succeed as student teachers.

In the next part of the workshop, Paula involved the class in working through these practical elements, such as setting realistic goals; reflecting on teacher stance, disclosure, and roles; and creating a conducive classroom climate. To get people thinking about teacher stance, Paula elicited reactions to the following statements:

Teacher should be neutral in classroom.
Teacher should challenge a pupil's view if they don't agree.
Teacher should challenge pupil's view if they think it's offensive.
Teacher should support a pupil's view if it's not being respected.
Teacher should play devil's advocate.
Teacher should express their own view.

Paula followed up with a slide on different roles teachers can take, such as neutral or impartial facilitator, devil's advocate, ally, and challenger. Students asserted that teachers must get across important points related to legal, ethical, and moral issues. For example, they must counter overt racism. Paula agreed that there are non negotiables, such as racism. But with most issues, teachers should present their own perspectives as well as critiques of them, which would make room for student dissent. She warned that pushing students to think differently depended on how well a teacher knew them.

Paula segued into the topic of conducive climate. Starting with a carousel conversation in which the class formed two concentric circles with people paired off, she prompted participants to talk about what could go wrong when teaching controversial issues. Paula gave concrete suggestions, such as proactively sending a letter home to parents, informing the department head, consulting with the mentor teacher, and asking for the principal's support. She showed a slide about how to create shared classroom agreements and provided a tool called FRED, which stands for (F) freedom of expression, within a (R) respectful environment, where everyone is seen as (E) equal, and (D) diversity is celebrated. FRED could be adopted as a metaphorical member of the class and used to filter discussion. The teacher might ask, "How can we discuss this in a way FRED would be happy with?"

Picking up speed due to time constraints, Paula talked about how to frame controversial issues, citing a human rights perspective as an example. She spoke about how to choose effective pedagogical methods. Turning to the citizenship curriculum, she said the next activity would focus on the concept of sectarianism, which was located in the theme of Diversity and Inclusion, and represented a crucial and potentially explosive topic. The following vignette shows how Paula taught the class to take up this topic in a "safer" way that contained the risks of teaching particularly charged material.

Paula modeled the use of a curricular resource that preservice teachers found quite intriguing. Small groups received a set of thirty cards bearing different symbols connected with the two main groups in Northern Ireland. They represented flags, murals, religious iconography, political parties, cultural activities, and historical events, and elicited reactions from students who, by virtue of their own identity, were unfamiliar with some symbols and provoked by others.

Each group had to decide how to sort the cards into categories. When Paula saw people automatically sorting into Catholic versus Protestant, she challenged them to think beyond religion. She said teachers should be prepared for visceral, negative reactions from students. She advised them to get students thinking about different viewpoints, rather than posing emotive questions such as, "Which symbol makes you most angry?"

Following the symbols activity debrief, Paula had the class work to develop a definition of "sectarianism," perhaps the most provocative term in the North. First she asked each individual to write down their own definition and identify the causes of sectarianism. Then she formed small groups and distributed the definitions. Paula asked each group to create their own combined definition and point out where they agreed or disagreed. She reminded the class to use FRED to govern their deliberations.

In a subsequent debrief, students read the definitions created by their groups. One group did not arrive at a "succinct definition." Andrew explained that the term's meaning is "very complex." He said the group agreed that sectarianism is not based on religious convictions, but is more about politics, culture, and national identity. Paula asked the class how the term is used in the media. Sean, part of Andrew's group, said it was "reductionist." It split the country into Catholics and Protestants, and did not address economic and political factors.

Paula said she would hear the word used to "demonize certain identities and expression of them." John pushed back, saying some expressions of identity serve to rub others' noses in it. Paula interpreted his comment to mean displaying identity in a "triumphalist way." Corinne argued that discussions of sectarianism come from "moderates" and "middle class" outsiders labeling certain communities as problematic.

Paula disclosed her own view: "I have to agree, and I'm laying my cards on the table. One use of the word is to demonize working class communities. We need to think about how we're passing on the dominant view to young people. . . . the assumption that expressing identity is sectarian." She asked how they would teach the complexity of a term that is used as a problematic label to Year 8's (12-year-olds). Students responded enthusiastically:

Student 1: Just the way you did. Bar none.
Student 2: Can I borrow your cards?

The activities Paula modeled and the debriefs, including her guidance, showed the class how the core issue of Northern Ireland's divided society could be approached through different discussion-based approaches. The card sort—with teacher facilitation—made students confront their initial reflex to divide symbols as Catholic or Protestant, pushing them to think past a binary division of society. Although the activity did not directly engage students in deliberation on a controversial issue, it provided a powerful entry point to a critical question: "Should potentially divisive symbols be displayed?" (Barton & McCully, 2007, p. 18).

In this second activity, students worked together to construct the best definition possible for a highly charged term. The debrief drew out the controversy embedded in the word "sectarian" as the class talked about how it gets used to "demonize" and drive wedges between groups. Paula disclosed her own views. Andrew, one of the preservice teachers I interviewed, used both of the activities during student teaching.

Paula talked later in the day about making time for students to "self-position"—whether publicly or privately—at the end of lessons and showed a variety of possible methods. But she was adamant that teachers not expose individuals by asking them to divulge personal information or opinions, something that could put young people at risk. And, notably, class participants did not talk about their personal experiences related to the conflict.

Human Rights and Controversial Issues

In subsequent classes, Paula built on the daylong teaching controversies session. The following week's class was devoted to human rights, utilizing a rich curriculum resource she developed for high school citizenship classes. Paula told students that human rights were "deeply controversial," and to take note of the controversies as they arose.

After exploring her students' knowledge of the topic, she modeled several activities from the curriculum pack. Following a discussion of human rights definitions and core principles, the class learned about the "historical antecedents" of human rights by teaching one another about worldwide historical contributors through a "Meet and Greet" activity.

Paula then presented the post-World War II context for development of the Universal Declaration of Human Rights (UDHR), asking students to look at the document critically and to identify potential controversies. Students pointed out tensions between state protections versus concerns about the role of states in suppressing human rights, special treatment for mothers and children versus equality for all, marriage rights versus religious beliefs, and freedom to protest versus security.

Paula asked the class to consider contradictions between the concept of universal human rights and the development of the UDHR out of a white, Eurocentric, Judeo-Christian individualistic worldview that clashed with perspectives of some other cultures. She noted that different places had their own concepts of human rights. When the United Nations tried to turn the declaration into a convention, which would have inscribed it as international law, the effort failed. Instead, conventions were written on specific issues, such as torture, discrimination against women, and rights of children.

One of the activities Paula modeled was a walking debate to think about balancing human rights when they conflict. Similar to the four corners activity that Mark modeled, people positioned themselves in relation to a statement the teacher made. Those who strongly agreed stood at one end of the room, those who strongly disagreed at the other end, and those who weren't sure in the middle. As the discussion proceeded, people could change their positions. Paula advised against using this approach with extremely controversial issues to avoid exposing students. Her use of the walking debate is illustrated in the following vignette:

> The room was filled with 24 standing preservice teachers waiting for Paula to begin. The first statement was about the right to freedom of expression, whether everyone should be able to say whatever they think. The class clustered on the Agree side, except for a handful in the middle. Paula asked those standing in different positions to explain their reasoning. One person said people should be

able to criticize anything, including religious doctrine. Another said people do not have the right to make racist comments.

Paula delved deeper, suggesting that context be taken into account. When she asked about free speech in a private space, people moved to the Agree side. When she asked about making racist comments in the workplace, everyone moved to Disagree. Paula further complicated the question by asking about freedom to make racist comments on the radio.

The next provocative statement was, "Everyone has the right to be free from torture." Students moved to the middle or the Agree side. Paula then relayed a scenario in which a bomb was primed, you knew the person who planted the bomb, but you didn't know where or when it was going to go off.

The preservice teachers shifted their positions. One justified torture on the basis of saving endangered human life. Others chimed in about torture being okay in extreme cases. The discussion got a bit heated as people questioned when someone should take the law into their own hands, why someone who took away the right to life should be protected, and what gave countries the right to go to war if individuals must be free from torture.

Paula told the class they'd be looking at the convention concerning war in February. She showed a slide that listed three types of rights: Absolute, limited, and qualified. She passed out a worksheet for students to record ideas from the walking debate. The sheet included spaces to note the human rights explored, circumstances in which they should be limited, and other human rights they should be balanced against.

The walking debate was different from previous activities I observed in Paula's course in that it asked participants to express their opinions. Paula modeled how to interject questions to push students' thinking. As usual, she bolstered the activity with a resource, in this case the worksheet, that scaffolded learning by eliciting written reflection and content knowledge.

Preparing to Think as Curriculum Designers

The citizenship curriculum resources that Paula and others had developed were critically important because the official curriculum was open-ended. In schools, preservice and beginning teachers have access to citizenship booklets and resources, as well as schemes of work (units) created by teachers at the school. Still, Paula wanted her preservice teachers to learn how to design new curriculum and respond to student interest in current events.

On October 31st, Paula had her students brainstorm about how to teach a legal case involving a Belfast bakery's refusal on religious grounds to fill an order for a cake decorated with "Support Gay Marriage." As shown in the following vignette, preservice teachers confronted the need to understand issues thoroughly and make them accessible and relevant to young people.

Paula gave the class a scenario: "Pupils say they want to discuss the Asher's Bakery case. What do you do?" In small groups, they were to plan a lesson or series of lessons. She stipulated, "I'm not asking what you think. I'm asking how you would go about teaching" the controversy. But to prepare, they should reflect individually about their stance on the issue. She reminded the class to think about how they would frame the issues, what were the key questions, what methodologies they would use, and what problems they should anticipate. Paula also said to remember that "FRED is part of your group."

After about twenty minutes, Paula addressed the class: "I think what's quite good is no one's gotten there yet. It's complicated." She asked each group to "feed back what's tough about this, the best way to approach it, what kinds of deliberations have you been having?"

Caitlin volunteered that one challenge was not knowing enough about the issue, the various perspectives on it, and the rationale for the court's decision. The framework could include religious conscience on one side and equal access to goods or freedom of expression on the other side. A question for their group was the age-appropriateness of the issue. Luke commented, "You're probably not going to come to a conclusion; that's not the point. It's showing people on different sides coming down differently."

Margaret said she wondered about the case's "impact on kids." Corinne added that it was "very personal." She explained her point: "Most likely someone would identify as gay or lesbian in your class." James agreed on the "whole complexity of it," and said it was "hard to frame our intentions" and "keep it safe."

Paula said student teachers would need to run their plan by their mentor teacher and/or administrator. She suggested using "simulation or role play" to give students different perspectives. And she advised that focusing on the legalities of the case was probably not as accessible or as interesting to young people as the issue of competing rights. This could lead to exploring the various debates around gay marriage to broaden the case beyond "gay rights versus evangelical Christians."

Paula then asked, "Where would you go at the end of it?" Margaret joked, "The pub!" The class laughed, and Paula added, "With your Year 8s!" She reminded everyone to "provide some opportunity to express what they think" without putting pupils on the spot with the question: "Do you think Asher [the bakery] was right?" Instead they could ask "What are the convincing arguments you've heard? What are the agreements and disagreements? . . . What have they learned?"

The lesson planning activity revealed some of the particular challenges of teaching controversial issues. Preservice teachers grappled with the gaps in their own knowledge about the bakery case and the difficulty of identifying the relevant issues. They raised crucial questions about how young people would be affected, depending on their identity and age. And they asked how these factors should shape their teaching approach.

Paula reassured them that their questions were well founded. She hoped the preservice teachers would conclude that this issue required a series of lessons. Later in the year, she showed them how to develop a concept map for each citizenship theme and how to create activities.

The focus of the February block was LGC at Key Stage 4 and the aim was to "support them in making links between the different (citizenship) concepts and developing a curriculum based on contemporary issues." She explained, "So what I'm trying to do is use a contemporary issue as a way of getting them to . . . see how you create a clear conceptual pathway for children through a complex issue."

Paula's commitment to addressing real challenges of classroom teaching was evident when she responded to the first student teaching placements. Based on her own and others' observations, she worried that student teachers were overwhelming their students with too much complexity. Paula told me she told her students, "'Strip that back. Your eleven, twelve, thirteen, four-teen (year old students), how do you take less and give a nice clear conceptual pathway through it?'"

In class sessions, she had them work in small groups on curriculum development related to immigration, refugees, and asylum seekers. Previously, she had modeled some planning on issues related to conflict, war, and humanitarian law. She acknowledged how difficult it was for her students to plan on their own. Yet she thought it was important that they be humbled by gaps in their knowledge. She wanted them to become aware of the developmental readiness of their young pupils and challenges of teaching a current issue that goes beyond asking their classes, "Did you see that last night in the news? Let's talk about it."

Paula extended the session on immigration with a deliberation (Structured Academic Controversy) on whether free movement of labor across international borders should be allowed. The class split into groups of four and then pairs within each group. Each pair read a short text and constructed an argument either in favor of free movement or against it to present to the other pair. Each side got two minutes for making their case, without interruption. Then the other side got two minutes to respond.

Paula called time and asked them to swap sides, construct a new best argument, and repeat the process. Finally, the groups of four had a few minutes to discuss their own perspectives on the issue. Paula advised that, with thirty-minute classes, teachers should devote one class to reading and thinking about the issue or watching a video, or they could have students read and highlight the text for homework. Then in the next class they could conduct a deliberation. Paula reviewed the benefits of deliberation for student learning and discussion dynamics, noting it was less confrontational than debate. As we will see in the next chapter, Margaret successfully tried it out in her first placement.

At the end of the year, Paula's preservice teachers wrote an essay, drawing on scholarship and their student teaching experiences, about the role of teachers when handling sensitive and controversial issues. This made them wrestle with tensions among neutrality, openness to all points of view, and taking a stand against hate and injustice. It made them reflect on their experiences and how they squared with theory.

PREPARING FOR THE CHARGED CLASSROOM

Paula's approach was permeated with her deeply held conviction that teachers need practical tools to do the following:

1. Teach controversial issues safely and pragmatically.
2. Address young people's developmental needs and interests.
3. Teach citizenship with intellectual integrity.

The model she taught married these tools with elements of reflective practice.

Paula wanted her preservice teachers to think through the risks of teaching controversy so they could contain them. At the same time, she wanted teachers to get students to wrestle with conflicting perspectives. She taught them about framing issues, a protocol for classroom norms, and discussion methods that engaged young people without exposing them, invading their privacy, or making them feel vulnerable.

To address the needs and interests of students, Paula stressed the importance of thinking about teaching from the perspective of young people. She showed her class many different tools that included curricular resources and pedagogical methods for motivating student participation. She had the preservice teachers think about how to teach challenging material to different age groups.

Paula demonstrated the intellectual grounding of the citizenship curriculum with the informative resources she used, the background knowledge she provided, and the teaching examples she gave. Preservice teachers learned new facts and concepts from the lessons she taught. Paula challenged them with curriculum design tasks to help them develop students' conceptual understanding with accurate knowledge.

Paula believed that all citizenship teachers would inevitably be teaching controversial issues because the official curriculum was saturated with them.

She connected her course to the interests, skills, and orientations of the 24 religious education, politics, and sociology majors in her class. Through modeling creative activities, empathic conversation, expert guidance, and intellectual challenge, Paula made her preservice teachers grapple with their anxieties, knowledge base, and stances on teaching controversial issues in a divided society.

Paula's approach addressed the tensions between educational ideals, such as giving students' voice, and classroom realities, such as time constraints, which in previous work I have characterized as the "charged classroom" (Pace, 2015). Although hopeful, Paula was realistic about the constraints of student teaching in particular. She told me, "I think what preservice teachers always struggle with in terms of learning how to be a teacher is learning how to be themselves in someone else's classroom, and that's very, very hard." Therefore, the model she taught was "less dependent upon classroom climate and relationships and more about the framing and the choice of methods"— elements over which they had control.

In the next chapter, we will see that Paula's preservice teachers took up conceptual and practical tools she taught them. Although each differed in what and how they taught, all asked students to explore hard questions. Paula's model of reflective practice in teaching controversial issues is a remarkable contribution to the education of both preservice and inservice teachers. Her contained risk-taking approach helps us navigate the charged classroom in politically turbulent times and polarized societies.

KEY TAKEAWAYS

1. Preservice teachers need a practical model for teaching controversial issues that includes teacher stance, realistic goals, public framing of issues, pedagogical strategies, and pedagogical risk assessment.
2. Risks of teaching controversial issues such as emotional reactions and exposure of identity must be contained through careful planning, proactive communication, and reflection to keep students and teachers safe.
3. Teachers need to use inclusive discussion methods such as walking debate, deliberation (Structured Academic Controversy), carousel conversation, and silent (written) conversation that encourage all students to participate.
4. Teacher educators must be realistic and prepare preservice teachers for teaching controversial issues under constraints such as short class periods and the low status of citizenship education in schools.
5. Preservice teachers need to practice developing curriculum around controversial issues that has intellectual integrity but is developmentally appropriate for young people.

Chapter 4

What Paula's Students Learned

How did Paula's preservice teachers make sense of teaching controversial issues? Which of the tools that she taught were applied in student teaching? And how were these novice teachers' efforts supported or constrained? This chapter looks at how a group of Paula's graduate students approached controversial questions in citizenship and other classes they taught. Importantly, it shows that even under institutional constraints, they took carefully planned risks to teach in ways that differed from how they themselves were taught in secondary school.

Margaret, Sean, Luke, and Andrew, all students in Paula's Citizenship course, were a diverse group, representing Catholic, Protestant, working-class, and middle-class backgrounds, and holding different educational interests and political leanings. Margaret and Sean grew up during the Troubles, while Luke and Andrew were too young to remember it. I interviewed Sean and Andrew in the fall, winter, and early summer. Luke was not available for the second interview, and Margaret was not available for the final interview, so I interviewed Luke in fall and summer, and Margaret in fall and winter. All the interviews took place after Paula's daylong session on teaching controversial issues.

PROFILES OF PRESERVICE TEACHERS

Teaching is shaped by identity, which includes educational backgrounds, professional interests, and sociopolitical orientations. Like Mark's preservice teachers, Paula's graduate students were a fascinating and diverse group.

Margaret and Sean were enrolled in the Social Sciences PGCE, which meant they took both Paula's Citizenship and Social Sciences methods classes. Their major subject was politics, and they stood out as educators committed to social justice. Both were raised Catholic in West Belfast, leaned to the left politically, and were already in their early forties—substantially older than the other students. And both teachers had childhood memories of growing up in Belfast during the conflict.

Margaret remembered security checks, harassment by British soldiers, and buses on fire. She had an uncle who was blown up in a pub and a cousin murdered by the Shankill Butchers, a vicious Loyalist paramilitary gang. Margaret had a nuanced outlook. Her religious, cultural, and national Catholic Irish identity was important to her, but she wished people in her country were not so fixated on religious and political identifications.

In her Catholic secondary school, Margaret encountered Irish politics and the Troubles through a politics teacher she regarded as "brilliant" at the time. He stressed the need for dialogue in Northern Ireland, but did not engage the students in any kind of discussion. Otherwise, teachers did not deal with controversial issues at all and students were expected to passively absorb knowledge.

Margaret studied politics at university, but had followed a career unrelated to politics. After having children, she became a special needs assistant teacher in a primary school and subsequently enrolled in the Social Sciences PGCE. Several weeks into the course, she described it as transformative, because as a mother and wife she felt she had lost part of her identity. The PGCE classes revived her keen interest in politics.

Sean also remembered the Troubles. He recalled regular searches on his way to school. Like Margaret, members of his family were killed. As a young adult, he volunteered for an organization that pressed for compensation for victims of state violence, which developed his interest in human rights and education. Sean said he attended a Christian Brothers grammar school and was influenced by three "very, very good" teachers, all politically left-of-center. However, he never studied controversial issues as a student. Irish politics was avoided and potentially controversial subjects were taught in a dry, factual manner.

Sean worked for years at an alternative school for Belfast youth where he taught Learning for Life and Work, which included citizenship, employability, and personal development. Sean said that teaching young people dealing with poverty and other obstacles gave him a strong orientation toward critical pedagogy.

Luke and Andrew were both enrolled in the Religious Education (RE) PGCE. Their RE tutor—Paula's colleague—also advocated the teaching of controversial issues and taught the relevance of religion to current events.

Luke, from a Protestant, Unionist family, grew up in Belfast. He did not have strong political views on national identity, but he loved Ireland as a country and considered himself "Northern Irish." Coming from a "pretty moderate" background, he said "the Northern Irish question" was something he needed to think about more. Like the others, Luke was not exposed to controversial issues at school, though it "naturally came up" in his high school politics class. In fact, his teacher had taught politics to prisoners during the conflict.

Luke identified as an open-minded evangelical Christian who had been taught that it was all right to question. He studied theology at university and, before enrolling in the PGCE, worked for a year at an affluent, multiethnic grammar school as an assistant to a special needs student.

Andrew also was enrolled in the Religious Education PGCE. He grew up in a middle-class area outside of Belfast in a Protestant, Unionist family. He said his character and humanistic values were shaped by Christianity and that overemphasis on different denominations in Northern Ireland was problematic. He felt proud of his "Northern Irish" identity, but had no objection to being called Irish, given that the island was a single country until the 1920s, when it was divided by the British. He said he favored remaining part of the United Kingdom because of the benefits of union, but did not "identify massively with Britishness."

Andrew studied politics, history, and religious studies during his last two years in grammar school. The teachers used a mix of approaches, but mostly the focus was on learning from texts and lecture. Andrew majored in theology and history at university.

Margaret and Sean's schooling predated the development of citizenship as a school subject. Both Andrew and Luke said that, in their school experience, citizenship was low status and not taken seriously by teachers or students. All four appreciated the opportunity to learn how to teach it well.

CONCEPTIONS OF CONTROVERSIAL ISSUES

Paula was one of two teacher educators in my study to explicitly define the term "controversial issues" to her class. Her graduate students said they developed conceptions of controversial issues, studied their relevance to contemporary life, and examined what teaching them entailed. They learned the importance of getting students to think critically about contemporary issues, form their own opinions, and express them respectfully. However, in some cases, their commonsense, rather than theoretically informed understanding of what were controversial issues, persisted.

Andrew defined controversial issues as Paula did, that is, "issues that deeply divide society or that deeply divide opinion in society." Although not discussed explicitly in class, he distinguished settled versus open issues (see

Hess, 2009), citing examples: "Like someone who publicly today in 2017 proclaims that, say, Catholics aren't equal to Protestants will likely be condemned, whereas . . . somebody who stands up and publicly states that abortion should be legalized isn't going to be widespread condemned. They're going to have support alongside those people who condemn them as well."

Sean acknowledged in the second interview that he had been confused about the concept of controversial issues, realizing he thought it had to do with *his* personal reaction to a particular issue. In a class session on developing curriculum ideas for teaching about immigration and refugees, Paula helped clarify his thinking. Sean learned the definition had to do with whether society is split on the issue and struggling with it, even if he himself were not. Sean said controversial issues in Northern Ireland included questions related to national identity, sectarianism, homophobia, and immigrants and refugees.

Interestingly, Margaret's understanding was somewhat different. She defined controversial issues as those that potentially provoke an emotional response, division among young people, and/or difficulty seeing different perspectives because of entrenched beliefs. When asked whether she had taught any controversial issues, she spoke about Islamophobia, sectarianism, refugees, and more, but acknowledged the absence of controversy in her approach to these topics. Margaret seemed to conflate sensitive and controversial topics with issues (Journell, 2016). It was not until I asked specifically about deliberation, having heard her mention it in Paula's class, that she talked about trying this approach with two different issues.

Luke defined controversial issues as those with conflicting perspectives that teachers should help students understand. He gave abortion and euthanasia as examples from Religious Education.

Like the preservice teachers in Mark Drummond's classes, these four students understood the contextual nature of controversy. What was controversial in one school community might not be in another. They espoused the idea, discussed in class, that school ethos and community culture should shape the approaches teachers adopt.

KEY LEARNING FROM CITIZENSHIP COURSE

Paula's preservice teachers learned an impressive array of active learning strategies for teaching controversial issues. They also got a conceptual grounding through class sessions and relevant literature, which they brought to bear in their end-of-year essays on the teacher's role in handling sensitive and controversial issues.

Pedagogical Tools and Principles

Paula's preservice citizenship teachers talked about learning the importance of approaching controversy in sensitive ways that open discussion instead of avoiding issues or treating them superficially. They agreed that teaching controversial issues revolves around facilitating active learning that challenges assumptions, explores diverse perspectives, and encourages students to come to their own conclusions. Sean said he was learning the pedagogical tools to facilitate a democratic classroom where student voices were heard, within the constraints of curriculum and timetable.

The teachers spoke about structuring activities so that students express an initial reaction, learn things that challenge their thinking, and have the opportunity to think and possibly re-position themselves. They most appreciated Paula's modeling of *structured small group discussion activities* that engage students in interactive learning, open dialogue, and allow room for students to develop their own positions.

A general strategy they learned to keep students and teacher safe was *asking students to analyze different positions* to encourage understanding of diverse perspectives. As Paula contended, they saw this approach as better than asking students to state their own views. Margaret believed examining different points of view would encourage them to question assumptions: "To really challenge their belief systems . . . you're forcing them to look at the other perspective. You're not asking them for their opinion [at first]. It's about looking at the other perspectives and understanding why people think what they do."

Each of Paula's students had their favorite activities. Both Luke and Andrew talked about how the small group discussion on defining sectarianism brought out the complexity of the question. Andrew spoke about sorting identity cards several times. He found it "eye opening" that despite being open-minded, he was unfamiliar with certain symbols of Irish identity. He tried the activity with his class and found it rewarding.

Both Andrew and Margaret were impressed with the "speed debate" on war crimes in which Paula flashed pictures of scenes from war and students had to quickly decide whether particular acts were within or outside the rules of war. Margaret explained, "Rather than going into your class saying, 'Here are the laws of war,' . . . You're saying, 'What would you do? Make a decision. Do you allow this? Do you not allow this?'"

Although the teachers did not highlight deliberations as a preferred tool, we will see that two of them conducted them during student teaching, although Andrew's deliberation was modified substantially because of time constraints.

Preparation and Planning

The preservice teachers learned the importance of *careful preparation* for teaching controversial issues. Preparation involves developing subject matter knowledge, finding rich resources, and reflecting on their own points of view about an issue. Before teaching an issue, teachers need to read widely and understand multiple perspectives. At the same time, teachers do not hold all the answers and should cultivate egalitarian authority relations that encourage students to form their own views.

Sean referred to a Paulo Freire quote about the need for teachers to know their subject inside and out before trying to foster a democratic classroom. He realized he needed to review and update material he had studied at university years before. Additionally, he learned that good preparation meant "putting yourself in positions you may not be comfortable with personally."

Andrew appreciated the class session on planning a unit on immigration and refugees. "So the whole idea of planning carefully and asking these questions, like why is this idea controversial and what should I expect from the pupils? How do I actually feel and how do I maintain the balance [between different perspectives]?" Sean noted the importance of thinking through goals for students and then figuring out which approaches best meet those goals.

Teacher Stance

The preservice teachers spoke about *teacher stance*, which they considered during class and focused on in their end-of- year essays. Margaret specified that teachers need to "make sure your bias doesn't come out, or that you allow the children to self-position without you influencing them." Sean said Paula made him think about how he would respond to students' potential questions about his political and ideological affinities, given his strong beliefs. Relatedly, Sean and Margaret spoke about being conscious of language they used in their classes that might reflect political affiliation.

Luke talked about learning to develop a posture of openness with his students. He tried to learn about students' preoccupations instead of making quick judgments. His final essay drew on Palmer Parker's (2010) concepts of openness, boundaries, and hospitality. He wrote about sharing a class contract with his classes that held both teacher and students to norms for respectful listening.

Over the course of the year, Andrew grappled with his initial belief that teachers must be neutral. In his final essay, he explained how he shifted from neutrality to "inclusive situated engagement" (Kelly & Brandes, 2001). He wrote about an incident in which "one pupil made a comment implying that he supported the viewpoints of the Nazi party regarding Judaism." Andrew said he made it "clear that to joke about an issue such as the Holocaust was prohibited" in his classroom, but that the teacher "could not change" the student's "personal viewpoints."

Later in his essay, he reflected critically on his approach: "This, to me, seems to have been a clear example of neutrality's limitations—if a teacher remains *truly* neutral, there exists the potential for unchallenged discrimination in the classroom." He spoke about his conceptual shift in our third interview. Andrew said, "Initially . . . I believed that it was possible to be neutral, but then I've realized if by definition neutral means not taking a stance at all, then you're not even allowed to take an anti-racist stance. . . . So I think for me to go into teaching a topic like that, actively encouraging the values of tolerance and respect, then I'm already sort of, I'm not neutral." It is important to note that Andrew was not advocating teacher disclosure of specific political views, but rather upholding democratic values in the classroom (Miller-Lane et al., 2006, p. 38).

STUDENT TEACHING EXPERIENCES WITH TEACHING CONTROVERSIAL ISSUES

All four of Paula's preservice teachers reported teaching at least one discrete lesson that centered on a contemporary controversial issue. According to Kitson and McCully's (2005) categorization of teachers, they took risks engaging students in these questions. They had students analyze resources that expressed divergent views and employed dialogic pedagogies, despite constraints over which they had no control. Andrew and Margaret consistently taught in ways that were very different from the teacher-centered, didactic methods they had been subjected to, utilizing active learning methods as much as possible.

Table 4.1 lays out the key controversial issues preservice teachers taught, the school subjects, and the tools they used.

Tackling Issues in a Race against the Clock

Andrew was able to teach more controversial issues than the other preservice teachers, but short class periods squeezed his lessons. He sent me numerous lesson plans and materials.

Although the curriculum at his first placement was prescribed, in religious education he taught a lesson on sectarianism and a unit on racial inequality. He used resources such as the community symbols card sort and the Black Lives Matter website. And he devoted a class period to a walking debate in which he posed controversial questions pertaining to sectarianism and related forms of discrimination in Northern Ireland.

Table 4.1   Student Teachers' Main Experience Teaching Controversial Issues

	Course	Focus	Curricular and Pedagogical Tools
Sean	Year 10 History	Good Friday Agreement: What elements are most important today?	Political murals, modified walking debate on elements of Good Friday Agreement
Margaret	A level Politics	Compensation for victims of the Troubles: Should former paramilitary combatants be compensated as victims of violence?	Research and deliberation on victims of Troubles and how to compensate
Andrew	Year 11 Citizenship	Racism on the Internet: Should racism on the Internet be censored?	Example of racism, UNDHR, deliberation in pairs
Luke	Year 11 Religious Studies	Euthanasia: How should end-of-life decisions be made?	Video clips, mini-white boards, case studies jigsaw

At his second placement, a higher-performing grammar school, Andrew had more autonomy over the curriculum and found that many controversial issues were part of the RE and citizenship curricula. In RE, he taught views of marriage, civil partnerships, divorce, and sexuality, as well as medical issues and animal rights.

Andrew said that in citizenship, the lessons on hate crimes, freedom of expression, and censorship of the Internet to prevent racism involved the most controversy. It was prescribed by the curriculum, and was packed with activities and resources. In a culminating lesson, the class watched a video about Internet use around the world. Then they read the United Nations Declaration of Human Rights article on free speech and discussed whether there are ever appropriate limitations. Next Andrew showed an example of racism on the Internet from Northern Ireland, borrowed from his department chair.

In pairs students deliberated on the question: Should the Internet be censored to prevent racist hate speech? Andrew told me, "There was a lot of good discussion about that because there were some who said that freedom of speech is a human right . . . and then there were others who argued that it should be censored. So that was quite interesting."

But, this discussion was constrained by the extreme limitation of a thirty-five-minute class period. Andrew explained, "It definitely met a goal for some pupils, where they were genuinely able to express their viewpoint and justify why they felt that way. But I think there were a lot of people who maybe didn't achieve that aim." Andrew had planned for students to write up their conclusions and then think about ways to fight racism as a whole group. But he never got to the final activity. Reading Andrew's lesson plan and listening to his report made it evident that he was racing against the clock.

Overall, Andrew taught lessons on controversial issues that utilized what he learned from university, met curriculum mandates, and fit the timetable. But time constraints prevented him from taking risks with more class discussion and providing time for students to take positions.

At the start of the year, Andrew had expressed anxiety about potentially having to deal with students' offensive comments. He learned how to tactfully challenge student attitudes without offending or indoctrinating:

> So, for example, maybe the pupils were discussing free speech and one pupil were to say, "Yes, I believe in free speech, and I believe I can say whatever I want," and I might say, "Well, what if what I'm saying violates some other human right. What does that mean?" . . . although I'm not necessarily telling them they're wrong to think whatever way they think, I'm just encouraging them to see another side of the argument.

Andrew's student teaching exemplified both contained and constrained risk-taking. He enthusiastically taught controversies using provocative resources and dialogic approaches, and carefully calibrated his responses to steer discussions. At the same time, an unforgiving timetable tightly constrained discussion.

Enriching Deliberation in a Supportive Environment

Margaret spent her first placement at a Catholic all-girls grammar school where she taught politics, history, and citizenship. Her citizenship classes met once a week for sixty-five minutes. She said she approached her citizenship classes in a relaxed, informal way. Each group created a class contract, but it was simply constructed by asking what made students feel encouraged to participate. Margaret attributed her success even with her most challenging group to building rapport by being herself instead of an authoritative figure and making her classes fun, while still holding high expectations.

Margaret was grateful to teach a double period, in contrast with the allotment for citizenship at her child's school, which was "half an hour on a Friday afternoon." She said she taught controversial issues from a global perspective, addressing Syria, refugees, and children's rights; Donald Trump; Islamophobia; and homophobia as well as sectarianism in Northern Ireland. Her responses to my questions indicated that she did not frame these topics as controversies, but instead taught them through social justice and human rights lenses. For example, she showed examples of sectarian violence inflicted upon Protestant communities to challenge students' beliefs and encourage empathy.

Margaret's understanding of controversial issues, like some others I interviewed, seemed to conflate controversial topics and issues. However, her report on two deliberations (Structured Academic Controversies) during her first school placement suggested impressive appropriation of this pedagogical tool (Grossman et al., 1999).

The first was with a Year 10 citizenship group in a unit on democracy and participation. She said it was "very simple—whether or not voting should be compulsory" and her purpose was to introduce students to deliberation, which she learned was much more effective than debate. In her school experience, debates were confrontational and arguments were often unsupported by evidence: "It was just 'I don't agree with that,' and 'How can you say something like that?' . . . whereas with deliberation, you're giving them all the arguments. . . . They do have to pick out which ones compel them the most, which ones they think are the strongest, and then they are forced to do both sides."

Margaret's second deliberation was in an A-level politics class, which met for 65 minutes once a week and 35 minutes four times a week. It focused on the struggle between the two main Northern Irish parties—Sinn Fein and the Democratic Unionist Party (DUP)—over whether victims of violence during the Troubles should be compensated if they had been members of paramilitary groups. This deliberation was much more complex, involving two class periods with homework in between:

> So I had printed out things like the proposed program for government. I had gotten them information from an actual question-and-answer time that had taken place in the [Northern Irish] Assembly between the politicians over the definition on what a victim is. And I had given them various envelopes with various resources in it. But, because they were sixth formers [16 to 18 year olds], I got them to use the resources to come up with their arguments and then they had to swap over and do the same thing. That took the full hour for them to actually prepare for it and then it was the next class that they did the actual deliberation. It meant, as part of their homework, they had to add to the resources I had given them or they had to support arguments that they had to come up with whatever they found.

The resources included the viewpoints of various organizations, such as charities working on behalf of victims.

Margaret learned about deliberation in both Paula's politics and citizenship courses. It involved "a lot of work" on the teacher's part, but promoted meaningful learning for students as they interpreted texts to construct their arguments. Although she said the issue was not emotionally charged, taking the other side was difficult for some students. Margaret encouraged them: "Some of the girls were going, 'I'm not doing DUP [Democratic Unionist

Party]. I'm not doing DUP. I can't. I just can't.' I was going, 'You can, because you don't believe it. You don't have to believe it, but you have to acknowledge that these are the reasons why there's so much division, lack of respect, whatever.'"

Margaret felt greatly supported by Paula's classes and confident as an older adult. She was ready to delve into issues with her students in her first place-ment. She talked about addressing issues in depth, not underestimating the ability of adolescents to handle tough questions, hooking student interest so they want to learn more, and warning students about upcoming discussions examining controversies. She benefited from teaching at a well-regarded school with an excellent mentor teacher and working under a timetable that allowed time to explore complex subjects.

Taking Risks at an Integrated School

Sean's first placement was at an affluent all-girls Catholic school where he, like Margaret, taught politics, history, and citizenship. He told me that Paula's class had changed his understanding of controversial issues. But like other teachers in my study, his ideas had not yet crystallized. When asked if he had an opportunity to teach a controversial issue during his first student teaching placement, he referred to a lesson he taught on poverty, noting his sense that it was a taboo subject and that he associated it with debates over class inequalities in the wider society. But he did not frame the lesson on poverty as an issue of contention.

Sean spoke about teaching lessons on immigration and refugees in which he provided knowledge, looked at specific cases such as the notori-ous Calais 'Jungle' refugee camp, and raised questions for discussion. He delved deeper into controversy during his second placement at an integrated school, particularly in a Year 10 history class he co-taught with the full-time teacher.

Sean explained that after they initially covered the Good Friday Agreement, he reflected on the lesson: "It's been a list of seven bullet points that they've noted in their books. They've regurgitated for an exam, but they haven't explored it in any sort of depth." He approached the teacher, requesting that he take the next class period to go into it more deeply.

The official curriculum, stated at the top of the lesson plan, mandated a unit on the partition of Ireland and its impact on Northern Ireland today. But Sean took this in a direction he said teachers typically avoided. Based on our interview and the lesson plan and materials he sent me, Sean's lesson involved significant risk-taking elements (Kitson & McCully, 2005). It linked present disputes with history, engaging students with provocative resources, discussion of the conflict's legacy, and evaluation of its political solution, the crucially important Good Friday Agreement. It examined the agreement's provisions, who benefited, and their importance today.

The lesson opened with a twenty-minute introduction focused on contemporary wall murals. Using a worksheet, students identified the community associated with each mural and linked the images to topics and themes they had encountered in their earlier study of Irish history. The class spent fifteen minutes reviewing what it had studied previously about the Good Friday Agreement and identifying the political parties currently represented in the Northern Irish power-sharing assembly.

Guided by Sean, students then spent twenty minutes on a worksheet outlining the agreement's key elements, such as the principle of consent (reunification with Ireland based on a majority vote), rights and equality, decommissioning of weapons, prisoner release, and normalization of security. Then, using a table divided into Nationalists versus Unionists, students were given ten minutes to discuss who benefited from each of these provisions.

Sean posted the seven elements and, using a version of walking debate, asked students to stand beneath the one they prioritized for contemporary Northern Ireland. He asked them to explain their position and allowed students to change their positions if convinced by someone else's argument. Finally, Sean told the class these issues were still controversial. He asked them to compare Northern Ireland before and after the Good Friday Agreement and discuss how the political landscape had changed.

In this lesson, time for deliberation was limited. But incorporating discussion in a classroom in an integrated school represented an important milestone for Sean. He wrote about the lesson in his final essay. Citing Kello (2016), he noted that in a classroom of mixed social, cultural, and political backgrounds, there was an "inherent element of 'risk-taking' due to the value-laden nature of the discussion." His preparation included "understanding where [he] stood on the issues." He explicitly advocated that students take a "rights-based stance," rather than remaining completely neutral. He made sure that "aspects of the agreement were examined from a multitude of perspectives, including those of non-state actors, often distanced from dominant narratives." Interestingly, Sean's lesson was as much about citizenship and politics as it was about history.

Sean thought that teachers should frontload exploration of controversial issues with substantive content. He realized he needed to trust students' ability to think critically and give them opportunities to arrive at their own conclusions. He had initially expressed confusion about what should be deemed controversial and concern about suppressing his strongly held political convictions. Paula's guidance and his student teaching experience helped him develop a clearer conception and the tools to challenge his didactic tendencies.

Beginning to Experiment

At the state secondary and grammar schools where Luke student taught, he mainly led religious education classes. His opportunity to teach citizenship was limited. However, at his second placement, a state-controlled grammar school, he was assigned one 40-minute Learning for Life and Work class, which included citizenship. He was expected to follow the department head's scheme of work (unit) on equality and social justice.

Luke's richest experience with teaching controversial issues was a series of lessons on euthanasia in his Year 11 religious studies (RE) class in the second placement. Previously he had taught the issue of abortion using the department's curriculum, but that fell flat. His university supervisor advised him he "needed to put more of [his] own stamp upon things."

Because it was his first time teaching about euthanasia, he initially used the department's materials, which were "quite standard." Luke said, "So those first couple of lessons were covering almost kind of, you know, just general reasons for, that might be given for the act of euthanasia and reasons against, and . . . legislation." He compared the U.K.'s policies with those of Switzerland and the Netherlands. Because it was RE, he brought in the Old and New Testaments. He commented, "But it was all quite—those first few lessons, it was all quite dry. It was still kind of filling in notes in a notebook."

What helped him be more creative, Luke said, was using individual mini-white boards, which allowed students to quickly express ideas in response to Luke's questions. He asked students to write down what came to mind when they heard the phrase "quality of life." Whereas they had previously been passive, content to just take notes on information presented, the white boards encouraged students to actively discuss the complexity of quality of life.

Luke showed a clip from the film *Me Before You*, a romantic drama about the relationship between a man who is paralyzed from an accident and his caregiver. He said that some students had seen the movie and the class had a "great discussion" about the conception of quality of life held by the main character, who ultimately decides to end his life.

The next phase was a "snowballing exercise" using mini-case studies, provided by the department, about people from the U.K. who had traveled to countries where they could "go through with euthanasia." In small groups, students read a case and became the "experts." Then they taught the group that followed them about the reasons for people's decisions. Following that, the class looked at cases that argued against euthanasia: "So we looked at Stephen Hawking as an example of someone who had been given a terminal diagnosis of a few years" and then had a remarkable life into his mid-70s.

They learned about Jean-Dominique Bauby, a French journalist with locked-in syndrome, which leaves most sufferers almost completely paralyzed. Luke recounted an activity he found impactful:

> I used the idea to get them to try to communicate to one another firstly with their hands using like an alphabet strip and pointing and then saying, "Okay, that was hard enough, but imagine if you didn't have any hands, and you can only blink," and then they did that. Quite a few of them were getting very frustrated and would say, "This is pointless." They gave up. The idea was to think, "Okay, we're going to look at a man for whom this is a reality," and yet he managed to write his memoir and advocated remaining alive despite his frustration.

Luke did not have time at the end of the euthanasia unit to ask students to self-position. He said it was not encouraged at the school. Instead, the aim was for students to understand different points of view. Luke said he would ideally want to include that final element.

Without prompting Luke said, "So I'll be honest. I mean the whole experience of being a student teacher, at the time . . . they had exams coming up, and a lot of what I was teaching them was 'You need to teach them this so that they can answer in an exam. So you need to teach them both sides, and if there's any time for discussion, then you can do that.'" Luke also acknowledged that part of his reluctance to delve into discussion, which both Paula and his RE tutor encouraged, came from not yet feeling comfortable as a new teacher.

CONTAINED, SUPPORTED, AND
CONSTRAINED RISK-TAKING

This chapter shows student teachers taking risks to teach controversial issues in both constraining and supportive school contexts. Andrew framed the issue of freedom of expression using the United Nations Declaration of Human Rights, confronted an example of racism on the Internet, and engaged students in paired deliberation. In other classes, he used methods learned in Paula's course such as the walking debate and card sort of political, cultural, and religious symbols.

Margaret conducted two deliberations, one on compulsory voting and the second on the issue of compensating ex-combatants for losses they suffered during the conflict. She creatively fleshed this out by asking students to carry out research supplementing the sources she provided.

Sean brought political wall murals to contextualize the Good Friday Agreement. He asked students to critically evaluate which groups benefited from its components and had them deliberate which component was most important. These three teachers, most notably Margaret, taught in ways that significantly differed from the didactic methods they had experienced as students.

Luke seemed to feel the most constrained by his student teaching placements. Still, he had two longer class periods to engage his RE students in the issue of euthanasia. Luke created a space for student participation while following his department's curriculum. He hoped it was a step toward more discussion in his own future classroom.

The preservice teachers noted several factors that supported or constrained their teaching of controversial issues. Time was the biggest constraint. Often, citizenship had a 35- to 40-minute weekly slot for part of the academic year in the school timetable. This made it exceptionally difficult to instill knowledge, explore multiple perspectives, and engage in discussion. Even though Sean had two 30-minute sessions per week over eight weeks at his first placement, he still considered the time insufficient.

Andrew's story about his Internet censorship lesson showed how the timetable squeezed his teaching: "So really you have maybe twenty-five minutes and thirty at best, I think. So it's difficult to achieve everything that you've planned." He continued, "And looking at my lesson plan, I know that we didn't spend fifteen minutes on the paired discussion because I probably overspent my time before that. So it was probably closer to ten minutes. By that time, it was difficult to actually write anything down. I think it would have been helpful to have more time to get them to actually think about it." The time constraint prevented Andrew from taking the risk of expanding beyond short, paired discussion in his lesson.

Other constraints were pressures to prepare students for exams and cover a broad curriculum. Luke expressed ambivalence about following the prescribed curriculum, and, specifically, the lesson plans developed by the schools. He spoke about the tension between learning the importance of discussing issues and the pressure to teach to the tests. In one of his RE classes, the teacher was "stepping in almost every lesson," presumably to make sure Luke was "giving them exactly what they needed for the exam." These constraints foreclosed involving students in sustained discussion.

Margaret said the citizenship booklets used at her schools were a constraint. The students hated them, so she stopped using them. She explained, "The only thing that I would say constrained is the booklet that they have, which I chose not to—I tried to use it. I tried, but the girls hate them. But it's just part of that statute requirement of having a tick, tick, 'We've covered this' or 'We wrote something.'" Margaret's decision showed an unusual willingness to buck constraining expectations and respond to students.

Sean and Luke spoke about particular school communities that made it difficult to address issues. Luke told me his first placement was in a rural, conservative, religious Protestant community that predisposed students to think there was a "'right' answer" to controversial questions and that teachers held these answers. In a wealthy grammar school, Sean found it challenging to teach poverty. Regarding his second placement at an integrated school, he commented that more work was needed to develop students' capacity to talk across socioeconomic, religious, and political differences.

Along with the obstacles were factors that encouraged teaching controversial issues. Andrew identified three supports at his second placement—the RE curriculum, which included numerous controversial issues, his mentor teacher, and established classroom rules. He was provided with resources but was also granted autonomy.

Importantly, Sean and Margaret's history and politics lessons benefited greatly from having significant time slots. Margaret's students were able to prepare for their deliberation by examining resources offering multiple perspectives. Sean's students were able to connect the past to the present and evaluate the significance of critical policies through different lenses. Longer class periods gave students greater opportunities to learn, think, and discuss complex issues.

Like Andrew, Sean and Margaret also benefited from supportive mentor teachers who gave them space to experiment. And because they had Paula for their social sciences tutor and student teaching supervisor, Sean and Margaret were supported by regularly occurring "chats" with her.

ADVICE TO TEACHER EDUCATORS AND REMAINING QUESTIONS

Paula's preservice teachers valued the robust toolkit she provided them. They recommended that teacher educators take up the key lessons they learned from her course, including:

1. The importance of embracing controversial issues.
2. Allowing students to self-position on issues either privately or publicly, depending on the sensitivity of the issue.
3. Using resources and creativity to show the relevance of controversial issues in the wider world.
4. Understanding it is not always possible to be neutral or impartial.

They also advocated modeling a range of active learning approaches, as Paula had done.

One suggestion for teacher education was that graduate students themselves engage in serious dialogue on controversial political issues. Over and over again, I learned that people in Northern Ireland have been socialized to be cautious when talking with people outside their own community. The title of Patrick Radden Keefe's acclaimed book on the Troubles, *Say Nothing,* (2019), underscores how a tight-lipped strategy for staying safe during the conflict permeated cultural norms.

Sean told me that learning to discuss issues openly was exactly what Northern Ireland needed, and he wished Paula's class had taken that risk. He felt it would have been helpful to directly tackle some controversies in course sessions so preservice teachers could experience what it is like to wrestle with them and prepare for potential classroom problems.

Luke said that teacher educators should prepare student teachers for dealing with challenges in their placements, such as the presence of a mentor teacher and the need to balance discussion with exam preparation and curriculum requirements. He added that preservice teachers should learn how to sense when students are upset and find ways to deal with it. Margaret also cautioned that teachers need to be prepared to handle "emotional responses" or a student "who you believe has stepped over that line from freedom of expression to being openly disrespectful."

Sean was left with a couple of questions. He wondered how to integrate his social justice commitments into teaching while still cultivating independent thinking. And he questioned the deliberation model for discussion:

> And again I don't know [about using deliberations]. I still have some degree of tension around it myself in that I'd like to see how it all plays out in real life because I don't want to create some sort of postmodern space where "You have this view, and I have this view, and everything's okay because we're different, and we disagree." That's part of it, but ultimately we can't just head down where everybody's right at the end, and there's no wrong answers. There are wrong answers, d'you know? And that I suppose is where I position myself.

Sean's comments represent a stance held by educators unwilling to teach social justice issues as open. As Paula McAvoy (2016) argued, structural inequalities "are empirical realities that need to be taught prior to discussion" about relevant issues, but "*What to do* about structural inequalities are open questions and are the type of questions students should be deliberating in the classroom" (p. 42). Having a deeper understanding of different types of issues would help teachers figure out which are suitable for deliberation and which are not. The book's final chapter expands on this point.

Sean, in our final interview, said he felt there had not been enough time in Paula's citizenship course to go in depth and reflect on practices such as lesson planning. In general, he wanted more time in his teacher education courses to "marry" practice and theory in order to develop a "living philosophy."

KEY TAKEAWAYS

1. Preservice teachers reported learning the most about teaching controversial issues from Paula's structured small group activities, emphasis on analyzing different positions, stress on careful curriculum design and preparation for teaching, and exploration of the teacher's role.
2. Student teachers embraced teaching issues located in citizenship and other subjects and adopted numerous tools, such as the symbols card sort, walking debate, and deliberation.
3. Student teachers' efforts were constrained by timetables and the low status of citizenship, pressure to cover curriculum and prepare for exams, and mentor teachers who interfered with autonomy.
4. Student teachers' efforts were supported by longer class periods, mentor teachers who shared resources and encouraged experimentation, and curriculum that included controversial issues.
5. Advice to teacher educators included more preparation for challenges such as exam and curriculum requirements that took time away from lessons, serious dialogue on controversial political issues in Northern Ireland, and more practice in lesson planning.
6. Teachers' remaining questions were about how to deal with difficult student reactions and how to balance openness to different perspectives with social justice commitments.

Chapter 5

Ian Shepherd

Teaching Sensitive and Controversial Issues through Historical Inquiry in England

Ian Shepherd is a history educator and genocide education scholar from England who brings unusual creativity and a constructivist philosophy to teaching. His commitment to education as a vehicle for building dialogue across differences is reflected in his domestic and international collaborations with educators and others in university, museum, and school settings.

Teaching controversial issues in history changes when we move from Northern Ireland, a society divided by a history of conflict, to England, where the fractures are deep, but less obvious. Connections between the past and present are not so keenly felt by most people. Teachers in England need to be more creative than their counterparts in Northern Ireland to link historical and contemporary issues.

Unlike Mark Drummond and Paula Barstow, Ian's approach to preparing preservice teachers to teach controversial issues is to embed the practice in class sessions rather than address it discretely. In this chapter, we look at Ian and his History course, located in a university's Post Graduate Certificate in Education (PGCE) program. Major influences on Ian's approach to preparing preservice teachers to teach sensitive and controversial issues in history are his early experience as a history teacher in an innovative department, university mentors who worked in the "alternative tradition" of the Schools Council History Project, and involvement in Holocaust education.

EDUCATION BACKGROUND AND PHILOSOPHY

Interviews with Ian revealed that his understanding and approach to what he termed "sensitive and controversial issues" differed from those of the other teacher educators described in this book. He thought everything in the curriculum had the potential to be sensitive and/or controversial, and did not make a "hard distinction." Ian gave the example of the Industrial Revolution, "which on the face of it, you think it's a fairly straightforward subject." He would encourage his students to explore child labor and link it to contemporary situations, so that their pupils would learn history's relevance and understand the historical roots of current problems.

Ian's orientation to controversy mirrors a book chapter by Andrea Libresco and Jeannette Balantic titled "Every Issue Is a Social Studies Issue" (2017). They advocate that "topics for classroom discussion are everywhere" and that teachers "have the power to inform themselves about a topic, tease out the controversial aspect of it, and formulate questions to nurture thoughtful discussion" (p. 14).

Ian's overall approach to preparing preservice teachers to teach controversy was to integrate controversial elements in course sessions and assignments. He continually provoked his students to think in new ways about teaching history by modeling activities that challenged their preconceptions. He taught them how to design lessons and units around key inquiry questions (questions that drive the inquiry process) and source work. To instill critical thinking, he showed the class how teachers question students effectively and ineffectively. Controversial questions were inserted in the imaginative lessons Ian used as vehicles to teach inquiry-based practice.

For Ian, teaching sensitive and controversial issues underpinned his own early teaching and was closely linked with getting students engaged with history. He taught 11-14-year-olds for over ten years and served as history department head during that time. The department was known for making history come alive for students. Importantly, the Schools Council History Project, which started in 1972 and served as Ian's model, had transformed conceptions of history education in the United Kingdom, emphasizing disciplinary understanding and inquiry-based learning.

In their important book, *Understanding History Teaching*, Husbands et al. (2003) explained an initiative, which began in the late 1960s, to promote an "alternative tradition" of teaching history that contrasted with England's "great tradition" and made teaching the subject much more complex. Instead of the teacher as a didactic deliverer of content, the teacher had to design and manage learners' constructivist engagement with the past.

The new paradigm emphasized issues and themes rather than chronological content, and it promoted student use of historical sources. It also embraced extrinsic purposes, or social aims of history education, such as preparing young people to participate in a democratic society. Ian's teaching, like Mark Drummond's, was shaped by these ideals.

Ian recounted stories of recreating historical contexts such as World War I trenches and the unsanitary conditions of medieval times through role-play, physical arrangements of the classroom, and special effects. He would tell students to imagine themselves in particular situations and ask them hard questions about what they would have thought and done. Then he would introduce new evidence or circumstances, and ask them to rethink their positions.

For example, he would announce the beginning of World War I and ask, "Would you enlist in the British army?" And then, knowing they would end up killing someone, "Would you still enlist?" He said he would teach students about the "sacrifice of young life" and the problem of underage soldiers, and compare that to child soldiers fighting in the Congo.

Ian first became involved with university-based teacher education while teaching school. In graduate school at another university, he worked with an important mentor who continually asked how they could engage young people in history. They developed ways to build the teaching of controversy into their teacher preparation program. One way was to challenge preservice teachers' and their pupils' preconceptions, to "shake them up" and "really make them think."

Along with his early teaching experience and work in teacher education, Ian's research in Holocaust education and teaching history in post-genocide societies such as Rwanda shaped his orientation toward teaching sensitive and controversial issues. He explained that this focus emerged from two sources. One was his own moral struggle to make sense of why people held such despicable views and did such incomprehensible things to other humans. The second was the designation of the Holocaust as a mandated topic in Britain's national curriculum and the need for teachers to approach it in constructive ways.

Ian shared that studying genocide confronted him with existential questions:

"Are they all culpable?" I suppose if Germany is culpable as a nation, then where does that place us in relation to some of the things that we're struggling with . . . now? In relation to when I was much younger, in terms of the invasion of Iraq and the wars in the Middle East that the British politicians had supported. Why wasn't I more vocal about that? Why didn't I do— . . . I don't think it's possible to sit on the sidelines anymore and just accept what is happening because I think the world looks a much darker place.

Ian found it emotionally difficult work, especially, when as a father of young children, he learned about what had happened to children in the Holocaust and the Rwandan genocide. Although he thought that expectations for genocide education could be overblown, he believed that young people needed to learn about the horrors of the past to develop as moral members of society who appreciated diversity and advocated justice.

UNIVERSITY PROGRAM CONTEXT

Following a university position in Education Studies, Ian moved to his current position in a different part of England with a racially and ethnically mixed urban center surrounded by suburbs, countryside, affluent villages, and depressed former mining towns. This region was politically diverse, with a large proportion of citizens who voted for Brexit.

Ian's History group in 2016–2017 comprised 18 students, fifteen from England and three from Northern Ireland, all white. The History course was in the university's secondary PGCE program, one of the university's two Initial Teacher Education routes to teacher certification. The other program, School Direct, was based in the schools, with one day a week at university.

The PGCE involved significant coursework but candidates spent approximately twice as much time in school placements as in classes. Teaching positions in England were not scarce as in Northern Ireland. Some 95 percent of PGCE students worked as teachers after completing studies.

The History course advertised on the university website that it would help preservice teachers make history come alive for their students: "You will be encouraged to utilise your passion for the subject to develop inventive ways to engage your pupils with the past. You will work with them as a teacher to analyse, interpret, evaluate and contextualise events and historical sources." In contrast with Northern Ireland, the website did not include anything about controversial issues, sociopolitical context, or extrinsic aims of history.

As in Northern Ireland, class sessions alternated with school placements throughout the year. The PGCE program started in September and finished at the end of June. During the first term, students attended classes at the university almost every day for six weeks. They spent six weeks at their first "School Experience" placement. A week of independent study built on their school experiences followed and helped prepare them for future teaching and assignments.

After Christmas vacation, classes resumed in January for several days before the second school placement, called "Teaching Practice," began. The students spent a total of fourteen weeks in their placements, returning to university classes for a few days during this time. They also had a week for independent study and three weeks for school-based inquiry. They attended their final class sessions and convocation in the last week of the term.

The majority of university classes was devoted to subject sessions in their course (i.e., History). Students also attended modules and tutorials in professional development, schools and society, aspects of learning, and inclusion and SEN (special educational needs).

In his faculty role, Ian's main responsibility was to coordinate the History course, teach class sessions, and supervise student teachers. He hired part-time instructors to help with supervision of school placements and course instruction. At the university, Ian also supervised master's and PhD students. He was involved in research and development projects on and offcampus.

PREPARING TEACHERS FOR SENSITIVE
AND CONTROVERSIAL ISSUES

Ian believed the first requirement for learning to teach sensitive and controversial issues was subject matter knowledge. This was important because teaching controversies meant approaching history through different angles and creatively working with disciplinary content.

Ian explained that, due to changes in university degree requirements, history majors no longer graduated with a coherent chronology under their belts. Instead, their knowledge went deep in particular areas, but was spotty overall. Ian had students complete a self-assessment at the beginning of the program so they could work on gaps in their knowledge throughout the year.

Second, it was vital for teachers to think about their goals for students' learning and the rationale for how they were teaching, particularly because teaching controversy involved "sticking [oneself] out on a limb": "What are going to be the learning outcomes? . . . How will they emerge? Why is it important that they emerge in this way?"

Subject matter knowledge and clarity about goals and rationale fit under the contained risk-taking strategy of thorough preparation and planning taught by all four teacher educators (Pace, 2019). At the same time, Ian, like Mark, enjoyed the spontaneity of free-ranging classroom conversations in which the direction of discussion was not certain, but was worked out extemporaneously.

Ian believed that teachers must be willing to experiment. He said, "There is a real danger of just playing it safe." Experimentation was aided by creative resources and group activities. At the same time, he wanted his students to become reflective practitioners who thought a lot about pupils' learning. Promoting engagement for its own sake was inadequate for effective teaching.

Ian modeled experimental approaches to teaching controversy, showing what it meant to make history come alive:

I'm always keen for . . . making history jump up off the page, and I think, if it's going to do that, it has to be at that kind of biting edge, . . . I think it has to be addressing a controversy, or it has to be dealing with issues that potentially are sensitive, but also student teachers need ways and means to be able to, to deal with those issues. So we're very much on the course geared up to exploring how inquiry-based learning helps students to investigate, discover, unravel, unveil, challenge orthodoxies.

For Ian, teaching controversy promoted highly engaged inquiry-based learning as well as social aims.

MODELING THE TEACHING OF
CONTROVERSIAL HISTORY

Ian said different approaches to issues were "built into the sessions that we run around lesson planning, subject knowledge, assessment and feedback." Ian gave the example of a session in which he enacted a lesson about the Derby Day race of 1913 and the suffragette Emily Wilding Davison who "allegedly throws herself onto the King's horse" and died. Her motivations were contested—was it an act of protest as some claimed?

Ian set the class up as a newsroom reporting on the arms race between Britain and Germany on the eve of World War I. Some students role-played news runners bringing in news on the ground. As the "reporters" were working on their arms race articles, suddenly a news runner came in to report an incident at Derby Day that occurred in front of royalty. Ian explained:

> I get them to take on the role of different types of news reporting. So some of them will be very right-wing papers. Some of them will be gentlemen's magazines. One of them will be a ladies' magazine. One of them will be an overseas paper, and they have to report this story with that political gender bias built into it. . . . We also compare it to actually what was reported . . . you go back to the idea, "What if this event hadn't happened or hadn't been of such a magnitude or if the editor had decided it wasn't front page news?"

The activity got the class thinking about how we know what happened in the past—particularly when the truth is uncertain—,who selects news highlighted by the media, and how it is reported. We will see in the next chapter that William, a preservice teacher in the history course, was impressed by this lesson as an example of how to teach controversial issues.

Ian used controversial events to show how an innovative, inquiry-based approach illuminates the complexity of history. At other times, inquiry was used to tackle controversial moral questions. The session I observed explicitly tied to teaching sensitive and controversial issues focused on the issue of the culpability of those who carried out orders to kill Jews during the Holocaust.

DISRUPTING ASSUMPTIONS ABOUT
HISTORY AND TEACHING

Ian was particularly interested in confronting student preconceptions about history and history teaching. During the first few class sessions, his activities and lectures made students grapple with the following questions: Why do we end up teaching the history we teach? Why do we teach it the way we do? Who thought it up? Have we always done it this way?

Initial activities included the following: Students had to select several images they believed were most important to teach and, in small groups, narrow it down to one. They worked collectively to identify the ten most important dates in history. Then they had to identify the five most important historical figures from 1800 to the present and before 1800. Students were asked to explain their reasoning and develop criteria. Ian pointed out the absence of women and people of color in their lists and noted that the choices would be different if the class were located in India or Brazil.

Ian asked people to think about how their own education had conditioned them to think in certain ways. He suggested they "look at how the history curriculum has developed": "What you've done is similar to what people have done to decide what's in, what's out. There's only a certain amount of time. Somewhere someone is making decisions." He reminded them that many young people stop studying history at age 13 or 14, and posed the question: "What are they getting?"

The next day, Ian modeled different approaches to teaching Hitler's rise to power, to show the legitimacy of varied teaching methods and get the preservice teachers to reflect on their reactions to each one. He had the class analyze sets of textbooks dating from the 1940s, lesson plans dating from the 1970s, and exam papers to consider changes in the curriculum. He then lectured about the emergence of the Schools Council History Project.

Ian explained that there had been consensus among historians, educators, and politicians on what history education should entail. But starting in the 1960s, the history curriculum came to be viewed as irrelevant. With more scholarship in social history, educators felt the curriculum stressing the greatness of the British Empire had to be reassessed. In truth, Britain was no longer "top dog" or an "economic powerhouse." Most of its colonies had gained independence.

Additionally, the dominance of "'white British history' could not continue in light of significant non-white immigration." Black, Asian, and other ethnic groups, having experienced a colonial system based on the "white man's burden," represented a growing share of the population. History was beginning to be studied from those positioned "below versus above."

Education scholar Martin Booth's 1969 book, *History Betrayed*, documented a groundbreaking study of history education. Ian presented its famous argument: "We are still wedded to techniques which tend to deaden rather than inspire; and so long as we believe that pupils must be told rather than discover for themselves, there is little possibility for uncovering their potential for creative, divergent thought." Booth smashed the consensus on history teaching and persuaded many history teachers that the subject demanded an inquiry-based approach.

Ian said that the Schools Council History Project, later known as Schools History Project or SHP, was formed in 1971. The journal *History Teacher*, a trove of resources and practical ideas, became a platform for the "growing voice of the teacher," who became the "dominant person deciding what will be taught." Ian said he would be distributing forms with a discount for joining the History Association, which he strongly encouraged. Many of the readings he assigned students came from the publication.

Ian told the class it was *Jackdaw*, a company that produced curriculum based on primary source documents, that "really got [him] interested in teaching history." He handed out a few Jackdaws to the class as well as copies of *Teaching History*. Ian said they would be working on teaching with documentary sources, which, contrary to popular belief, could be engrossing even for Year 7 pupils.

Ian picked up his lecture with the turn to conservatism during the 1980s and the 1990s under the governments of Margaret Thatcher and John Major, who said there had been an "insidious attack" on traditional British history, and that the "transmission of facts about Britain's heroes and victories should be the prime purpose." The Great Education Reform Bill of 1988, sponsored by the Conservative government, was passed. Ian said that, in 1991, when he headed his school's history department, "a huge document arrived on my desk"—the new national curriculum that stipulated what and how to teach, in what order, and how to assess. Teachers went from the freedom of the Schools History Project to a prescribed curriculum.

With the proverbial swinging pendulum, the 2000 and 2007 versions of the national history curriculum once again included teacher voices. But time for history was squeezed as math, sciences, and literacy were prioritized. Ian explained that, in 2011, Secretary of Education Michael Gove, "an unashamed traditionalist," pushed for the "transmission" of a "grand narrative" of British history that would eliminate inquiry-based teaching. A backlash from academics and educators resulted in a 2013 version of the history curriculum that included knowledge of Britain's past, Britain's place in the world, and challenges of the 21st century.

Ian closed with a quote from C.P. Hill: "History, properly taught, can help men to become critical and humane, just as wrongly taught it can turn them into bigots and fanatics." Images projected on the screen included a headline from the *Daily Express*, "Muslim Schools Ban our Culture," and a face with the following labels: Terrorist, Muslim, Saddam, Al Qaeda 9/11. He asked how we can challenge the rise of the far right, showing images of signs saying, "Stop the fascist BNP." Ian said that in white mining towns, the British National Party (a minor far-right political party) was trying to proselytize at schoolhouse gates and the police had to be called in. He posed a rhetorical question: What is the role of history in tackling this problem?

Ian's lecture portrayed the history curriculum as a political football in which teacher influence rose or fell depending on the prevailing political winds. He advocated the Schools History Project model that focused on inquiry questions, analysis of sources, historical thinking skills, and the engagement of young people in examining relevant issues. Ian prodded his preservice teachers to rethink the purposes, content, and processes of history education. Through modeling different approaches, immersing the graduate students in lessons and activities, and presenting historical context for Britain's history curriculum, he challenged their prior conceptions of teaching.

A few graduate students told me the first few class sessions had completely changed the ways they thought about history. He had successfully "scrambled their brains" and conveyed the idea he expressed to me about teaching history through inquiry-based methods to disrupt traditional ways of thinking. Ian clearly advocated a risk-taking approach to teaching history (Kitson & McCully, 2005). In the next chapter, we will learn whether new ways of thinking translated into classroom practice during student teaching placements.

HISTORY, MORAL QUESTIONS, AND THE HOLOCAUST

Based on my observations and interviews, the centerpiece of Ian's preparation for teaching sensitive and controversial issues was a two-day sequence on teaching the Holocaust. It revolved around an all-day field trip and a classroom lesson, both of which generated strong reactions from the preservice teachers.

What Is Controversial about the Holocaust?

Ian's perspective on teaching the Holocaust as a controversial topic was provocative, yet relevant given contemporary incidents of antisemitism and the persistent voices of Holocaust deniers around the world:

People will say, "Yeah, I understand that it's sensitive, but it's not controversial. It happened, and that's the last thing I would expect you to say." I'd say, "No, no, it is controversial. You've got people out there who would deny it existed. And you've got some countries that have problems with the way that it's become a dominant discourse in some records." So it is controversial in that sense, and we have to explore those controversies. We should not hide away from those things. I'm a great believer in tackling Holocaust denial and Holocaust deniers head on. I think kids really do need to know about that.

In Ian Davies's 2000 volume, *Teaching the Holocaust: Educational Dimensions, Principles and Practice*, Ian Gregory asked how we can teach the "outrage" of the most significant event in the twentieth century in order to examine what it means to be human: "Effective teaching about this most sensitive and controversial topic draws upon the range of perspectives that different disciplines afford us and encourages young people to reflect deeply and unflinchingly on the implications of what is presented" (p. 50). He continued, "The study of the Holocaust is shot through with controversy," for example, the debate between intentionalist versus functionalist explanations that focused on the Hamburg Reserve Police Battalion 101—the most thoroughly researched "killing unit" of the Nazi State (Kuhl, 2017). We will see how Ian took up this debate in a lesson he modeled for the class.

Ian approached the Holocaust by bringing his class to the National Holocaust Centre and Museum, where we met in small groups with museum volunteers, visited the main exhibit, had lunch with and attended the presentation of a Holocaust survivor, and toured a new exhibit. The following day, Ian led a full debrief of the field trip and modeled a lesson that explored a critical question: Why were ordinary people willing to commit mass murder?

During our first interview, Ian gave me a preview of what he called "Police Battalion 101"—an activity he co-created with a teacher colleague—before he brought it to his History class. It referred to a group of 500 policemen who were sent to Poland during the German occupation and participated in the killing and transport to Nazi death camps of thousands of Jews.

Ian explained the activity's purposes: "What I'm trying to explore is how do you again begin to challenge people to really think about what was happening, the decisions that individuals made, whether they had to follow orders, whether they could have stepped aside, did they need to, to shoot?" He specified, "Is it good enough to say, 'Oh, it was down to Hitler,' or, 'It's down to a few of these henchmen. It's down to the SS or it's down to . . .' Well, really? But here we've got this Major Trapp. Who's saying, 'You don't have to carry out these shooting orders . . . Nothing's going to happen to you.'" Ian suggested that the Battalion 101 activity could lead to deliberation on just consequences for the shooters.

By asking questions about why the battalion members carried out the order to shoot, Ian explained that while students would be "shocked" by what they learned about the Holocaust, he wanted to almost "humanize an inhuman situation," and explore deeply the hard question of why the reserve officers carried out such horrific orders. Students would say, "Well, but wouldn't they feel peer pressure?" Ian hoped that teachers would then impart moral lessons: "You don't always have to follow the crowd. . . . You can stop things happening."

Ideally, teaching sensitive and controversial issues would lead young people to take action around contemporary situations. He spoke about challenging preservice teachers' rationales for studying the Holocaust, asking: "[I]s that all you want them to come out as having done, to know and understand? . . . [H]ow do you become an active person in this?" Ian wanted his graduate students to take on the extrinsic, social justice aims of history teaching.

Modeling the Police Battalion 101 Lesson

On September 23, Ian asked his class to critique the exhibits at the Holocaust Centre and reflect on the visit. They had much to say about exhibit strengths and weaknesses, the survivor's argument that other genocides in addition to the Holocaust need to be taught, and a volunteer's provocative comment that the Holocaust could have been prevented if individuals had made different choices.

Ian transitioned to a lesson that modeled teaching sensitive and controversial issues. First he presented survey findings that revealed teaching of the Holocaust was often problematic due to inadequate preparation, unclear purpose, and lack of focus. He told the class he would offer a different approach, "based on historiography," that showed how to address significance and complexity in history for pupils in Key Stage 3 (ages 11–14).

The following vignette describes his demonstration:

Ian introduced the lesson, which revolved around the 1942 massacre of 1500 Jewish men, women, and children from Jozefow, Poland, by the German reserve police force Battalion 101. Its focus was the debate between two scholars— Christopher Browning, author of *Ordinary Men: Reserve Police Battalion 101 and the Final Solution in Poland*, and Daniel Goldhagen, who wrote *Hitler's Willing Executioners: Ordinary Germans and the Holocaust*—over what drove Germans to kill Jews. Essentially, Browning argued that the shooters were ordinary men who, under extraordinary circumstances and because of several factors, succumbed to the pressure to follow orders. Goldhagen challenged Browning's book, arguing that the ideology of antisemitism in Germany made many Germans support the killing of Jews. Students would consider the significance of various factors, taken from the authors' arguments, to answer the question, "Why did they shoot?"

Along with a one-page narrative about the massacre, Ian distributed a packet that included the key question, photos with facts and lesson objectives, a page with a line representing a spectrum from "Unlikely to have been a major influence" to "The greatest influence," a table with sixteen possible influences, four pieces of "New evidence" from various sources, and brief synopses of the two scholars' arguments. Essentially one argument was that perpetrators were ordinary people victimized by extraordinary times. Another argument was that perpetrators were antisemitic and willingly killed Jews.

Ian directed the class step by step through the activity. On the basis of the information they had, students in small groups discussed reasons for their placement of influences along the spectrum. Ian asked for "feedback from the groups" on what they thought was least influential. The groups agreed on "They were mad," "They were evil, bloodthirsty men," and "They were cowards." Groups disagreed on "Hitler had the answers to make Germany great again." Ian then asked about factors they thought were influential and compared responses. He queried, "So the sense of right and wrong goes out the window. It's times of war. You're shaking your head, saying you agree with that?" A student responded, "We also said it was safer to carry out orders rather than fighting at the front."

Next Ian had everyone look at the first piece of "new evidence," taken from 1960s court cases in which reserve officers were tried. He read aloud testimony about battalion commander Major Trapp's speech the morning of the massacre. Ian instructed the students to revisit their choices: "But based upon that new evidence now, do you think you need to reappraise some of your factors? . . . . in the light that he doesn't like these orders, but this is helping to win the war quickly." The class again compared responses across the groups.

Ian then made them consider a provocative new piece of new evidence: Major Trapp allowed men to excuse themselves without punishment; 12 out of 500 men did so. The small groups buzzed with conversation and moved around their factors. When discussing what they changed, Ian asked where they put antisemitism. One group had decided its influence was low, while another group said it was fairly high. Ian raised a general question: "How deep-seated was antisemitism in Germany?"

The Battalion 101 activity made students wrestle with a profound question about culpability for mass murder through a novel, structured process. Ian demonstrated how its process "unlocks good thinking" as confrontations with new evidence and probing questions compelled students to evaluate ideas. He modeled careful facilitation, providing direction and questioning to push students' thinking. Ian's question about antisemitism in Germany implicitly challenged those who did not consider it an influential factor, although there wasn't enough time to discuss it. It showed how questions could be posed in a non-confrontational, yet thought-provoking, way.

The lesson included two more rounds of evidence and the outcome of the 1960s trials. Ian asked the students to write two or three brief statements about why Battalion 101 killed the Jozefow Jews and then debriefed:

> The students wrote private reflections for a few minutes and volunteers shared with the group. Ian asked their reactions to knowing that very few out of the 100 put on trial were punished and whether they thought that following orders reduces guilt. Tom mentioned being in the army, and William quickly asked, "Do you mean Abu Ghraib?" He stated that when someone interviews for the military, the first question is, "Are you prepared to kill someone?" and the next question is "Would you go against a commanding officer?"
>
> Time was short and Ian stepped in with comments about teaching: "You can see as a teacher dealing with this, you need a great deal of skill. . . . pupils might not be comfortable discussing . . .This is controversial." He asserted, "I don't want my students to be comfortable. I want to disrupt, get in their face, make them think."
>
> Finally Ian asked everyone to get up and position themselves along a spectrum with one end representing Goldhagen's argument and the other side Browning's. Seven stood with Browning, eight went to the middle, and a couple sided with Goldhagen. He quickly asked a few people to explain their positions and how people felt about teaching this activity.

Ian's lesson modeled how powerful sources, structured small group activity, and close facilitation can open up morally profound controversial questions while guiding student interactions. Ian moved from small group deliberation to reporting out to the whole group and then from private to public disclosure of students' conclusions. I surmised this felt safe because the Holocaust did not hit close to home for this group, as discussion of the Troubles might for students in Northern Ireland.

William's astute remark about Abu Ghraib brought the essential question much closer to home. Discussion of his point might have been extremely powerful. Ian did not address the comparison, presumably because he was rushing to finish the lesson. Taking it up might have led to a more nuanced understanding of the well-researched Jozefow massacre example.

The Battalion 101 lesson called on students to use what they knew about history to answer difficult, yet essential, questions about culpability and justice. This ambitious activity, which took approximately an hour, raised the pervasive problem of insufficient time for in-depth examination of controversies while holding out the powerful possibilities for doing so. The conclusion might have entailed putting the debate into context. For example, the students could have learned that, despite its popularity, Goldhagen's book was strongly criticized by historians, and that recent sociological analyses had moved past binary arguments about responsibility (Kuhl, 2017). Additionally, it could have made the connection to contemporary antisemitism in Britain and elsewhere.

At the same time, Ian taught his lesson within the real confines of a time-table that also would constrain his preservice teachers' lessons. In this way he prepared them for the charged classroom, where the great potential for teaching controversies coexists with tensions (Pace, 2015). Teachers typically fear that conflict in the classroom will undermine their authority and disrupt their agenda for student learning (Britzman, 2003). The lessons Ian modeled conveyed the critical role that conflict plays in learning and how it can be structured into lessons that foster constructive and equitable dialogue (Bickmore & Parker, 2014).

SCHEME OF WORK (SoW) ASSIGNMENT

The culminating assignment for the History course was to develop a scheme of work consisting of six to eight one-hour lessons and write a 3,000-word evaluation of it. The History PGCE Handbook stated, "The scheme of work should be based around the broad theme of teaching sensitive and controversial issues in history. Whilst there are some obvious contenders in terms of topics, we would suggest that with most topics these angles can be developed." Mentor teachers would visit the university to provide guidance in choosing the topics. Preservice teachers were to read literature over the winter break that would help them "shape the nature and the scope" of the unit.

In the 3,000-word evaluation, preservice teachers were directed to cite "relevant literature about teaching and learning in history in general and also teaching sensitive and controversial issues." The evaluation should address learning theories and their connections to "history specific literature around teaching sensitive and controversial issues and the approaches that should be taken." Students were instructed to assess the scheme of work in light of the literature according to subject knowledge and understanding, planning and teaching, and assessment. And the evaluation needed to address how the student teacher dealt with the sensitive and controversial nature of the chosen topic and issues that arose in the classroom.

The final part was an appendix that included "SoW lesson plans, resources, evaluations, lesson observations, work samples from pupils, any data pertaining to pupil progress." We will see a few examples from the SoWs in the next chapter.

Ian said that the best schemes of work were those of student teachers with the strongest mentor teachers who were well read, thoughtful, and articulate about their own practice. Ideally, there would be a series of meetings in which mentors would help student teachers not just decide on their focus, but think creatively about more interesting ways to explore their topics. Ian realized that the quality of mentorship his preservice teachers received was variable. He also gleaned that some schools were rigid about what student teachers had to "deliver" to their pupils.

CONSTRAINTS AND CHANGES

Ian identified several constraints, located at the university and in schools, on student teachers' teaching of sensitive and controversial issues. He also spoke about programmatic changes he planned to make for the History course.

Constraints on Teaching

The first constraint Ian identified was insufficient time for their preparation. Ideally, his program should be two years instead of nine months, and the PGCE tried to accomplish too much in those nine months. More time should be spent on pedagogical thinking and planning, including the formulation of inquiry questions that would drive lessons.

A second big constraint was "the reality of schools." Ian explained, "Some schools have really tied down the way the teachers can operate. And so trying to do what we're talking about here is tricky. . . . So it takes either a brave head at the department or a brave mentor that's going to give a beginning teacher a bit of a head for them to be able to do these things."

Ian spoke about the obsession with accountability and competition along with a political culture of conservatism that seeped into schools. For example, some religious schools would oppose discussion of same-sex marriage. Other schools would not be happy with discussions of Islamophobia. Ian believed that teaching controversies about the British Empire was important. But the nation as a whole was "not comfortable with a kind of colonial past," and certain politicians wanted a "very positive spin" put on it. Schools varied, but, in general, tended to "play it safe" because they did not want bad publicity. Teachers were expected to be politically neutral and not disclose their views to students.

To illustrate the volatile sociopolitical context of schooling, Ian referred to the 2014 "Trojan Horse affair" in which some Birmingham schools were suspected of running an Islamic program to radicalize young people. A news article from 2017 said that, for some, it represented a "confected scandal promoted by right-wing newspapers" while for others, it symbolized the "failures of multiculturalism and the threat that hardline Islamic ideology poses to the future of the country" (Shackle, September 1, 2017).

In our interview, Ian contrasted the taboo on sensitive and controversial issues with the introduction of *Understanding History Teaching* (Husbands et al., 2003), which took up the question of what history teachers should do the day after 9-11. Ian commented, "Do you carry on talking about the three-field system, when you've got kids in front of you fired up with so many questions about, 'Well, why did they do it? Where did they come from?' . . . Exactly the kind of key questions that you're trying to get out from kids, and yet you're closing all of that down because you think, 'No, no, that's politics. That's sensitive.'"

Another challenge to taking up sensitive and controversial issues during student teaching was the number of classes teachers were assigned. Ian explained that because some classes met only weekly and pupils took many different classes, teacher workloads were heavy. Student teachers were supposed to teach roughly two-thirds of the inservice teacher's timetable. Typically they would see two groups of Years 7, 8, and 9, which generally consisted of 25–30 pupils; one group of Years 10 and 11; and one sixth form group. Although they did not teach each class every day, that meant preparing lessons for at least six different classes in the course of a week.

These demands made it vital that teachers share SoWs, lesson plans, and resources with their student teachers. But, Ian said that curriculum changes, marking student work, and required data input from exams and course grades were leading to teacher burnout.

Course Changes

A reality of teacher preparation programs in the U.K. was that more of preservice teachers' learning took place at school sites from school personnel rather than at the university. The ability of university faculty to supervise the student teachers was limited. Typically, faculty visited the student teachers four times during the year. In our final interview, Ian said that, because the university's history cohort was going to be much larger the following year, visits would be reduced to three per year.

To help remedy the problem, Ian said a significant change was going to be made in the History course. Instead of student teachers going to their school site every day during the second, longer placement, Fridays would be reserved for meetings at the university. Hopefully, this would decrease the dichotomy between the two teacher preparation settings and faculty could play a larger role in shaping student teacher learning.

Despite a conflict-averse climate in schools, Ian encouraged his preservice teachers to teach sensitive and controversial issues through his own example and the SoW assignment. In our final interview, Ian responded to questions about how the SoWs turned out that year and what he might do differently to support them. First, he said, he would be more prescriptive about the readings they needed to do and check during class sessions they had completed these readings. Second, he would have them do a peer review of their evaluations earlier in the process to give them formative, rather than summative, assessment.

Regarding close-to-home topics such as the British Empire and terrorism, he said the history program had work to do in these areas: "[There are] teachers in schools who are saying, 'Kids really want to know about this. They're coming in with burning questions around why are these terrorist attacks happening around the world.' . . . [W]e need to find some time to explore what's there . . . and how might we add to it." Ian recognized the potential for connecting British history to contemporary concerns such as racism, terrorism, and immigration (Kitson & McCully, 2005).

We learn from Ian Shepherd that exploring controversial questions in history requires a disciplinary, inquiry-based approach in which teachers design lessons to unsettle preconceptions and make students grapple with evidence. To prepare his preservice teachers for this approach, he tried to disrupt their understanding of history teaching. Despite the popularity of the Schools History Project, its impact had been variable when Ian's students had been in school. As we will see, the four candidates interviewed had also experienced traditional history teaching.

Ian gave them tools to enact the SHP's alternative tradition. He modeled risk-taking through the use of provocative sources and innovative activities. His attention to perennial questions about the Holocaust encouraged exploration of difficult questions of morality and justice.

In the next chapter we will see how Ian's preparation influenced preservice teachers' understanding of teaching controversial issues in history and their creative efforts to design curriculum. We will learn about their successes and struggles with teaching controversy during student teaching placements and compare these experiences with those of their counterparts in Northern Ireland.

KEY TAKEAWAYS

1. Many topics in the history curriculum can be taught as sensitive and controversial issues if their significance, complexity, conflictual nature, and relationship to the present are examined.
2. To be prepared to teach controversial issues, preservice teachers need to develop their subject matter knowledge, learn to formulate sound goals and a rationale for what they are teaching, be willing to experiment with provocative sources and experiential methods, and reflect on teaching and learning in their classroom.

3. Teaching controversial issues involves designing curriculum that grows out of the Schools History Project tradition—curriculum that is highly engaging for young people, gets them to tackle hard questions using inquiry-based learning, uses evidence to challenge conventional thinking, and is motivated by social aims.
4. Teacher educators prepare preservice teachers for teaching controversial issues by disrupting their preconceptions of history and teaching, making them think about how and why certain history should be taught, demonstrating a variety of innovative approaches, and providing tools for developing curriculum such as key inquiry questions and source work.
5. Preservice teachers should work out for themselves what it means to teach sensitive and controversial issues by trying it but they need support from school mentors and at the university.

Chapter 6

What Ian's Students Learned

Both England and Northern Ireland are part of the United Kingdom. Nevertheless, Ian's preservice teachers had much different orientations toward teaching controversial issues than their Northern Irish counterparts. In England, the practice was less urgent and less risky, because the country is not torn by a history of conflict between two major groups of people. Still, like the preservice teachers in Northern Ireland, Ian's graduate students were prepared to teach in ways that challenged their apprenticeships of observation. Their exposure to inquiry-based history teaching in secondary school had been limited, but they embraced the new ideas they learned from Ian's history course and tried to put them into practice.

This chapter looks at four student teachers' efforts to teach controversial issues in history in the face of competing curricular demands and factors that either assisted or hampered them. They taught lessons using inquiry questions, provocative resources, and source analysis, applying tools learned from Ian's course. The chapter is based on a series of three interviews each I conducted in fall, winter, and summer with William, Harrison, Ben, and Cathy. All four were in their twenties, from a range of social class backgrounds and different parts of England.

As we know from the previous chapter, Ian wanted his graduate students to figure out for themselves what it meant to teach sensitive and controversial history. Therefore, they were not provided with specific and explicit definitions, principles of practice, and modeling of numerous strategies.

At the same time, for their second student teaching placement, Ian assigned them to develop and teach an entire scheme of work (SoW) that revolved around a sensitive and controversial issue. The ways they fulfilled this assignment varied significantly. The preservice teachers sent me lesson plans and materials as well as reflective essays from the assignment, which nicely supplemented our interviews.

PROFILES OF PRESERVICE TEACHERS

Harrison identified himself as a working-class, left-leaning, "white British atheist" from an urban area south of London. His undergraduate degree was in politics. After a job unrelated to education, he spent a year working in the special education department of an all-girls Catholic school. Harrison said he was excited about teaching history and politics because these subjects had great potential for discussion and debate.

For Harrison, studying history in school was a "mixed bag." It included a lot of book learning and exam preparation with a smattering of fun and interesting activities, until he went to a two-year "college" for his A-levels, where more discussion took place. He said that "source work," analysis of sources using historians' methods, "was a massive thing." Since the start of the PGCE Harrison had come to realize he needed to learn a lot about content and pedagogy.

William grew up in an affluent town near London. He identified as a white Caucasian male, not religious, and without strong political, cultural, or ideological affiliations. William went to boarding school starting at the age of six. His father was a career military officer and he had planned on the same, but after an injury he left on a medical discharge.

Before university, William's history education focused on "battles and wars." The most memorable part was playing a strategic board game at the end of one class and watching videos. When studying issues he understood to be controversial, such as the slave trade, the Holocaust, and civil rights in the United States, he had one teacher who "opened up" these subjects by asking open-ended questions, soliciting student opinions, and disclosing his own views.

Ben was from a "very white" former mining town with a lot of anti-immigrant sentiment. He identified as atheist, British, white, middle class, and "Northern," as well as having Scottish heritage. He lacked exposure to diverse populations until he got to university. Ben said his interest in politics made him sensitive to inequality and exploitation. He was inspired by some of the teachers he had as an adolescent—particularly a politics teacher—but not his history teachers.

His own education in history involved a lot of "textbook exercises" and lessons were often traditional and boring, so he did a lot of learning outside class through books, films, and even video games. Ben earned a degree in history and politics, and earned a master's in history. He had worked in classrooms as an observer and aide, and during his second undergraduate year visited a primary school in a "deprived area" to teach a few history lessons each month.

Cathy was from a middle-class town in southeast England. She identified as white and Christian, and considered herself "unpolitical." She had worked with children since she was sixteen. During university, she was a substitute teacher and involved in an outreach project that offered history workshops at "deprived" schools. Cathy wanted to teach religious education as well as history. She was interested in different cultures and felt strongly about challenging students' Islamophobic misconceptions.

In her all-girls secondary school, Cathy had good history teachers who used different approaches, but she did not remember studying controversial issues. At university, she took a course on the Holocaust, which was controversial in that it challenged conventional views of Hitler's role. Like other preservice teachers, Cathy told me she needed to improve subject matter knowledge.

KEY LEARNING FROM THE HISTORY COURSE

The preservice teachers' preparation for teaching controversial issues was embedded in their learning about teaching history. The key lessons they shared with me reflected Ian's adherence to the "alternative tradition" that emerged from the Schools History Project (SHP) of the 1970s.

As explained in the previous chapter, the alternative tradition made teaching history more complex (Husbands et al., 2003). Instead of didactically delivering content, the teacher had to facilitate learners' constructivist engagement with the past. The SHP emphasized issues over chronological content, the use of historical sources for student inquiry into historical questions, and social aims of history education. Ian's teaching, like Mark Drummond's, was shaped by these ideals.

As Ian noted, preservice teachers were surprised, somewhat overwhelmed, and humbled by what they learned during the course's first few sessions. They had thought teaching would be relatively easy and that the course would start off with "nuts and bolts." They said their minds had been "scrambled" because they saw the complexity of teaching history.

The initial class sessions raised many questions ranging from broad to specific: How do you make the content accessible and interesting to individual students? How much freedom did teachers have given politics, curriculum, schools, departments, and so on? How do young people understand history? What should be the balance between skills and content? Should disturbing photographs from the Holocaust be shown to children?

Approaching Controversial Questions through
Imaginative Structured Inquiry

The preservice teachers spoke about learning to formulate key inquiry questions to drive lessons, make historical sources the core of lessons, and engage students through questioning. Ian's modeling of particular lessons compellingly demonstrated these elements.

Ben analyzed Ian's general approach: Ian teased out conventional knowledge from the class and worked with it for a while. Then he introduced new information and a different perspective. The idea was to address students' preconceptions and challenge them in a sort of "progression." Ben explained, "He gets your brain and mashes it around a bit. He tricks you into thinking— he lulls you into a false sense of security about how you think and then flips it on its head and says like, 'Well, actually you probably should think about it this way.'"

Ben, William, and Harrison were impressed by Ian's modeling of the Police Battalion 101 lesson as a structured approach to a difficult subject. To briefly review, the lesson taught students about the massacre of over 1,000 Jews from Jozefow, Poland, and posed the key inquiry question: "Why did they shoot?" In small groups, they ranked the factors that contributed to the reserve police officers' actions and then re-ordered the ranking based on additional evidence.

Harrison said the lesson gave students the opportunity to "watch modeled pedagogy" and discuss it. Specifically, the lesson showed "how to approach something in an inquiry-based fashion" and kept the class focused on "a point of contention." He also said it left him "morally questioning." He most appreciated Ian's asking what they thought about the outcome of the trials and the fact that perpetrators were not convicted.

Ben remarked on the psychological concept of "crowd mentality": "I thought that that activity we did today actually was very good in making you think about psychology in these controversial situations because it's not just about history. That plays a big part, but it's also about understanding the human condition, and that's really made my head think about what would I do in those situations?"

Ben said the Battalion 101 lesson showed him how a lesson can be designed to foster a bit of empathy, even with evildoers. He made a connection to Bernard Schlink's *The Reader*, which implicitly asks, "Can you put yourself in the shoes of someone in Nazi Germany who is working . . . as a guard, and they've got to make these decisions on whether they follow the crowd?" He believed crowd mentality was "really powerful."

As a teacher, Ben learned about the role of discussion. He said, "We were talking after every bit, what . . . factors had gone up or down, what we thought about the new piece of evidence, and I think that's really how a lot of people learn is by sharing ideas and talking to other people because through talking to someone, you have to synthesize your own thoughts into words." He also remarked on the pedagogical structure's effectiveness in getting students to think and rethink based on new evidence: "It taught you to think in logical steps. It clarifies one bit of information you have, and you think a certain way, and then he throws another bit of information at you, and you think a different way. That sort of progression I think is quite powerful."

William described the lesson as an information-ranking activity that was "very clever" and got him thinking about use of evidence and sources. Another example of modeling controversial history teaching that William appreciated was the Derby race incident in which suffragette Emily Davison was killed.

In that exercise, the class simulated a newsroom in which reporters were researching the pre-World War I arms buildup. Ian played their editor. He suddenly asked them to change stories and write news articles for various magazines on a suffragette who was killed after throwing herself in front of the king's horse. The reporters continued to get new information as the story unfolded and had to make real-time decisions about what was reliable. They also had to tailor their articles to their respective publications. William found this such a good lesson that he emulated it with his own class when teaching about Thomas Becket, the archbishop infamously murdered in 1170 after a conflict with the king.

Ben said that critiquing videos of other teachers was a useful demonstration of "what not to do." It got him thinking about how to frame questions and use language during lessons. Other videos made him think about how to make lessons more inquiry-based. Ideally, a teacher wanted to ask open-ended questions that raise different perspectives and link them back to the key inquiry question. Ben acknowledged this was a "really difficult part of teaching."

Approaching the Holocaust through a Museum Visit

Three of Ian's preservice teachers remarked on the value of the September field trip to the Holocaust Centre. It yielded lessons about the importance for young people of educational design, individual stories, and historical context.

The visit to the Centre, along with the class's reflection on it the next day, prompted them to think about a new exhibit, carefully designed for young people, that Ian showed them. The exhibit displayed the places inhabited by a Jewish family in Nazi Germany, and everyone thought it was more effective than the main exhibit. Harrison told me he learned to see a museum space, activities, and exhibits through the eyes of a student.

In our interviews, the preservice teachers said the main exhibit over-loaded information and lacked discernible organization, making it difficult for young people to appreciate. Ben articulated why the new exhibit worked better:

> It was almost like a lesson in the sense that it started with some objectives, and then from there, it went from activity to activity, each activity almost like the room, and then you get towards the end, and you come to a conclusion . . . or some historical knowledge. . . . it's inherently narrative. You're going from one area to the next, course, consequence, chronology, all that thing that flows through. . . . It got you thinking about progression of the hate and anti-Semitism, and the building, whereas the exhibit was just, "Here it is."

The survivor gave a speech to visitors that was especially instructive. Harrison learned about the power of individual stories to humanize difficult-to-comprehend historical events. The survivor helped the teachers realize that the Holocaust should not be taught as a separate topic, but approached in a broader context of "genocide as a whole."

Planning a Scheme of Work

By the end of the school year, Ian's preservice teachers had planned and taught an SoW. The assignment was aimed at developing a coherent set of eight lessons that fed into a broader inquiry and goals for student learning. Ben told me in our second interview that each lesson needed a "good inquiry focus throughout" and "a good hook" that "gets them thinking about the issue." Then students would "develop their understanding" and be assessed on it. Each lesson "links on to the next one," and all of them feed into the whole: "They all sort of mesh together like a jigsaw."

Learning to do source work with students during Ian's course sessions contributed to SoW planning and teaching. In December, the graduate students gave mini-presentations on analyzing sources that made them think about effective versus ineffective practice.

CONCEPTIONS OF CONTROVERSIAL ISSUES

As discussed in the last chapter, Ian merged sensitive and controversial issues and did not explicitly define them. Consequently, his preservice teachers lacked clarity about the distinction. When asked to define the term "controversial issues," they tended to confuse them with controversial topics—those certain stakeholders deem problematic to teach (Ho et al., 2017), or they thought of them as sensitive issues—those likely to upset young people.

Probably because Ian focused on the Holocaust and because it is a mandatory topic in the English history curriculum, the preservice teachers cited it as an example of a controversial issue. When I probed, they explained that, while its historical reality was not controversial, it could be taught with a controversial slant as Ian did in his Battalion 101 lesson when he raised the question of guilt.

Harrison defined controversial issues as "anything that could be deemed as controversial, emotionally challenging, introducing new ideas that might upset their [students'] current perceptions. So challenging their status quo. . . That's a really broad definition. [laughs]"

He said that context mattered, especially student identity. For his rural working-class students, issues around class and social mobility might be most controversial.

William began by saying controversial issues were topics that students might not want to learn about or that parents might object to. On further questioning, he explained that if there were consensus on whether and how an event happened, then it was not controversial. If there were disagreement, it would be deemed controversial. And if one has to be careful about teaching an event based on student reactions, say, because it was violent or pupils have some family or cultural connection to it, those were sensitive issues. Examples of controversial issues included whether England should pay reparations for its role in the slave trade, responsibility for the Holocaust, and Oliver Cromwell's brutal conquest of Ireland.

Ben defined controversial issues as a topic that elicits a reaction when you talk about it because it's part of the "public psyche." In our second interview, he admitted, "it's quite hard to define what a controversial issue is. I mean, everything could be controversial . . . I think the sort of things like taking away people's freedoms, killing people, those sort of topics, they tend to be the ones that seem to be controversial." He gave Nazi Germany, the Holocaust, and slavery as examples. In our final interview Ben said his understanding had progressed. He now understood them as subject matter about which society disagrees.

Cathy defined "sensitive and controversial issues" as issues that have the potential to offend people or where there are competing schools of thought that can't be reconciled. She gave the Holocaust and slavery as examples, but said "you have to put a slant on it to make it controversial." Like others, Cathy seemed to view controversial issues as debunking established views of history.

Ian's graduate students emphasized reasons for teaching controversial issues that were somewhat different from their Northern Irish counterparts.

They stressed the importance of teaching rational inquiry, challenging the status quo, and grappling with the mistakes of the past. Harrison said examining controversies "force students to think, engage with the debate, and have an opinion" rather than be "spoon fed a correct answer," and that having an opinion on issues "shapes your identity." Cathy said teaching controversy was important because "history is all about different cultures," and understanding different perspectives was key. This group did not talk about teaching controversial issues as a path toward social or political change.

STUDENT TEACHING EXPERIENCES

The preservice teachers' accounts of their student teaching and the lesson plans and materials they sent me revealed their efforts to apply important tools learned from the history course. They created lessons that made the study of history engaging, complex, and inquiry-based through key questions, source work, and stimulating resources. They worked to make lessons accessible to young people, scaffold small group work, and try out innovative methods. Harrison and William in particular spoke about raising moral questions through their lessons.

Accounts of student teaching also revealed challenges. Student teachers struggled with classes of mixed ability, limited time, and traditional school cultures. Dealing with student behavior and heavy class loads were also challenges. During their second placement, student teachers worked in about eight different classes, of which seven differed in age level, performance level, or subject. As in Northern Ireland, although they shared teaching responsibility with teachers of record, their many classes and limited time in each spread them thin.

Also as in Northern Ireland, when asked about teaching controversial issues, the student teachers talked about lessons that did not actually revolve around controversial questions, but rather included provocative content. This indicated some confusion about the concept of controversial issues and perhaps also a desire to respond positively to my research questions.

Table 6.1 represents the most robust controversial issues lesson each of the teachers reported, the class in which it was taught, and the tools that were used.

Exploring Moral Complexity with Rich Resources

Harrison had a rewarding experience with his first school placement at a "state-run academy" in an "upper working-class to low middle-class" area. Academies are state-funded schools independent from the local educational

Table 6.1   Student Teachers' Main Experience Teaching Controversihal Issues

	Course	Focus	Curricular and Pedagogical Tools
Harrison	Year 9 History	Shot at Dawn: Was Henry Farr a coward or casualty?	Newsreel clip on war neuroses, Analysis of testimony, *Not Forgotten* clip, photo of war memorial to executed soldiers
William	Year 8 History	Cromwell and the Massacre of Drogheda: Could Cromwell defend the indefensible?	Song and film clip about Cromwell in Ireland, Belfast mural, source work
Cathy	Year 9 History	Who deserves credit for D-Day?	American History Channel clip on D-Day, card sort, written conclusions, discussion
Ben	Year 8 History	Did Charles I deserve to be executed?	Film clip on Charles I trial and execution, source work, speeches

authority and not required to follow the national curriculum. Most secondary schools in England, which are non-selective, are now academies.

His second placement at a small, "very working-class" rural school was more challenging. But Harrison enjoyed crafting history lessons using compelling and varied resources. After he taught about Great Britain's reactions to the Spanish flu and to AIDS, he had a terrific opportunity to observe other teachers teaching the same lesson, using his resources, to another class. He said, "I watched them teach it far better [laughs], which is obviously going to be the case because they are experienced and know exactly what they're looking for as opposed to me who is muddling through."

What impressed him most was their ability to target the "key points" of the lesson. They managed to cover content for exam requirements and work in discussion of moral questions about society's response to AIDS: "You are dealing with issues of persecution of the homosexual community, lack of understanding, huge levels of ignorance, people being withdrawn from classes because parents are scared of it, issues of blood transfusions and screening and things like that." The lesson also addressed the inadequacy of Britain's response to the Spanish flu: "This killed more people than the First World War."

Harrison learned the necessity of making content accessible and relatable to students by using developmentally appropriate language and resources. He said, "You can be brave and courageous, but if they can't understand what you're saying, there's no point in talking . . . let's be honest." He added, "[V]ideo sources are brilliant. I think that is because it's accessible and everyone can get them, so long as they're appropriately pitched because what I've learned from other lessons is I might think they're cracking, kids might think, 'What is this?'"

Despite muddling through the first time, Harrison said he enjoyed teaching that lesson, although he had to cover a lot of content in a short time: "It was pacey because covering two epidemics, giving the context, and showing the big thematic links as well as getting into video sources and concept cracking that, within an hour with a mixed-ability class is incredibly difficult."

Teaching an academically heterogeneous class was particularly challenging: "That is really tricky particularly when you have got such a chasm of difference in ability in the class. . . . That's one of the things I'm also struggling with just generally . . . I've got twenty odd kids who are A to D grade, bottom end, and then I've got three or four who are going to be A star top end."

Harrison was proud of a lesson he taught to Year 9s titled "Shot at Dawn: Coward or Casualty? A Case Study of Henry Farr." It was about a well-known case of a soldier who was executed for cowardice during World War I, even though he showed signs of shell shock (now called post-traumatic stress disorder). The British army executed 306 people by firing squad for cowardice during World War I. Harrison characterized this topic as offering multiple controversies and lots of opportunity for debate.

Harrison began by introducing soldiers hospitalized for shell shock through a "wonderful bit" of 1917 newsreel on war neuroses from British Pathé, which claimed they were treated successfully. He followed by posing the key questions: "Why was Henry Farr shot at dawn? Was he a coward who deserved to be shot? Or a casualty of war?" Fortuitously, testimony from Farr's court martial case was contained in the textbook. The class read the evidence put forward by the prosecution and defense. Students took notes in a table with two columns: Evidence of Cowardice versus Evidence of Casualty.

Harrison showed a video clip of an interview with Henry Farr's descendants from an addendum to *Not Forgotten,* a British documentary on the impact of World War I, and a photograph of the Shot at Dawn memorial to the 306 servicemen executed during World War I for cowardice. The students wrote their own conclusions, using these sentence starters:

"I believe that Henry Farr ____ because ____.
Although there is evidence to argue ____ (evidence).
However, I still believe ____ because ____ (evidence)."

For a "stretch," students were given the following prompt: "Can you think why the Army, even when knowing about psychological issues, may still want to execute the likes of Harry Farr? Note down your thoughts." Harrison relayed the gist of the brief discussion that ensued in his class. No one argued Farr deserved to be shot. However, some argued he was a coward.

He recounted an exchange with the group:

"Even if they knew he was shell-shocked, why do you think they shot him?" They went, "They can't afford to treat him, so they shot him?" But once you start developing the question beyond that, it's going, "Well, look back to the testimony. What was it saying his effect was on other men?" . . . We developed to the point of, "Oh, they shot him as an example, and it sent a very strong message to everyone else that you're not getting out." Through questioning Harrison guided students to the understanding he wanted them to get. Harrison was disappointed there was not more time to expand the discussion.

Harrison had an hour to teach a morally profound lesson about an episode in military history that remains controversial to this day. He selected a variety of resources to impart some knowledge about shell shock, the case of Henry Farr—one of many soldiers believed not to have received a fair trial—, and the memorial created in 2000 for the families of soldiers executed for cowardice. The lesson plan states that students had ten minutes to write their conclusions about the case, which, as we have seen with other student teaching lessons, left only a few minutes for discussion.

Harrison's scheme of work was on life in Nazi Germany. The topic was chosen for him by the school. The key question was why 13.5 million Germans voted for the Nazis. Although it included a look at war profiteering, the lessons were not framed as controversies.

Examining Controversies through Popular and Historical Sources

William student taught at a school that had just become an academy and served mainly white "middle- to lower-class pupils," a major contrast with the wealthy school where he did his first placement. He said that despite the school's insufficient funding, and student and parent antipathy toward outsiders and the government, he "absolutely loved" the experience.

William's scheme of work for Year 8s was on the English Civil War, a conflict fueled by religious turmoil. William explained the war's context—massacres and clashes between Catholics and Protestants in mainland Europe and Ireland had long had repercussions in England. The controversy he taught, concerning the trial for treason and execution of King Charles I of England, was whether fault lay with Charles I or Parliament, which had indicted him. The class held a mock trial of Charles, with students role-playing the prosecution and defense. The trial prompted a forty-minute debate that William characterized as "really quite rewarding."

William described at greater length a lesson he designed and taught on Oliver Cromwell's massacre of Irish Catholics and English Royalists during the Siege of Drogheda in Ireland. Had the lesson been taught in Northern Ireland, it would have exemplified Kitson and McCully's (2005) risk-taking criteria, but in England it did not hit so close to home.

William sent me his lesson plan, PowerPoint, and graphic organizer for source work. The lesson's KEQ (Key Enquiry Question) was "The Drogheda massacre—Could Oliver Cromwell defend the indefensible?" The rationale included the following: "This lesson will look at one of the most controversial moments in Cromwell's life and how it has influenced English and Irish relations even today. Pupils will be charged with evaluating the validity of the sources with particular focus on the provenance of the source."

The lesson began with listening to a 1989 song by the Pogues, "Young Ned of the Hill," which curses Oliver Cromwell for the horrors he perpetrated on Ireland. The song was followed by a short clip from an Irish docudrama called *Cromwell in Ireland,* which stated that Cromwell headed an English army that killed 25 percent of the Irish population. Students were asked to "write down two things [from the video] about Cromwell's legacy in Ireland." William introduced the KEQ and the main objective of the lesson: "To investigate what happened at Drogheda and why it is still seen as a controversial moment in English and Irish History today."

The next PowerPoint slide showed a 2002 Belfast mural depicting the massacre. Above an image of victorious English soldiers, an image of Cromwell bears the caption "Oliver Cromwell Protector and Defender of the Protestant Faith." Below, two quotes from Cromwell explain the need to "crush" the Catholic church because Protestant churches had been "desecrated" and Protestant people "slaughtered."

The heart of the lesson was a "source analysis task" in which students filled out a "fact finder sheet" by examining six sources placed around the room after William modeled the task using the first source. The sources included Cromwell's account of the capture of Drogheda to the House of Commons, an eyewitness account that appeared fourteen years later, an excerpt from a 1980 textbook, a statement written by a historian in 2002, and a nineteenth-century illustration of the massacre in a 1986 book on Irish history published in Dublin. The graphic organizer had students notate the source's provenance, reliability, and what it told about Cromwell's actions at Drogheda.

The lesson culminated in a fifteen-minute discussion and the school's mandatory ten minutes of writing on two questions:

1. "In your opinion, does Cromwell deserve the title 'The Curse of Ireland'? Explain your answer."

2. "Do you think we can **trust** all of the evidence we have seen today? Explain your answer (Consider the provenance caption of each source: who wrote it, when and why was it written?)."

William said the lesson took more time than planned, and he was reluctant to cut it off because students were engaged and making connections. He asked the head teacher if he could extend the class period and she agreed. This vital support for teaching controversy, which we saw with Sean in Northern Ireland, counteracted time limits that so often squeezed lessons.

William said the discussion was "really interesting"—many students "were saying that Cromwell was a war hero during the Civil War, but Ireland damaged him spectacularly, and that was what I was trying to get at really." He thought the lesson was highly controversial because it made students realize that historical events from centuries ago are still playing out today and challenged their view of Cromwell as a heroic figure.

He also considered that it successfully taught "historical literacy" because students found discrepancies among sources and realized that even now people interpret the facts differently. William commented, "It got the pupils to suddenly realize that history is not something about the past. It is still going on today where these events are no longer just consigned to the pages of history. They are genuinely being debated . . . it allowed pupils then to fully engage and form their own opinions, and actually the material I gave them was quite challenging."

William, like Harrison, demonstrated his use of "initial stimulus material" to get students engaged. He seemed confident in orchestrating classroom activities in which students examined sources on Drogheda and debated Charles I's execution. Importantly, he modeled the source analysis task to set up students for success. The lessons he described served valuable goals such as learning to think critically about history using tools of the discipline. Despite extending the class period, there still was not enough time to discuss connections between history and contemporary politics.

Wrestling with Controversial Questions and Complex Tasks

Similar to the other preservice teachers' placements, Cathy's second placement was at a secondary school in a former mining community with mostly white working-class students. She sometimes struggled there, for example, when designing her scheme of work on World War II. But she worked hard at successfully completing the program.

In our second interview, she spoke about wrestling with whether it was possible to frame World War II as a controversial issue. Cathy said she was preparing lessons on whether the war was inevitable, the role of children on the home front, Nazi and British propaganda, and the Battle of Britain. She was considering a culminating lesson on how the war should be remembered and memorialized: "Should soldiers display their medals proudly?" She explained, "I found a really good blog that was saying that you shouldn't wear medals for battle because you've killed people basically. . . . It's meant to be remembrance, but how much remembrance and how much celebration we got one up on Germany?"

At our third interview, Cathy described the lesson from the SoW she taught that she considered most controversial. It was titled "Do the Americans Deserve to Take the Credit for D-Day?" Our interview was supplemented by the lesson plan, PowerPoint, and essay she wrote about how the lesson went.

After providing context about D-Day, Cathy presented a short video called "America the Story of Us: D-Day Invasion" from the American History Channel. Without telling students who had made the video, she had them write on a handout how the video portrayed the roles of the Americans and the British. She hoped to provoke student reactions because they would have nothing to record on the British side of their paper. In her reflective essay she wrote, "Pupils were outraged by this account." She recognized that she could have discussed with them the source's bias, but did not have time.

Next, she distributed cards with military tactics, which students had to sort first according to whether Germany, Britain, or the United States was represented and then identify "positives and negatives of each country." Then students organized a set of facts that Cathy gave them about troops and armaments. Finally, students wrote a paragraph on the question, "Do the Americans deserve to take the credit for D-Day?" supported by more specific questions: (1) Why would some people say America was the main reason the Allies won D-Day? (2) Why would some people say it was Britain? (3) Whose tactics meant the Allies won?

Cathy said the students "wrote loads," much more than usual. They "used a lot of evidence." Then she "flipped it over its head for the plenary," by asking, "What would have happened if America had not contributed any men?" The discussion moved to "What if they had refused to participate at all?" and went on for about ten minutes. If she had more time, she would have asked students to revisit their paragraphs.

Cathy said she deliberately intended her lesson on D-Day to lead students to follow one narrative until a different version was revealed by additional facts. She believed the British were generally unaware of the U.S. role in WWII and its contribution to D-Day in particular. She wanted students to "rethink their ideas" by "looking at it from a different angle." Cathy wanted to set up the kind of progression that Ian modeled to promote conceptual change in which students would initially respond to a question, confront new evidence, and then revise their understanding. Her reflective essay said that while the video evoked the negative reaction she wanted, the main activity involving evaluating evidence was difficult for students.

In hindsight, Cathy said that instead of having them work silently, which "led to a lot of confusion," they should have "bounced ideas off each other." Also, she should have read through all the instructions before they started so they wouldn't have had to ask procedural questions. Cathy wrote that students were confused about whether to classify something as a country's weakness or strength, and thought she should have simplified the table they had to create. She noted there was not enough time to practice source analysis, as she had intended.

From teaching about D-Day, Cathy said she learned how important it is to frame open-ended questions in emotive and engaging ways. She also became aware of how she used language, in particular her use of "we" and "our" in connection with British history. Cathy wanted to do her SoW assignment on World War II because of important roles played by members of her family. But she concluded the topic did not lend itself to teaching controversial issues:

> I found that it was quite hard for me to think of controversial angles. I know that sounds really silly . . . but World War II is such a known thing . . . It's all so British. . . . I wanted to look at how Dunkirk was portrayed in the media . . . as a massive success, but we lost a fifth of soldiers, and we were cornered, and we nearly lost the war. . . . But obviously I only had an hour, and even that was pushed and just trying to get through knowledge, and then look at the controversial side was just impossible. I really struggled with that.

Cathy openly acknowledged the challenges she confronted, which included a teacher who made her feel unwelcome. Cathy said that in general she had difficulty imparting sufficient knowledge and exploring controversial issues in an hour-long lesson. She added that talkative students made it hard to teach. My sense was that she wanted to engage students in controversy, but needed scaffolding from mentors to create clearly thought-out and accessible lessons for her students.

Constrained by Expertise and Insufficient Time

Ben enjoyed his second placement at a well-regarded comprehensive school. (Comprehensive schools offer grammar school, technical school, and secondary school curricula.) Despite his plan to develop a scheme of work on the Holocaust or slavery, Ben ended up focusing on the British Civil War for Year 8 History. Well into his placement, he went to a pub with other teachers from his school site and talked about curriculum. The British Civil War had not been taught, despite its importance, and they encouraged Ben to teach it so that they could utilize his SoW the following year. He had written his undergraduate dissertation on it and the teachers gave him freedom to do as he liked.

In our final interview, Ben said he read the articles on teaching sensitive and controversial issues Ian provided, but did not feel he addressed such issues sufficiently. He would begin class with controversial material to "entice" students, but did not follow through on making controversy a focus of lessons. He thought he would include "Cromwell in Ireland . . . which is a massive controversial part of it." Ben said that people in England were talking about Northern Ireland again because of Brexit, and "get very irate about it." He explained, "All of that stuff started during this period of time." But because of "logistical sort of constraints," he did not get to teach that part.

Ben explained that his familiarity with the period was a problem: "It was almost like a blessing and a curse . . . I've already got all these ideas that I've developed over the years around specific historical things." He speculated that being so knowledgeable "constrained" him from thinking "outside the box" and taking a "few more risks."

Ben thought that his lesson on Charles I's trial and execution did revolve around a controversial question: "Did Charles I deserve to die?" The lesson plan, which detailed the first day's activities of the three-day lesson and the resources Ben created, was carefully conceived. It started with a clip from *The Devil's Whore*, a popular drama set during the English Civil War, to help students visualize the trial and execution and begin to organize information. Then students worked in small groups to analyze an evidence sheet with short quotes from five sources, by color-coding arguments for and against execution and ordering them according to their strength.

The class was split into the prosecution and defense. Students wrote speeches stating arguments for and against their side. Ben's lesson plan stated that, through this assessment, students would "evaluate which interpretation of the past is more appropriate based on their own judgments derived from discussing with other students and their analysis of the evidence available."

In a "plenary" that culminated the first day's activities, individual students took a position by writing yes or no on a Post-it and placing it on the appropriate side of the board. The teacher picked these up to "push for explanations" and check for understanding. In the following class five days later, students continued to work on their speeches. Nine days after that, they delivered them (unfortunately Ben was not able to be present that day).

Ben said that the speeches were only partly successful, because the students lacked sufficient historical knowledge to argue effectively. Ben concluded, "I didn't give enough modeling of what I think they needed to look at. And I needed to give them more time as a group and more structure and guidance on what they needed to be talking about as opposed to 'Here's a load of things you need to do. You need to get writing it now.'"

He planned to redesign the lesson with these takeaways in mind. The materials he sent me actually provide clear and well-organized instructions. For Year 8s, developing an understanding of the different sources on their own seems challenging, despite having a list of key words to help them. And the lesson plan shows that, due to the number of activities during the first day, each was allotted only five or ten minutes. It is understandable that Ben felt pressed to cover a lot of ground in a short time given the constraints of a one-hour weekly class session.

In his Year 9 class, Ben was given a scheme of work that revolved around the question, "Did people actually like living in Nazi Germany?" He found that pupils had a hard time addressing the question's substance, in part because they were learning source analysis skills and being assessed on them.

Ben said it was challenging to juggle the multiple demands he faced with a large, talkative class: "Remember I only see them once a week for an hour. . . . I'm trying to get them thinking really deeply about that question, but then also they've never done a proper source analysis before, and I've got to basically do that for them." It was a "top set class" with "a couple of pupils that really got it" because they understood how to do the source analysis and could then contemplate the question. But others really struggled. Ben said they complained, "'I don't get the questions we need to ask the source. I don't really get what we're looking at.' Some of them were just like, 'I don't know what the source says.' And with that initial struggling, they can't then really think about that question in great detail."

Dealing with student behavior while studying sensitive issues also was challenging. Ben recalled that from his own school days: "You'd be talking about something like the Holocaust or slavery or whatever, and they're just all laughing and giggling and whatever, and not focusing on it. And trying to get across to them that this is really important for them to learn, to deal with, not just for them, but for society as well." At the same time, he did not want to scare 13-year-olds: "It's quite a young age, and making sure that what you're doing is not going to give them nightmares is something to consider as well."

Ben's reflection on his student teaching experience speaks to the expertise and experience demanded by both the alternative approach to history teaching and the practice of teaching sensitive and controversial issues. Institutional constraints made these even more difficult.

CONSTRAINTS AND SUPPORTS

The English preservice teachers experienced different constraints on teaching controversy than their counterparts in Northern Ireland, although there was some overlap. Exams and timetables interfered in both locations. But instead of the challenges of teaching in a divided society, particularly in communities that had been hot spots during the Troubles, preservice teachers in England spoke more about time constraints, a traditional school culture, and student behavior.

Ben, Cathy, William, and Harrison all taught at schools located in a former mining area that was economically depressed. They told me that some students seemed quite alienated from school and the mix of academic levels posed challenges. There were cultural and political differences between school communities and student teachers. Both Harrison and Ben student taught at a school with a rigid traditional pedagogical culture that conflicted with what they had learned at University.

Harrison, during his second placement at this school, chafed at the "chalk and talk" teaching style justified by the rationale, "This is how kids here learn." During most of the placement, Harrison "knuckled under" and felt like a "cog in the machine." His Year 11s were doing "controlled assessment" under an "old examination system" during the final eight class periods of the year. Ben described classes at this same school as focused on textbooks and tests. He said, "I hate to say it, but there wasn't much sort of like people interaction in the way that it got them generating their own ideas. It was more like 'This is what you need to learn and copy it down,' that sort of thing."

William said some of his lessons were "constrained" due to a school requirement that he reserve ten minutes in every lesson for writing. It limited his ability to engage in deeper analysis and debate with students. Also, at the end of term, Year 10s were doing mock exams, which made it hard to explore content in any depth.

The number of classes the student teachers taught spread their attention in many directions and made it difficult to focus. For example, in our second interview, Ben told me the daunting range of subjects he was teaching, including medieval history, ethics, and philosophy in Year 7 Humanities; the Industrial Revolution in Year 8 History; Nazi Germany in Year 9 History; law and justice, and jobs and employability in Year 9 Citizenship and Personal Development; World War I medicine transitioning to Weimar Germany in a Year 10 GCSE module; and America in the 1930s and 1940s. The frequency with which he saw classes ranged from once every two weeks to twice a week. Ben let me know he was very tired: "I'm spinning a lot of plates."

Cathy too said she struggled with jumping "from one to the next" and not having enough "head space." She had to be very organized: "I print everything out that I'm going to need for the next day and put it in folders that are labeled like Lesson 1, Lesson 2, Lesson 3, Lesson 4, so I can literally just grab it and go and not have to think, 'Have I got everything?' because I know I have." Cathy told me during our final interview that she had a "mini breakdown" because she was working with a team of teachers for a new GCSE (General Certificate of Secondary Education) class who were directing her in conflicting ways.

Like the competing curricular demands I described in *The Charged Classroom* (Pace, 2015), tensions between the two traditions of history teaching were evident in the experiences of these student teachers. The 2000 national history curriculum was much less prescriptive than previous iterations, "enabling teachers to plan creatively and flexibly" (Husbands et al., 2003, p. 14). But in one-hour classes that met once or twice a week, pressures to cover content, assign writing tasks, teach source analysis, and in some cases prepare for exams meant that teachers were pulled in different directions and time for discussing significant questions was constrained.

As we saw in a previous chapter, history teachers in Northern Ireland confront contentious issues in the curriculum whether they want to or not, whereas those in England may not. Kitson and McCully (2005) question to what extent their category of Avoiders—teachers who do not embrace social aims of history and avoid controversy—pertains to history teachers in England: "Might similar teachers in England shy away from teaching about immigration, the legacy of empire and issues, past and present, of racism and intolerance?" (p. 35).

The preservice teachers in England did teach about slavery, the U.S. civil rights movement, and racism as these topics appeared in the curriculum they were teaching, but they did not focus on controversies within these topics. They did not report teaching other aspects of Black, Asian, and Minority Ethnic history; immigration; or the legacy of empire. Based on their reports, these topics were not part of the curriculum at their schools.

Harrison and Cathy each taught a citizenship lesson in which they challenged rampant Islamophobia in the media. Harrison and Ben said they would like to teach immigration and class issues. The aforementioned topics, however, did not make their way into history lessons on controversial questions.

The student teachers in England reported notably fewer supports than constraints. They said that although student behavior could pose challenges, a supportive factor was students' receptiveness to their lessons. William noted the autonomy and encouragement he received from mentor teachers and department heads. Cathy valued the positivity of her university supervisor, especially when she struggled at her second placement.

A particularly strong source of support was the history cohort. Student teachers texted each other often to ask for ideas and share resources. They gathered together for dinner every so often. It was helpful that they taught some of the same topics.

ADVICE TO TEACHER EDUCATORS
AND REMAINING QUESTIONS

Ian's graduate students admired and appreciated his expertise and felt encouraged to teach controversial issues in history. They learned important practical tools for designing curriculum and teaching inquiry-based lessons. Still, three of them said they were unsure of the best ways to approach controversy. They advised that teacher educators explicitly model different ways to teach issues. Also, William and Ben would have liked greater clarification with examples on what is a controversial issue versus what is a sensitive issue. Ben suggested discussing with preservice teachers the various definitions of these practices.

Two preservice teachers wanted more on how to question students most effectively. Cathy suggested getting preservice teachers to practice: "I would get them to work on their questioning and how to bounce ideas off of each other, because that was hard." Like Aoife in Northern Ireland, she wanted to learn ways of formulating questions that get to the heart of a controversy but do not inflame students.

Although students' responses to history were not emotionally steeped in collective identity and lessons learned from family and community, the student teachers still were concerned about reactions to sensitive and controversial history. They said that teacher educators should model how to vary activities to engage students, encourage their cooperation, and prepare them to make contributions. Harrison and Cathy felt they needed more preparation on facilitating discussion, and establishing norms and rules. Cathy wanted guidance on dealing with disruptive students and Harrison wanted modeling of "how to deal with abhorrent views."

Having to write an evaluation of their SoWs made student teachers reflect on their curriculum design and practice. To strengthen the SoWs, Ben suggested assigning a group project in which the student teachers developed a scheme of work together: "We could have picked a sensitive or controversial issue to look at. And then we could have brought that in session and talked about it and then talked about how we would have taught it, and then maybe done that as a group." He said that student teachers could plan and co-teach a controversial issues lesson. This advice reinforces the idea that teacher preparation courses should provide opportunities for practice teaching. In the next chapter, we will see a university course designed to do just that.

Finally, Ian's graduate students advised that teacher educators prepare their students to teach controversial issues in ways that fit the demands of schools. They had evidently been prepared to design rich, interesting lessons that revolved around inquiry questions, provocative resources, and source analysis that held great potential for exploring historical—and moral—controversies. These lessons were difficult to complete in one-hour class periods with young adolescents. The student teachers wanted a bridge between university ideals and the real conditions of the charged classroom.

KEY TAKEAWAYS

1. Preservice teachers learned that teaching controversial issues involves structuring a progression of conceptual change in which the teacher elicits students' prior knowledge, introduces new evidence that challenges that knowledge, gets students to wrestle with inquiry questions that often are moral, and helps students arrive at new understandings.
2. Student teachers designed and taught rich lessons on controversial issues in history and adopted key practices such as forming key inquiry questions, selecting stimulating resources, orchestrating source analysis activities, and questioning students.
3. Student teachers' efforts were constrained by school timetables, curricular demands such as coverage and exam preparation, and a traditional school culture.
4. Student teachers' efforts were supported by the SoW assignment, communication with their peers, students' receptiveness, and encouragement from mentor teachers and department heads.
5. Advice for teacher educators included clarifying conceptions of controversial issues; explicit modeling of different approaches to teaching controversial issues; providing opportunities to rehearse questioning students, curriculum development, and teaching of lessons; modeling ways to deal with challenging student behavior; and preparing preservice teachers for the real constraints of classrooms and schools.
6. Teachers' remaining questions were about the difference between sensitive and controversial issues and the best ways to teach controversial issues given constraints, develop classroom norms, facilitate discussion, and handle disruptive students or those who expressed "abhorrent views."

Chapter 7

Liz Simmons

Teaching Controversial Issues through Democratic Discussion in the U.S. Midwest

The teacher education course I studied in the United States was different from the other courses described in this book because of its timing, its focus on civic discourse, and its opportunities for practice teaching. This chapter looks at Liz Simmons and her course on democratic discussion in social studies. It is one of two electives that follow four other social studies methods courses in the teacher education program at a Midwestern university and begins in March when student teaching placements are ending. Social studies preservice teachers in the program are earning both their teaching license and master of education degree.

We start by learning about Liz's background in teaching and research, her philosophy, and the aims of the course. The chapter describes class sessions in which Liz models different approaches to discussion and students practice leading discussion-based lessons, many of which revolve around controversial issues. Liz offers abundant resources and emphasizes process and reflection. Over time, her class grapples with the issue of free speech versus protection against discrimination and threats to safety—a perennial issue raised by contemporary controversies in the United States.

EDUCATION BACKGROUND, BIOGRAPHY, AND PHILOSOPHY

Liz Simmons is a deeply knowledgeable, dedicated, and open-minded veteran social studies teacher educator and scholar whose primary interest is politics. She taught secondary school for a few years before going to graduate school and becoming a university professor and researcher. Liz's research focuses on democratic citizenship education for adolescents and encompasses a wide range of projects. She has also researched topics related to race and gender in education. The scope of her expertise in educational research and practice is broad and deep.

Although she has worked on international projects, Liz's conception of controversial issues is informed mainly by U.S. scholarship. She distinguishes between open and settled controversial public issues (Hess, 2009), and between controversial issues and difficult histories. And she is committed to teaching controversy through discussion because she believes teaching civic discourse is fundamental to educating for democracy.

Scholars argue that discussion of controversial political issues is an essential part of preparing democratic citizens (Hess, 2009). To fully participate in a democratic society, students must learn to deliberate with others on significant issues—such as war, education policy, and reproductive rights—about which people strenuously disagree (Gutmann, 2000). When students express their own ideas, they manifest the ideal of civic equality, which upholds the idea that every person is a legitimate participant in discussion and decision-making. Done well, classroom dialogue about controversial issues teaches political tolerance—the disposition to grant civil rights such as freedom of expression to all (Avery, 2002). It also strengthens student political knowledge and interest (Hess & McAvoy, 2015).

Unfortunately studies in the United States have found that, despite its crucial importance, such discussion occurs infrequently in social studies classrooms, particularly those designated lower-track or populated by Black, Latinx, immigrant, and/or low-income students (Kahne & Middaugh, 2008). Many teachers avoid it for reasons such as the challenges it poses to classroom management and to their own pedagogical capabilities. Because leading discussion is so challenging, it is difficult to teach others how to do it. Walter Parker and Diana Hess (2001) take up this problem and challenge teacher educators not only to teach *with* discussion as a pedagogical strategy, but also to teach *for* discussion, that is, focus on its value, purposes, types, and processes.

Liz took up this challenge in her course. She was well versed in the literature on classroom discussion in social studies. And she was dedicated to preparing her preservice teachers for discussion of controversial issues by ensuring they understood its vital role in democracy and had the tools to facilitate it in their future classrooms.

When asked about her background and identity, Liz replied self-effacingly: "Just think WASP, Midwest WASP." She was introspective and said she worked hard to reflect on her gut reactions and implicit biases. As if she were responding to Ian's lesson on Police Battalion 101, which posed the essential question, "Why did they (reserve police officers) shoot (1,000 innocent Jews)," she advocated taking responsibility for racism and the capacity to tolerate or even perpetrate evil:

I mean, personally I think it's part of all of us, that we are very susceptible to these things and if we don't recognize that . . . then that's the danger. So when I hear people say, "Well, I would have been one of the people that rescued people," maybe, but let's consider that you might not have been, you know? We all like to think that we're in that group, right? So let's take it to a situation where you observe somebody being bullied. That happens in adult circles, too. Did you rise to the occasion? . . . We are constantly trying to do better, but if we don't recognize how some of our innate tendencies are anti-democratic, then we're going to have a big problem.

Liz openly engaged in self-examination in light of social psychological insights about human nature.

Liz had been teaching the democratic discussion course for the past few years. Her practice of teaching controversial issues began as a social studies teacher who had majored in political science. Her high school classes would discuss current events and social issues. She "exponentially increased" her knowledge of different methods during her graduate studies with a very influential mentor. Liz also "tripled" her commitment to discussing controversial issues, and remembered being particularly inspired by Shirley Engle's article "Decision Making: The Heart of Social Studies Instruction," originally published back in 1960 and republished in 2003.

In her early years as a faculty member at the university, Liz taught a one-unit course on the National Issues Forums, in which students attended a workshop that included a Town Hall meeting. The group developed frameworks for teaching controversial issues in the classroom. The classroom discussion course was developed years later by colleagues who taught it for a few years. Eventually Liz took over the course and revamped it. She included sessions on teaching difficult history (Gross & Terra, 2018) as well as controversial issues.

It is interesting to compare Ian Shepherd's merging of sensitive and controversial issues in teaching history with Liz's distinction between controversial issues and difficult history. While making the distinction, she nevertheless believed the two had important similarities in their demands on teachers:

I do differentiate between . . . difficult histories and controversial public issues because slavery is not a controversial issue obviously, but talking about slavery in the classroom is very difficult, or it should be. . . . There is some overlap in that . . . it can be very emotional. It has some impact on people's identities, social identities, and in that sense, there's enough overlap there, the sensitivity that's required, the preparation that's required, the thinking that's required in sequencing discussion and instruction.

In the U.S., social studies includes history, civics, economics, and geography. At the high school level, these disciplines are often taught separately, but social studies teachers typically are responsible for teaching more than one of them. Therefore, teacher education programs prepare social studies teachers, as opposed to history or geography or other discipline-specific teachers, as in the U.K.

UNIVERSITY PROGRAM

University-based graduate-level teacher education programs in the United States are overseen by state agencies and vary in duration and structure. Liz's program takes 13 months to complete. Instead of one year-long course in their discipline, as teacher education students do in England and Northern Ireland, students take four courses that combine social studies theory and methods. They also take courses in educational technology, child and adolescent development, special education, and academic literacy for English learners.

Candidates in Liz's program complete two school placements. One involves half-days of co-teaching with a teacher of record for eight weeks. The second consists of teaching full days, with less assistance from teachers of record, for twelve weeks. One placement is in a middle school and the other is in a high school.

A short description on the university website describes the program as designed to develop "inquiring, analytical, and reflective professional educators" prepared to teach middle (grades 5–8) and high school (grades 9–12). One of the aims is to create "advocates for young people and the social studies" who help students become "thoughtful and active citizens in a culturally diverse, democratic society." The combined master of education and teaching license program is intended for students with bachelor's degrees in anthropology, sociology, history, political science, geography, economics, or psychology. The program is aligned with standards adopted by the state's commission on teaching.

At Liz's university, full-time teacher education instructors are "professors." Along with the classroom discussion in social studies course, Liz was teaching a doctoral seminar, advising graduate students, chairing doctoral dissertations, supervising student teachers, and collecting data for a research project.

Liz's course began in March as student teaching placements were wrapping up, meeting weekly for ten three-hour sessions. The racially diverse class included ten students, primarily from the Midwest. Only two were women. Preservice teachers had done their student teaching at two placements, one in middle school and one in high school.

COURSE AIMS

Liz had five main goals for the course that demonstrated her commitment to teaching with and for discussion. First, she wanted preservice teachers to think deeply about the *role of discussion in a democracy*, because that would motivate them to teach controversial issues. Developing a strong sense of democratic purpose in discussing controversies would sustain that motivation in the face of difficulties. She explained:

> If you're doing it so that you can have an engaged classroom, so that your students are developing critical thinking, so that they learn more academic content, but you're not tying it to their role as citizens in a democracy . . . then it's not going to sustain you when the going gets rough . . . . So I hope that they walk out with some sense of a mission that this is important, not only for students' academic and social development, but . . . their political development.

Second, and related to the first goal, Liz wanted preservice teachers to know some of the *scholarship on discussion*. To help ground them in a philosophical, purposeful orientation, she assigned a book on principles and practices of classroom discussion and research articles on the connections between classroom discourse and democratic participation.

Third, Liz wanted teachers to obtain *practical tools* to ground their teaching. Liz said her approach involved providing tried and true models and resources. Her fourth goal was for graduate students to *practice discussion facilitation*. When asked how preservice teachers learn to teach controversial issues, she replied, "By actually doing it, you know? And getting practice and putting them in situations where they need to come up with, 'What am I going to do now?'" She would assist them in preparing their lessons and debrief about how these went.

Fifth, Liz wanted to get preservice teachers to *grapple with tensions* related to teaching controversial issues and difficult history. Tensions reflected the avoidance of talking about controversial issues in the wider society, polarized communities, lack of school support, student resistance, and teachers' own political beliefs and identities. She explained, "[I]f you're someone who tends to be more political, then you probably have some strong viewpoints. Can you [give a fair representation of different views]? And then with difficult issues, if you're a white person, which . . . many of our teachers are, then what do you need to think about in terms of teaching about slavery, you know, for a racially diverse class or a homogenous class?"

Liz thought that although educators sometimes exaggerate the potential dangers of teaching controversies in conservative communities, there were real risks. She said that "knowing who you are, why you are doing what you are doing, and having a very well thought out rationale for what you're doing,

I think can take you a very long way." She hoped her preservice teachers would have the confidence and tools to know "what to do when tensions get too hot—because that's one of their biggest fears."

Liz's explicit attention to the potential threats of teaching controversial issues prepared her preservice teachers for contained risk-taking. She understood if her students, in the first year of teaching, started off with Structured Academic Controversies on "issues that are not quite as hot" and then integrated "a little more controversy" and current events the following year.

PREPARING FOR DEMOCRATIC DISCUSSION OF ISSUES

Liz planned to develop preservice teachers' familiarity with four approaches to civic discussion: Structured Academic Controversy (SAC), Socratic Seminar, Case Study, and Town Hall. In addition, she wanted teachers to know about the wide range of resources and materials available to them. Liz spoke about their need for "practice, practice, practice," both to rehearse different approaches to discussion and to prepare them for future challenges. Liz told me that along with making suggestions to student leaders during their lesson preparations, she injected questions during class discussions to hopefully get everyone thinking more deeply about teaching.

Grossman et al. (2008) argue for pedagogies of enactment in teacher education in which teacher educators identify core teaching practices, teach novices how they are connected to theory, and provide opportunities to decompose (Grossman et al., 2009), rehearse (Lampert & Graziani, 2009), and reflect on these practices (Lampert, 2009). As described in this book's introductory chapter, Walter Parker's (2003) and Diana Hess's (2001, 2003) essays on preparing preservice social studies teachers to conduct discussions represent this vision of teacher education.

Liz's approach was oriented toward the purposes of the practice-based model but was not as systematic or focused. It did not involve preservice teachers in decomposing or analyzing discussion facilitation moves, but it did teach them how practice was aligned with theory. It was not focused on one or two types of discussion, but it involved preservice teachers in rehearsal and reflection on practice, with student discussion leaders receiving feedback from instructor and peers.

Creating a Rigorous and Warm Climate

While the democratic discussion course heavily emphasized practice, it also had rigorous expectations for academic work. For each week of the carefully designed syllabus, at least two journal articles, book chapters, and/or podcasts were assigned. Students submitted a "ticket for discussion" before class in which they responded to a few questions related to the texts. Liz collected feedback at the end of each class session on what students found most engaging, helpful, confusing, surprising, or concerning.

At the same time, Liz created a warm, personal classroom atmosphere. The graduate students all knew each other from previous classes, including one they had taken with Liz. American cultural tendencies were evident and decorum was polite yet informal. Authority relations were less hierarchical than in the English and Northern Irish courses I studied. Students and professor often boosted each other's self-esteem and emotions. Liz brought treats every week. Students felt free to take the discussion where they wanted. The pace of lessons was relaxed and discussions sometimes went on for much longer than planned.

On March 21, the first day of class, Liz randomly paired up the students and asked them to articulate what they appreciated about their partner. The effusive appreciations were about how brilliant, collaborative, dedicated, and so on their classmates were. As she frequently did, Liz asked why she had them do this, emphasizing the importance of trust.

She then introduced the course and the programs they would be using, such as the National Issues Forums. Liz said if there were an issue on the syllabus someone did not want to discuss for personal reasons, they should email her. She explained that she chose the National Issues Forum on end of life because it tended not to divide people along politically partisan lines. She said students might not always feel comfortable discussing certain issues, but should not "feel really devastated either." She did not want "high anxiety or nightmares."

Liz modeled a strong concern with equity. She was solicitous yet unapologetic in saying she would sometimes call on people to speak. To ensure that students understood her motives, after asking the class for reasons, she said that if the teacher did not call on students, it would end up being the "same people talking" and sharing the "same thoughts." She added, "I want to hear from all of you. Each of you has something to give."

Liz referred to the lack of women and people of color in "upper echelons of government, business, etcetera." She continued, "If we can encourage everyone and develop skills of speaking up and articulating their opinions we may see some changes." She promised that it was fine if on a particular day someone let her know they did not want to be called on.

A Citizenship Test? Structured Academic Controversy

Two weeks later, Liz conducted a Structured Academic Controversy on whether a citizenship test should be required for high school graduation in their state. The SAC model of small group deliberation has been successfully utilized by teachers in numerous national contexts (Avery et al., 2013).

Liz's thorough lesson began with an interactive lecture on classroom discourse, which drew on the Parker and Hess (2001) article on teaching with and for discussion. She reviewed the difference between IRE (recitation) and discussion, and then the distinction between deliberation and seminar. She asked the class to talk about where deliberation is found and what the definition of civic discourse signifies. Liz gave two examples of current public issues: Should convicted felons be allowed to vote and should recreational marijuana be legalized?

Liz distinguished between debate, with its goal of winning, and deliberation, with the goal of arriving at the "best possible solution based on our best thinking and shared interest." She clarified that the SAC was one kind of deliberation, and referenced David and Roger Johnson's 1979 article, "Conflict in the Classroom: Controversy and Learning," that introduced the methodology.

After this prologue, Liz distributed a handout with the SAC Issue at the top: "All (name of state) students should be required to pass a civics test in order to graduate from high school." She organized the class into two groups and gave them name tags with "Side A" and "Side B." Then she organized two groups of four (in one case, five), composed of people representing both sides. Liz reviewed the directions: Each side would have two minutes to present and one minute to answer clarification questions from the other side. Then they would reverse positions and present the other side. After that, everyone would drop their assigned positions and deliberate the question. Finally there would be whole class discussion and debriefing.

Before starting the SAC, Liz taught the class "a little more about the citizenship test" proposed in their state. She showed a map of the United States indicating where bills have passed or been considered and then had everyone fill out a "pre-deliberation ballot." Then students were directed to click on a link that connected them to a citizenship quiz.

Liz asked what people thought of the questions on the quiz. Students criticized that it was multiple choice, trivial, and hard to read. She went over guidelines for deliberations, such as listening carefully, encouraging people to speak, and remaining "engaged and respectful when controversy arises." The vignette below describes the actual deliberation. It shows the process of a SAC and facilitation of it.

For this SAC, students worked with a pair of commentaries by Sam Stone, director of the Civics Education Initiative, and Joseph Kahne, professor of education policy and politics, published in 2015 in the practitioner journal *Social Education*. The essays argued respectively for and against a required citizenship test. Groups were given time to identify the main arguments in the articles and take notes in the graphic organizer on their SAC handout. Liz said they could "add arguments not in the article." She recognized that the side they were presenting "may not be your personal position," but they should "try to get into why someone would feel this way." They had fifteen minutes to prepare.

After Side A and Side B presented their arguments, Liz gave everyone five minutes to "huddle, elaborate, and come up with more arguments for the other side." When they presented the other side, they would not refer back to the articles because they were supposed to have "listened very carefully" when the original arguments were presented.

After the reversal of sides, students were instructed to drop their roles and deliberate in their small groups based on what they really thought. Then the class reconvened and each group summarized their final deliberation. One group thought a meaningful citizenship test should be required, because "if others need to take it to become citizens, we shouldn't give those born here a pass." The other group was "all leaning towards absolutely not." They did not want to impose barriers to high school graduation. They asked if the test took into account cultural differences, for example, between those living in a major city versus those living in Native American communities or rural areas.

Liz asked a series of questions to debrief the SAC: "What were some of the most compelling reasons for each side? What did your group decide? How and why did you arrive at that decision? What was the most difficult aspect of this issue for your group? What values underlie this issue? How does the SAC process relate to democratic principles?"

After students spoke, Liz disclosed that she went "back and forth" on her answer to the question. She did not like the idea of a paper and pencil test, but wondered, "with the denigration of immigrants and refugees," would a required test "develop appreciation of what folks need to do and empathy for them?"

The above description demonstrates the structured nature of the SAC approach. The teacher guides the process with instructions but lets students deliberate on their own. Students' presentation of arguments in the text is brief. Their final deliberation is vital because it affords the opportunity for students to formulate and exchange their opinions. The debrief allows for more exchanges and, in this case, for the teacher to disclose her own thinking about the issue.

Liz continued the lesson by asking everyone to put on their "teacher hats" while she presented "learner outcomes" for the SAC, research findings on benefits of SACs, suggestions for using and adapting SACs, and reasons why students and teachers liked them. By the end of the class session, everyone had dived deeply into the discussion model and the issue under deliberation.

Importantly, Liz had the luxury of flexibility with time. She made adjustments to her syllabus as needed. The lesson described above modeled both immersion in content knowledge and deliberation (Simon, 2005). As we will see in the next chapter, preservice teachers interviewed from the class cited this class session as particularly valuable for their learning because they liked the SAC model.

Freedom of Speech, Tolerance, and Protecting Targeted Groups

On April 11, Kenji and Nick were the first students to lead a discussion. They used a lesson plan Liz had selected from *The Choices Program*: "The struggle to define free speech: From Skokie to Paris." *The Choices Program*, developed by Brown University's history department, offers curriculum units, lesson plans, and instructional materials for courses in history, current issues, geography, and electives. The lesson plan on free speech included a short introductory text on human rights, an article titled "Freedom of Expression in Skokie: A Case Study on Human Rights," a graphic organizer titled "Contrasting Views on Human Rights," and source excerpts on "Skokie, Illinois, 1977" and "Paris, France, 2015."

The *Skokie* case involved a 1977 Supreme Court decision about whether a group of neo-Nazis called the National Socialist Party of America had the right to march in a town inhabited by thousands of Holocaust survivors. The lower courts had issued an injunction against wearing Nazi uniforms and armbands with swastikas. The American Civil Liberties Union argued that the injunction violated the First Amendment rights of the marchers. Ultimately, the case was so contentious that the group's leader decided to hold the march in Chicago instead of Skokie.

On January 2015, two gunmen attacked the Paris headquarters of *Charlie Hebdo*, a French satirical magazine, killing 12 people. Presumably the attack was retaliation for the magazine's publication of controversial cartoons depicting the Prophet Muhammad. Millions marched with posters and banners that said "Je suis Charlie" to show support for the magazine and free speech. But many criticized the magazine for publishing offensive cartoons that antagonized Muslims, especially given intense anti-Muslim feeling in France and Europe.

The following vignette describes the lesson and Liz's assistance at critical moments. She helped the student leaders provide clarification and context when they distributed sources materials, and tried to ground the discussion and connect the issues to events close to home. The vignette shows the challenges of leading rich, focused classroom discussion, even when the students are thoughtful preservice social studies teachers.

At the beginning of the lesson, Kenji and Nick projected a slide posing an essential question: "Should freedom of expression be prioritized above the right to be free from discrimination, intimidation, or threats of violence?" They allotted almost fifteen minutes for an opening activity that asked students if they had ever experienced limits on their own expression, how those limitations made them feel, and whether the restrictions were fair and justified.

Kenji passed out the *Skokie* case study, which situated the decision in the context of the broad interpretation of freedom of expression in the United States compared with other countries. He asked class members to annotate the text, noting they would be discussing the following questions: Is freedom of expression a human right? How is the United States different from other countries in this regard? When one set of rights infringes on another, how should we decide which rights take priority? Liz prompted, "What are the rights that are in conflict? I'm trying to understand the question." Kenji replied, "Oh yeah! If we're looking at Skokie, if one group claims another group is inciting violence or infringing on their rights, how do we decide which rights take priority?"

Now the class, divided into two groups, worked with the sources on the charting activity set up by the graphic organizer, which included "Arguments in favor" and "Arguments against" limitation of freedom of expression in certain cases. After about ten minutes, the class gathered for discussion of the following questions: What are the major arguments in favor of freedom of expression in Skokie? How do you know? What are the major arguments against? After an exchange about sources' arguments, Liz gestured to the student leaders to move things along. Nick handed out several more sources, and suggested people jigsaw within their groups.

Liz reminded Nick to say something about the sources. Nick explained that they were about the *Charlie Hebdo* case. He gave some background and projected an image of protesters with signs that said, "Je suis Charlie." Students discussed the sources in their groups and then came together in the whole group. Nick asked for the main arguments in favor of limiting the magazine's right to publish the cartoon and then the arguments against.

The *Choices* lesson plan framed the essential question as a conflict between two distinct human rights. It reminded me of how the teacher educators in Northern Ireland framed their lessons on human rights and the marching controversy in the Citizenship curriculum. They posed scenarios that made students wrestle with conflicting rights and which ones should take priority.

Kenji and Nick had followed the lesson plan with fidelity. It involved juggling the projection of a few slides, the opening activity, the cases, source material, and the graphic organizer, plus questions to guide student thinking and discussion in small groups and the whole class. Liz occasionally provided reminders to clarify and contextualize the assigned tasks. She signaled that Kenji and Nick should quicken the pace as the lesson bogged down between the opening activity and a series of exchanges about source arguments.

In the next segment, the class expressed their personal views about freedom of expression when it conflicted with other human rights:

Nick asked for similarities between the *Skokie* and *Charlie Hebdo* cases and directed everyone to the essential question: Should freedom of expression be prioritized above the right to be free from discrimination, intimidation, or threats of violence?

Liz pointed out "recent incidents" on campus. Earlier in the year, the university's Republican student group painted "build the wall" in an area devoted to student clubs, sparking protests. Liz said, "A lot of people thought it never should have been written" because it was "threatening to Latinos in particular." Instead of taking up this example, students began talking about federal agencies "not using the term climate change" and spreading "alternative facts." Kenny referred to a quote by Oliver Wendell Holmes about the "best truth" being the one that wins in the "competition of the market" and questioned that premise with the example of Nazi Germany.

As the conversation drifted further away from the cases under discussion, Liz asked point blank, "Do you think Charlie Hebdo should be able to publish images of Muhammad?" Joshua replied that "they shouldn't have the right." He had shared earlier that Islam prohibited images of religious prophets, which should be respected. Nick implicitly challenged this idea by paraphrasing, "Legally the French government should stop it." Joshua repeated his point.

At this point, the discussion gathered steam as students took up the challenge posed differently by Kenny: "Government protects religion?" He drew a parallel to Kim Davis, who made national headlines when, as a county clerk in Kentucky, she refused to issue marriage certificates because of her religious opposition to same-sex marriage. Joshua replied, "Does it defend discriminating against religion?" Ashley brought up "contraception and Hobby Lobby," a Supreme Court case that decided for-profit companies cannot be forced to provide insurance coverage for birth control that conflicts with their religious beliefs. Kenji asked, "Should religion be protected at all?"

Joshua continued, "This nation" protects "freedom of religion." Liz replied, "Or none at all." Ashley commented that she had learned in a constitutional law class that there was "no protection for atheists."

The discussion points to the challenge of co-constructing exchanges that build depth over breadth. No one took up Liz's reference to campus events, although students raised other campus incidents the following week. The group appeared to struggle with focusing on the essential question, although Joshua responded directly to Liz's question. Although others did not agree that Islamic religious beliefs should limit *Charlie Hebdo*'s freedom of expression, Joshua's contribution expressed the key idea that, in some cases, free speech should be limited.

When time ran out, Liz asked students to fill out feedback forms noting "strengths of the discussion" and "suggestions" for Kenji and Nick. She gave them time to express their feelings and thoughts about the lesson. They began by saying, with so much material, they were very limited by time. Nick listed what had gone well: There were "no silent moments." He and Kenji were "over prepared." He said they had a lot of content and this was an "edited version of what we prepped last week." Liz said that with such a small group, the lesson could have moved faster.

She asked what they thought of the case study approach. Nick thought that contextual knowledge was important for addressing the essential question. Liz concurred that this involved learning history at the same time as deliberating an issue. Kenji said the case study gave time to analyze sources in small group work and discuss in the large group.

Liz asked them to compare today's lesson with the SAC on citizenship. Nick said he preferred the latter. He liked the intentional "look at all the angles and swap." The case study approach "jumped into personal" views more quickly. Liz commented that this topic more directly "hits people's social identities." She said, "We can all identify" with questions about religious beliefs, attacks, and freedom of expression. In subsequent class sessions, the class would continue to grapple with the perennial question of whether and how free speech should be limited.

The Meaning of Tolerance? Socratic Seminar

The following week, Liz conducted a Socratic Seminar on a short excerpt from Michael Walzer's book *On Toleration*. She explained that Socratic Seminars focus on a written, visual, or multimedia text. Twelve chairs were set up in a circle and she asked everyone to bring the handout, the text, and a pen. The description below traces how the discussion evolved as participants connected abstract ideas to concrete examples that raised hard questions about the meaning, and limits, of tolerance. These questions bear on recent controversies about freedom of speech as well as treatment of marginalized groups.

> The discussion began with noting abstract ideas, such as making a better world, mutual respect, and the connection between tolerance and unequal power relationships. Ashley brought up recent antisemitic "hate crimes on campus" and a "Town Hall forum" on the incidents, with the FBI, residence life, and police, but she had not seen any follow up. Dan said someone was arrested, adding that antisemitic posters had appeared around campus.

Kenny linked these incidents to the text, suggesting that "one angle on the situation" was to frame the problem as, "these people are not tolerating" different groups, versus there being a problem with "not tolerating antisemitic expression." He interpreted Walzer as saying that "some ideas are not worthy of tolerance and mutual respect," suggesting antisemitism and racism were examples. He asserted, "I think . . . as social studies teachers, we can have dialogue and debate but there are some sides of issues we have no business" giving a fair hearing to. He said he had "battled" this kind of speech a lot at his last student teaching placement. We will learn more about Kenny's experience in the next chapter.

Liz allowed the discussion to continue. People wrestled with the meaning of tolerance versus acceptance and respect and its relationship to power and equality. They attempted to link the Walzer text to the civil rights movement, treatment of refugees, and accommodation of students with specific needs. The discussion returned to antisemitism on campus. They talked about the places slurs had been posted, including outside a Jewish student's dorm room.

Liz summarized the big ideas that had been exchanged: They had talked about tolerance as a starting point for mutual respect and about power dynamics. Sometimes they might not be able to respect the words or actions of particular groups. She gave the group a couple of minutes to "write down what you're thinking now about this quotation."

Liz saw perplexed looks on people's faces and said that questioning, thinking differently than you thought before, and seeing concepts as more complex were desirable. "We want to be mucking around in ideas a lot." She warned, "As a facilitator if you have something specific you want students to get, you're going to be disappointed. Students will take you in directions you hadn't anticipated." She noted that her preparation for the seminar included a long list of questions, but she asked only a few because the students had taken the lead.

After a break, Liz debriefed the seminar, asking the class to compare the seminar approach with other discussions they had had. Kenny pointed out that there was not a lot of structure, which made it different from the case study. Liz asked how the lack of structure felt. Tanya and Ashley said it felt much more organic and natural compared to the SAC. Eli added that "the SAC ideas were there for us" and that ideas in the seminar "went way beyond the questions." He noted there were pros and cons to both approaches.

Liz acknowledged that she should have ended the discussion ten minutes sooner to prevent it from going in circles. She said that ideally students would generate their own seminar questions. She referred to three handouts she had given them on assessing seminars, which included a rubric, observation form, and self-evaluation. Students asked questions about whether to have a fishbowl and what size class would be too large for a whole class seminar.

Through the Socratic Seminar, the class constructed a new understanding of tolerance, its implications for relationships between groups, and limits on freedom of expression. Along with the ideal of mutual respect, they concluded that intolerance toward targeted groups should not be tolerated. The students dug into the text, connecting it to the past and the present, and to distant issues and those closer to home.

Liz modeled careful listening, allowing students to take the lead and allowing time for ideas to evolve. Time was devoted to debriefing the seminar so that preservice teachers made the connection between their learning experience and teaching. Liz also modeled reflective practice through self-critique. The second-to-last class session took up the question of free speech again, this time in the context of classroom discussion.

Dynamics of Discussion in Diverse Classrooms: Case Study

On May 30, the class's theme was opportunities and challenges for discussion in culturally diverse classrooms. Assigned readings included articles on LGBTQ and racial classroom dynamics, and a case addressing school tensions related to Donald Trump's campaign and election.

In the first half of class, the leaders worked with other students on what it means to create a safe classroom space when conflicts arise. They presented "de-escalation techniques" for emotionally charged incidents, which included taking a moment of silence, reiterating discussion rules, taking a break for written reflection, splitting up into small groups, clarifying problematic comments, and meeting one on one with offending students.

After the break, Ashley and Joshua led the class in examining a case titled "Walling Off or Welcoming In? The Challenge of Creating Inclusive Spaces in Diverse Contexts" (Calleja & Kokenis, 2017). The case features a meeting of a "School Culture Committee" grappling with troubling student behavior linked to Donald Trump and his policies. It also considers a parent's criticism of teachers' efforts to create safety for targeted groups.

The following vignette shows how the class tackled more deeply the question of when the right to free speech should be limited. The salience of the case about a school that reflects the deeply polarized and contentious U.S. political climate following Trump's election was palpable.

In a dramatic reading to review the case, individuals played different roles and brought the School Culture Committee meeting to life. Ashley and Joshua provided two prompts for discussion in pairs. Then they asked people to share thoughts with the class. Eli spoke to one prompt: "Compare protected political speech to bullying and harassing speech and identify clear cases of each as well as ambiguous cases in a gray zone." He said there was a lot of ambiguity, but he and his partner decided an example of protected political speech would be a general statement like, "Undocumented immigrants take jobs away from U.S. citizens," while harassment speech sounds something like, "We don't want you here."

Tanya brought up the importance of intention, and Kenny expanded on her idea: "Like 'strengthening the border' might be a disagreeable policy solution. It's targeted . . . but it's not explicit about who it's talking about, whereas 'build the wall'. . . has an association . . . with Mexico, and then there's like 'Go back to Mexico!' which is very explicit targeting of individuals in the classroom."

Liz referred again to the "build the wall" mural on campus and said "a number of people saw that as hate speech." She asked provocatively, "Is it? . . . When your presidential candidate is making that his mantra?" Kenny asked if all speech that offends or marginalizes someone should be considered harassment. Nick commented that a statement said by first graders doesn't impact anyone, while when the president says it, people are incited to action.

Corey said they needed to consider the meaning of "build the wall" based on the president's prior anti-Mexican remarks which targeted a specific group and constituted harassment. Kenny stated that federal civil rights legislation prohibits discrimination on the basis of national origin.

Sparked by the case and the student leaders' prompt, the class's focused discussion entered politically charged territory. It directly addressed the difficult question of where the line is between acceptable and unacceptable speech. The "gray zone" highlighted its ambiguity, yet students thoughtfully posed general principles to consider, such as intentionality, targeting of specific groups, and impact. Liz helped push their thinking by raising the "build the wall" incident on campus again. Individuals expressed a range of opinions and the reasoning behind them.

Over three lessons—the *Choices* case study on free speech in Skokie and Paris, the Socratic Seminar on Walzer's tolerance, and the case on free speech at school in the era of Trump—the class co-constructed an understanding of a crucially important issue. It took time, patience with nonlinear discussion, thought-provoking questions, and rich resources to get there.

REFLECTING ON PAST TEACHING TO LOOK AHEAD

During our final interview the following winter, Liz noted several ideas for improving the course. She said that next time: "I would develop more role

plays that would put them in difficult situations" and "work a lot harder at trying to get them to really get into that role and grapple with" the perspectives
and situations. Her idea reminds me of the simulation Mark enacted with his
citizenship class.

Liz said she would also cut back on student-led discussions. The quality
was uneven, and she felt they needed more modeling of discussion facilitation by someone with more experience. She also would have the preservice
teachers reflect more deeply on their facilitation by listening to an audio tape
of their session and writing about how the discussion went.

Liz was considering restructuring the course's content to focus on several
issues "that really divide us as a country," such as race, the environment,
the military, patriotism, immigration, and religion. That would encourage
students to "do a deep dive" and struggle with their own and dissenting viewpoints. In sum, Liz imagined how she could take more risks.

When asked about modeling for the class, Liz reflected on the importance
of being explicit about her "instructional decisions." She spoke about need-
ing to "break down for them" why she chose particular resources, how they
connected to her learning goals, and the reasons for what she did in class.

Liz talked about the transition from graduate school to inservice teaching.
She hoped her graduate students would be "very thoughtful" teachers with
a "repertoire of tools" to employ with knowledge of "how and when to use
those tools." She hoped they would not be "too scared" to lead discussion of
controversial issues. She understood they might proceed with caution as they
got to know the community and became more settled before taking significant
risks.

Regarding the school conditions that supported or constrained teaching
controversial issues, Liz spoke first about the research pointing to the impact
departments have on teacher effectiveness. Then she referred to conversations with recent alumni who told her that challenges to teaching controversy
had "much more to do with standards and coverage" than with feeling they
could not "broach particular subjects." There was a perceived pressure to
"meet these benchmarks." Additionally, in some schools, class periods were
only forty-five or fifty minutes, which made it difficult to deal with the "ebb
and flow of emotional exchanges."

In the next chapter we will learn about the supports and constraints on
teaching controversial issues experienced by three of Liz's preservice teachers. Each felt equipped with pedagogical tools she had provided and wanted
to put them into practice. For Kenny in particular, school and departmental
constraints impeded his teaching of controversial issues, despite his passion
for and deep knowledge of politics.

Liz was the only teacher educator in my study who explicitly taught with
and for discussion. She immersed preservice teachers in discussion through

(1) modeling, (2) studying, and (3) practicing discussion preparation and facilitation. Liz modeled formats that ranged from very structured to open-ended. She brought an array of curricular resources to support teaching. After every lesson, she engaged the class in debriefs and collected feedback to encourage reflective practice and connections between the university and their own future classrooms. Liz modeled how to encourage participation of all students, listen carefully, allow students to take the lead, and at the same time, guide the process.

The class studied the purposes, principles, and practices of discussion as well as challenges to discussion such as polarization, confirmation bias, and social inequalities. Students read assigned texts that informed class sessions. Liz and the student leaders engaged the class in activities that made everyone think critically about characteristics of high-quality discussions, equity concerns, and techniques for de-escalating conflict.

Most notably, Liz had her students prepare for and lead at least two discussion-based lessons. The issues they addressed included end-of-life decision-making, freedom of speech in controversial cases, reparations for slavery, and policing in Black communities. Although she decided, upon reflection, that they needed more modeling beforehand, the element of practice was, as we will see in the next chapter, an important vehicle for teacher learning.

Liz created a trusting community in which preservice teachers could take risks to lead the class in discussion of controversial issues involving questions of morality, human rights, and social justice. She provided the texts, assisted them during the planning stage, and carefully inserted minor suggestions and questions to enrich the discussion during their lessons. But essentially she let students take charge so they could practice teaching and develop some measure of confidence in leading discussions of issues in their future classrooms.

KEY TAKEAWAYS

1. Teaching controversial issues and teaching difficult history are distinct practices, but both are served by making classroom discussion the central pedagogy and content of a teacher preparation course.
2. To be prepared to lead discussion of controversial issues, preservice teachers need to understand the role of discussion in a democracy, be familiar with scholarship on classroom discussion, learn practical tools, practice leading discussion, and wrestle with tensions that accompany discussing controversial issues.
3. Practical tools include discussion models such as Structured Academic Controversy, Socratic Seminar, Town Hall, and Case Study, as well as

curricular programs such as the *National Issues Forum* and Brown University's *Choices*.

4. Preservice teachers need explicit modeling of discussion facilitation, opportunities to practice discussion preparation and facilitation, and feedback as well as self-assessment on their practice.

5. Given the tensions that accompany discussion of controversial issues, such as the friction between free expression and inflammatory classroom discourse as well as challenges to equity, a university-based methods course should raise awareness and help preservice teachers work out ways to manage them.

Chapter 8

What Liz's Students Learned

This chapter on Liz's graduate students provides an important complement to the chapters on preservice teachers in England and Northern Ireland. First, Liz's course focused on discussion as a pedagogical method and on scholarship examining its value, purposes, and dynamics in social studies classrooms (Parker & Hess, 2001). Second, the timing of the course was different from the others.

Because the course was offered toward the end of the teacher education program and started as student teaching placements were concluding, final interviews with Liz's students took place several months into their first year of inservice teaching. That meant they were able to speak about how they approached teaching controversial issues unconstrained by the limitations of student teaching. However, other constraints came into play.

Because of the pressures of job interviews, teacher performance assessments required to earn their teaching license, work and family obligations, and long commutes, only four of Liz's ten graduate students volunteered to be interviewed. One was a woman of color who had taken an administrative position for the following year, so she would not be able to report on her teaching experiences following Liz's course. In the end, the sample did not reflect the racial diversity of the class, but did show political and social class differences.

The three first-year teachers worked in extremely varied school contexts. One taught at a high-performing high school on the line between suburbs and farmland, where 90 percent of students were white and 11 percent qualified for free or reduced lunch, Another was at a credit recovery alternative high school, also majority white, with over 50 percent qualifying for free or reduced lunch. The third was at a pre-K through twelfth grade charter school. 91 percent of students were Asian American, Latinx, and Black, 85 percent were qualified for free or reduced lunch, and many were the children of immigrants.

PROFILES OF PRESERVICE TEACHERS

Liz's graduate students who volunteered to be interviewed were an interesting group from different parts of the United States, with varied educational backgrounds and political orientations. Kenny identified as a white, middle-class, straight male from a town in the same state where the university was located. He was a politics major who was passionate about public policy. During his undergraduate years, he had worked in a legislative office and served as an "elected student leader who ran the advocacy" for higher education students. He wanted to teach U.S. Government and was excited about working with young people who could make a difference.

Most of Kenny's own high school social studies experience was predominantly lectures with PowerPoints and textbook readings, although in tenth grade the class engaged in debates. He was a very successful student with a traditional mode of teaching and looked up to his teachers as role models. Now, though, he realized that the approach he had experienced would not be effective for many students.

Nick identified as a white, cis-gendered, straight male who grew up in low-income areas in the western United States. Nick had pride in his working-class identity and Scottish heritage. He told me his father had immigrated from Scotland with his family when mines closed in the 1980s. Nick spent two years at a military high school. Like Kenny, his social studies experience was heavily based on lectures and textbooks. After working for a few years, he attended a continuation high school and obtained his GED (General Education Diploma) so he could enlist. Nick served in the military from 2008 to 2012, was a "human intelligence collector," and earned an MLS (Military Occupational Specialty).

An interest in anthropology motivated Nick to go into teaching. He taught fifth grade at a charter school for a year on a temporary teaching license. He had enrolled in the university's elementary school teaching program and switched to social studies. Nick said he was "more conservative than the average person" in his program. He did not affiliate with either Democrats or Republicans, and said that he favored smaller government but was not socially conservative.

Eli identified as a white, upper-middle-class male from the Midwest. He said that growing up in a Jewish family and going to Hebrew school taught him to ask questions, and he wanted his students to ask about why things were the way they were. In his secondary school, social studies mostly revolved around the textbook, except for Socratic Seminars in AP (Advanced Placement) Government.

Eli was a history major. After college, he worked as a youth camp program coordinator for a year, and then as an AmeriCorps coach for low-income juniors at a public high school preparing to apply to college. Eli said that during the teacher education program, his political orientation had shifted from moderate liberal to the left, which made him want to bring "more marginalized" perspectives into his teaching. He had become more politically engaged since the presidential election, in part because many of his students were affected by Trump's anti-immigration policies.

CONCEPTIONS OF CONTROVERSIAL ISSUES

The preservice teachers had read a conceptualization of controversial issues from Diana Hess's (2009) book in a previous course and in an article by McAvoy and Hess (2013) in Liz's course. My observations did not include the class session that addressed the latter text. But we will see that Kenny remembered its impact on his understanding.

Kenny said that the definition of controversial issues had been "part of our class discussion," which involved "the framework of like open versus closed issues, and then there's like a public nature to these issues." He explained there were "four quadrants, maybe like closed private issues, open private issues, closed public issues, open public issues." He remembered talking about "how closed versus open issues varies by context, and in some areas with some classroom environments, in some schools, in some districts, in some states, in some areas of the world, issues that might be closed somewhere might be different and be open in a different context." He gave gay marriage as an example of an issue that had moved from open to closed.

Kenny said he could "list out seventy issues" he thought were important to teach young people. His first example was what to do about income inequality and how to respond to historically marginalized groups, for example, affirmative action or reparations.

When asked in our second interview to define controversial issues, Nick said they were contextual and included anything he was inclined to notify parents about before teaching. When asked for examples, he said while very little was controversial to him personally, he thought "anything that's going to step on people's cultural or religious toes, so to speak" or that "families would have a rigid stance on." He then, like Kenny, gave the example of gay marriage as an issue that was considered open for some while legally closed. Nick was most interested in teaching issues that were relevant to the students he would be teaching.

Eli defined controversial issues as something up for debate or "conversation with multiple perspectives that are on the table." They could be connected with "values" and "fundamental principles." He said they had talked about open versus closed questions "a little bit" in Liz's course and in a previous course. Eli thought that an important issue to teach his future students included undocumented immigration. He was also intrigued by teaching issues such as same-sex marriage and abortion and the role of religion in exploring them.

Kenny and Eli embraced the democratic aims of discussing controversial issues. Eli said, "We want our students to form their opinions and back them up with evidence and arguing and kind of preparing them for their future roles in society." Kenny thought it was vital that students develop skills to examine issues and grapple out loud with diverse viewpoints given the great demographic diversity of the United States. Nick, as we will see in more detail later, did not adopt the aim of preparing young people for democratic decision-making on public issues.

KEY LEARNING FROM THE DISCUSSION IN SOCIAL STUDIES COURSE

There was significant overlap between Liz's aims for the course and key takeaways reported by the teachers I interviewed, but there also was an interesting disjuncture. Liz wanted her graduate students to embrace the democratic mission of discussing controversial issues—to cultivate more knowledgeable, engaged, and tolerant citizens. She wanted them to learn different models and curricular programs with robust resources for teaching controversial issues. And she wanted them to grapple with challenges of teaching controversy. The three teachers embraced the second and third aims, but Nick questioned the first one. He had his own conception of citizenship and aims for his students, which influenced his approach to controversial issues.

Classroom Community

Kenny, Nick, and Eli said they learned how to build a classroom culture conducive to talking about controversial issues, which is the first strategy for contained risk-taking taught by teacher educators (Pace, 2019). From this course and others, they learned about the importance of getting to know one's students, creating community, and developing norms. Eli said he had learned about being culturally relevant and thoughtful about his own identity so he could be more authentic and understand how he might be perceived by others. Kenny spoke about recognizing his privilege and blind spots.

The three teachers found the second-to-last class session on dealing with challenging classroom dynamics and creating a safe space, described in the previous chapter, to be quite helpful. Kenny and Eli spoke about the nuances of safe versus comfortable, and about allowing students to express opinions but not make racist or other offensive comments. Eli said he learned he could ask students to stop and reflect, perhaps through writing, to prevent discussions from "spiraling" out of control or getting too "heated." From this session, they learned to proactively address potential emotional conflicts, another strategy for contained risk-taking.

Engagement with Discussion Models

Like the teachers in Northern Ireland and England, the three teachers valued studying different discussion approaches. Kenny said he appreciated learning tangible, useful teaching practices: "So I think teachers always like really concrete things, so like a Structured Academic Controversy (SAC), a National Issues Forum. Those discussions give us a lot that we can work with right now in the now, if we don't know exactly how to tackle something." Nick spoke about the value of engaging with different methods instead of just reading about them. Eli said they had learned to approach teaching controversial issues in "careful, deliberate, intentional ways" that included Socratic Seminars, SACs, and Town Halls.

Kenny, Nick, and Eli all described the SAC on requiring a citizenship test for high school graduation as a standout session, although Kenny and Nick did not remember the formal name of the method. Kenny thought it was an effective way to "scaffold into discussion skills." He thought the citizenship test SAC was "a fascinating conversation" and "really relevant to my life as a social studies teacher." Nick commented, "I liked how once again, it forced students to take multiple sides, but then it also allowed for kind of the personal opinion piece at the end." He added, "I think that's something I could definitely see myself not just using, but trying to make a routine out of."

Eli enthused, "It was really fun, and the structure I think will be really helpful for me, for students. . . Switching from one side to the other is also really I think a valuable skill in our society because it allows students to see both sides and argue for both and why maybe others would think one way while they think another." He thought that discussing an issue "in a respectful way . . . rather than in an argumentative debate" was "validating" for students.

Kenny had tried the SAC model during his student teaching after hearing another instructor talk about it. Eli was making it a regular feature of his economics class his second semester of teaching. All three teachers' comfort with the SAC, a highly structured small group activity, pointed to this method as an exemplary approach to controversial issues that embodied contained risk-taking (Avery et al., 2013).

All three said that discussing issues every week in class helped them understand their own views and those of others, benefiting their teaching. Kenny noted that learning to disagree was an important step for him. They also learned facilitation skills from Liz. Nick said he appreciated how Liz jumped into discussions with comments and questions, because she had a "lot more experience" than they did. He learned that a teacher's role in a discussion is "a lot more active than [he] previously thought." For example, teachers listen to understand where students stand on issues. They can be intentional in grouping students, to build in diversity of opinions. Teachers need to move around the class and sit with students during their conversations.

Kenny framed a key lesson in general terms: "So we're learning practices that ask us to ask students to step into the world of someone else or to gain a window into a different perspective or to argue from that perspective." He also understood that students needed to be taught how to have productive discussions.

Preparation and Practice Teaching

The previous chapter looked at how Liz made practice teaching a centerpiece of her course. In our interviews, Nick and Eli stressed the benefits of practicing discussion leadership. Eli learned how to step back from a traditional teacher role. Specifically, rehearsing discussion facilitation helped him learn pedagogical moves such as deciding when to pause and wait for students to speak, and when to move on. He learned not to rush, but to be deliberate about addressing sources. He thought about formulating questions instead of providing answers. And he practiced creating focused yet complex questions.

Eli's report suggests he was working on two important elements of discussion facilitation—engaging students as sense makers and orienting students to the text (Reisman et al., 2018). Additionally, he said that positive feedback from Liz and his peers built his confidence.

Although Nick said that teaching grad school was "mildly inauthentic," he was glad to learn about the "planning end" of discussions. He praised Liz's guidance during the planning process: "She came in and was helpful by kind of redirecting our thinking about some of the theories . . . she just made sure we refocused on kind of the kernel, what was important and all that." Like the other preservice teachers I interviewed, the three teachers learned the importance of thorough planning.

Eli spoke about the teacher's need to read extensively and be intentional about planning the discussion but open to letting it evolve in unexpected ways and tying it back to an overarching goal. He also said it was important to allow space for students to reflect and write after discussions, perhaps answering the following questions: "What have I learned? Have my values changed? How have they changed? What are they now? What else am I wondering about?"

Nick said he had significantly changed his mind about the need for teacher and students to prepare for discussion. Previously he had a laissez-faire approach: "Let's just have a conversation about it, man, see what you like or whatever, see what goes." He came to realize that "if we're going to take our time to have those high-quality conversations, there needs to be some kind of direction." That meant giving students a reading, points to think about, and/or questions to answer.

Dealing with Reprisals

The teachers worried about getting pushback on teaching controversial issues from parents and administrators, perhaps because of the conservative suburban district where they student taught. By the end of the semester, they had learned the contained risk-taking strategy of proactively communicating with parents and administration. They spoke about the importance of having a clear rationale for teaching a controversial issue for parents and of giving a "heads up" to administration to get support. Kenny, recalling a comment made by Nick, said that leaning on standards for justifying his lessons was insufficient.

Purposes of Discussion

Kenny and Eli seemed to embrace Liz's democratic citizenship aim for discussion of controversial issues. They spoke about developing a capacity for civil discourse, students' understanding of diversity, media literacy, and political analysis and engagement. Nick said he held a different view about the purposes of teaching controversial issues. He said, "I think teaching controversial issues is about knowing that there are issues out there with which you are not ever going to really agree with, but still need to learn about, live with, and respect other people for."

Nick perceived that people in the program had another agenda in teaching controversial issues: "I think sometimes people who . . . [are] very liberal . . . really want to change people's minds. . . . I think they have people at heart when they do that and trying to improve people's lives. But I think conservatives sometimes are much more like 'live and let live,' and if we disagree on stuff, that's just going to happen." He said that teaching controversial issues contradicted teaching for social justice because the latter advocated "right answers," but the former did not.

Nick also disagreed with the idea of educating engaged democratic citizens advocated by the course. He explained, "I think the class is considering an effective citizen somebody who's going to really take part in the national discourse surrounding any number of topics and be able to be effective at that and come away with a decision that was made critically. I think that's great and well and good, but I don't think that's the only way to be an effective citizen."

He was more interested in citizenship at the local level. He spoke of his father, who had not graduated high school and did not vote, but was very involved in his union, as a role model. Nick said he thought in broader terms: "How are we just giving people good life skills to have as opposed to this very like, 'We're trying to build good citizens.'" These ideas were reflected in his teaching of issues.

FIRST-YEAR TEACHING EXPERIENCES
WITH CONTROVERSIAL ISSUES

Student teaching placements were drawing to a close when the Discussion in Social Studies course began. The first placement consisted of co-teaching with an experienced teacher for half-days over eight weeks. The second placement involved teaching four periods a day in a twelve-week trimester. Kenny, Nick, and Eli student taught for one of their placements in a large suburban district with a conservative reputation, although individual schools within it varied. Their other placements were in the city where the university was located.

Although they did not have time to apply lessons learned from Liz's course to their student teaching placements, their reports about dealing with controversial issues in those locations illustrate challenges to teacher practice.

Final interviews with Liz's graduate students were conducted in winter of the following academic year. By then, the three teachers were working in very different school contexts and locations. All three were able to cite an example of teaching controversial issues, the ways they contained the risks of teaching controversy, and supports and constraints that shaped their practice. Compared with England and Northern Ireland, class periods were longer and classes met more frequently, so that overall the U.S. teachers were less squeezed by timetables than their U.K. counterparts. But in one case, unexpected constraints, such as a first-year teacher evaluation, were a major impediment.

Table 8.1 presents the key controversial issues lesson the teachers discussed with me, the corresponding course, and the tools employed.

Table 8.1 Teachers' Main Experience Teaching Controversial Issues

	Course	*Focus*	*Curricular and Pedagogical Tools*
Kenny	Ninth grade human geography	Refugee crisis: What should U.S. policy be on accepting refugees?	Research, jigsaw deliberation, policy letter
Nick	Eleventh and twelfth grade economics	End of Life: How should end-of-life decisions be made?	National Issues Forum video, discussion
Eli	Twelfth grade economics	College tuition: Should college be free in the United States?	Readings, SAC

Teaching Social Justice Issues under School Constraints

Kenny struck me as a promising candidate for teaching controversial issues thanks to his knowledge, enthusiasm for politics, and participation in class discussions. He said he had learned from the teacher education program's emphasis on social justice the importance of reflecting on his white male identity and role in creating an open classroom climate: "So I think it's to acknowledge the privilege that I have and to acknowledge that there are perspectives and views and ideas that I don't have because of my position and to allow and create an environment where people can bring in those perspectives that I might not have."

Kenny had taken risks during his student teaching placement in a suburban high school where he taught four sections of 12th grade U.S. government and politics. During a unit on criminal justice, he explored the issue of prison pay equity using the SAC model, which he had heard about in a previous course. He learned about the need to structure debriefs to allow for shades of gray on issues that do not have clear yes or no answers. Kenny realized that breaking down binaries was an important skill because policymaking should be dealing with the "gray area."

When the issue came up spontaneously in class, Kenny had tried to challenge students' favorable views of Donald Trump's 2017 executive order on immigration seeking to ban people from several Muslim countries from entering the United States. He said his students were saying that "public safety is the number one thing and, if we can't guarantee that they're not going to be terrorists, we should not let people into this country."

Kenny tried to "prod their historical thinking," asking if they could remember a time when the government banned people from coming to the United States and the consequences of doing so. He told them about Syria's civil war to "introduce some complexity into their minds," but students seemed set in their thinking. Kenny said he did not "feel equipped to develop something quick" because he was on a deadline to cover "five units of stuff" in twelve weeks. He felt badly about missing the chance to help students examine such an "intense" and important public issue but concluded, "I know the community in my class wasn't ready to have that conversation."

Another risk was showing the 2016 documentary *13th* created by Ava Duvernay and nominated for an Oscar. The title refers to the Thirteenth Amendment, which abolished slavery, and the film argues that a new form of enslavement has emerged through mass incarceration of Black Americans. Kenny said that although students were willing to analyze it from a media literacy standpoint, they resisted considering the film's content. In their written reflections, some individuals expressed the racist views highlighted by the film.

Again, Kenny said he did not feel equipped to "coax a conversation" about the issues. He said that more time to read widely and support from colleagues and administration would have encouraged a discussion in face of the challenges. He explained, "I didn't want to have a twelve-minute conversation on the last day when there was only that time left in class and then just put students back in their trenches, I think."

In our final interview, Kenny told me about his first-year position. The school was 90 percent white, and only 11 percent of students qualified for free and reduced lunch. He taught human geography and economics, but unfortunately, was not assigned to teach government. Classes ran for 53 minutes. Additionally, Kenny met with his professional learning community (PLC), which consisted of himself, an economics teacher, and two geography teachers.

When asked if he had the opportunity to teach controversial issues, Kenny talked about a human geography lesson on refugees that involved a couple of days of research and discussion in small groups. The final product was "a clear statement to Rex Tillerson about what the U.S. policy should be towards accepting refugees." Kenny's description sounded like a jigsaw approach, in which students collaborate in groups on becoming experts on a particular topic and then reorganize into mixed groups to teach others about their topic.

Kenny said that the research groups looked at the numbers of people displaced by global crises and compared that with the number of refugees the United States admits. Focusing on eight crises around the globe, each group assessed the needs of people affected by one of the crises. Then in "summit groups," which represented the eight crises, they deliberated how the United States should respond and wrote individual letters. The controversial question was, "How should the U.S. policy be changed or should it be changed?"

Kenny said that he had a "social justice purpose," which entailed "looking beyond your own experience to see if there are parts of the world that you need to learn about . . . and how you can advocate for those without a voice or without power in the decision." The second purpose was to teach how to "find the facts that can be behind certain conflicts in the world." The third purpose was to deliberate a "pretty heavy topic" in order to build consensus around a solution.

Kenny said deliberations were brief in the summit groups: "Students got through discussions so quickly that it was 25 minutes in, and . . . they thought they were done." They were focused on their research notes and had difficulty thinking analytically. He reflected, "I think that asking better questions and then scaffolding better discussion skills" would help the next time. He imagined starting with a trial discussion with an issue that was "goofy or zany" and then coming back to policy on refugees.

Kenny said his geography classes would soon be exploring the benefits and drawbacks of genetically modified organisms (GMOs), whether the government should "force companies to label their GMOs" and "if they should use GMOs at all." Kenny said he planned to use the resources Liz had provided as he became more comfortable with the content he was teaching. He anticipated doing a SAC in the spring semester.

Kenny was candid about his own learning curve and the limitations of his teaching of controversial issues. He spoke about learning how to enforce classroom norms for attentive listening without constantly "calling kids out." Kenny's PLC and the school's teaching evaluation process limited his teaching of controversy. We will examine these constraints in the next section.

Teaching Decision-making in an Alternative School

Nick did not report teaching or dealing with controversial issues during student teaching placements except for a simulation on NAFTA with eighth graders. He did not consider it significant because the issue "wasn't genuinely controversial" to the students. In our final interview, he spoke about teaching at a small alternative school for struggling students that offered a program for quickly earning high school credits. He taught government, economics, and an elective he designed in physical anthropology. Classes ran for 45 minutes plus ten minutes for silent sustained reading, and included mixed grade levels. Class size varied tremendously, but the maximum number in attendance on a typical day was 15.

The students were mostly white and two-thirds were male, and 52 percent qualified for free and reduced lunch. One of Nick's classes was designated specifically for students working on "staying sober from whatever they were addicted to." Nick said that low engagement was a problem, so he was willing to diverge from his lesson plans if a discussion evolved about a topic that interested students. In his government classes he initiated impromptu conversations about Black Lives Matter and gun violence in the wake of mass shootings that made national news, but had decided to use a project-based curriculum that did not lend itself to teaching controversial issues.

Nick's economics course revolved around the fundamental question of how people make choices. He taught a two-day lesson on end-of-life decision-making, after proposing the topic earlier to make sure students were on board. Nick used the National Issues Forum Institute's video (he did not remember the name of the curriculum) from Liz's course as an introduction. The video set up three potential choices—maintaining quality of life, preserving life at all costs, and letting individuals decide.

For the remainder of the class period and the next day, Nick led a whole class discussion sparked by the video. On the first day, the class discussed the pros and cons of these systems. Nick provided information that supplemented students' prior knowledge. Nick said the students were treating the issue as philosophical and moral, until he connected the issue to economics by asking, "[W]ho gets to choose to either extend the care being given to them in the hospital or choose to kind of cut your life short?" They connected the dots and replied, "Oh, the rich people."

Students realized, "'Well, wealthier people are going to be able to choose more expensive treatments and choose to be able to extend those treatments for longer,' whereas if folks have to pay for their own care, they are more likely to say, 'You know what? I can't afford two years of chemotherapy' or 'I might choose physician-assisted suicide to avoid financial issues.'" Nick said that students "had their minds blown" by thinking about the issue from the "economics angle."

That led to larger questions about what was "economically fair" and "morally fair." Students shared anecdotes, such as, "Well, you know, I had an aunt who had to do chemotherapy, and they lost their house." One 17-year-old with a child talked about his employer charging $600 a month for health care, which helped others realize their families were paying a lot for health care too.

Nick put the students into groups to discuss which end-of-life option they favored. They continued with whole class discussion the next day, and it evolved organically, focusing on the legislative implications of choosing continued care or physician-assisted suicide. The students brought up complicating factors, such as "What if you got a really greedy kid who's pushing you to kill yourself so he can get your money?" Nick said that Liz's class had discussed that problem as well. The discussion evolved into identifying solutions to potential problems. Overall, Nick was pleased that students seemed to understand that "economics is really about making choices" in "any aspect of life," and that three-quarters of the class seemed highly engaged by the issue.

Nick talked about another "out of the box" controversy he was teaching in the economics class: Are cryptocurrencies like Bitcoin good or bad? To spark students' interest, he led with "the illicit angle," which involved talking about "secret Internet money buying cocaine and weapons." He planned to raise questions about legitimacy and regulation: "So the controversy is, one, it's being used for criminal purposes. . . not 100 percent of it, but it definitely got its start there. And then, two, it's kind of thumbing the nose at the Fed, and the kids like that angle to it, too [laughs]."

Nick enthusiastically explained that he hoped to extend the cryptocurrency conversation for another week by linking the discussion to stocks, bonds, and investments. He wanted students to think about making "deliberate choices" and understand "different economic reasoning principles" that could inform those choices.

Nick's plan for the lesson suggested he interpreted teaching controversial issues in ways that fit his pedagogical motivations and his students' interests. His approach raises the question of whether the cryptocurrency lessons "count" as teaching a controversial issue. If students deliberated whether or not cryptocurrencies should be outlawed or regulated, the answer is yes. By contrast, deliberating on what are good investments does not address a controversial public issue, although students might develop their financial literacy and learn important skills.

Nick offered lessons on creating discussion norms and reflecting on practice. He said that before teaching a controversial issue, he set up classroom and discussion norms through role-plays: "I gave the kids a really stupid, simple question like, 'What's your favorite pizza?' and then I kind of acted as the foil to them in terms of bad discussion skills, and we just pointed them out and talked about what did we think as a class were 'good' discussion skills, right?" He provided "some poking and guidance," for example, to ensure gender equity was one of the norms.

Nick said he would like to make controversial issues a little more academically structured, with more reading and writing, and a final product. Such expectations were challenging because his students moved slowly. In this situation, one form of risk-taking would be to make more academic demands on students, which could spark resistance.

Conducting Deliberations with Racially and Linguistically Diverse Students

Eli's second student placement was teaching global studies at a middle school located in the same district where Kenny and Nick ran into student resistance and a school culture of avoidance. He too felt stifled by a suppressive environment, especially when he wanted to discuss Trump's travel ban with students. When he asked his cooperating team, they said that "as a social studies teacher, your goal is to stay politically neutral on topics."

He brainstormed with one teacher about how they might approach the issue in a neutral manner: "Maybe we could talk about some of the checks and balances where they had the judge who overturned it . . . but not to necessarily go into whether this ban was—evaluate whether it was good or bad or something like that."

Eli's first year of inservice teaching was at a progressive charter school that served a racially diverse, low-income student population that included 25 percent English-language learners. In the fall, he taught multiple sections of tenth grade world history and an 11th/12th grade elective called history through media. In the spring he taught 12th grade economics and an elective on historical fiction.

Many of Eli's students were newcomers to the United States or were the children of immigrants. In our second interview, he said that teaching about undocumented immigrants was important, especially because he hoped to teach at this school the following year. But once he got there, he chose not to risk a deliberation about immigration out of fear it would be too "contentious."

During the first semester he did not teach any controversial issues, because the world history curriculum included a lot of pre-history and ancient civilizations and the previous teacher had left detailed lesson plans and materials. By early March, in his economics classes, he had conducted two SACs—one on whether states should limit the number of months that people get food stamps and another on whether college should be free.

In our interview, Eli spoke in more detail about the free college tuition deliberation. He chose it because students expressed interest in this issue and he thought it was important for them to formulate their own opinions. He also wanted students to learn about related economics concepts such as tax impact, scarcity, and trade-offs. He followed a colleague's SAC structure that included guidelines and purposes for the deliberation, its relevance for citizenship, and an assessment scheme for earning points.

Students were divided into groups of four and asked to analyze an article, participate in small- and large-group discussion, and write a reflection. Eli walked around the room, listened, and assigned points for each activity. In the small group, he gave points for engagement in the SAC. In the large group, points were awarded for asking questions and citing sources. Eli found it "tricky" to assess participation. He used a spreadsheet to keep track of the categories and found it got easier after trying it the first time.

Eli said that, for the deliberation on food stamps, he provided a "cheat sheet" with statistics and information on both sides of the argument as a scaffold for students. He did not provide a similar scaffold for the college tuition deliberation. He noted that both deliberations were most successful with higher-achieving students because they could more clearly state their opinions. He perceived that the assessment made students nervous and the conversation a bit forced. Eli said he was figuring out how to tweak the assessment structure to make participation less artificial and reflection deeper.

Eli was surprised that only one student said college should be free, even though many of his students would benefit from zero tuition. Arguments against the policy included lack of incentive to work hard in college, higher taxes, and an absence of people to do menial jobs that did not require a degree.

When asked what he learned from doing the SACs, he replied, "That they are addicting [laughs]. . . . I think the students really are excited and curious about what we're going to talk about next. I love the fact that they want to keep getting better. I saw a lot of—maybe a handful of the students . . . struggle in the first one and do much better in the second one. And seeing that growth has been awesome." Eli's plan was to make them a regular feature of the class. He wondered how to vary the format so it would not become routine.

Eli's account of his teaching indicates his efforts to scaffold deliberation of issues for his students, who represented a population that receives significantly fewer democratic learning opportunities than their affluent, white counterparts (Kahne & Middaugh, 2008). His enthusiasm for using SACs is shared by many teachers working in diverse school and national contexts (Avery et al., 2013).

CONSTRAINTS AND SUPPORTS

The three teachers from Liz's course did not all get to teach controversial issues during their student teaching placements, but they did so in their first year of teaching. They went about it in different ways, shaped by their individual preferences, the curriculum, and their students. At the same time, several factors constrained their teaching of controversy.

My final interview with Kenny was surprising. He seemed like a natural candidate for teaching controversial issues, given his knowledge of and enthusiasm for politics. In our initial interviews, he said he was "really excited" and thought it was "so so so important." However, his teaching assignment, professional learning community, and teacher evaluation held him back. The reasons why were clear to him:

> I think the biggest thing that constrains me is my school. I think it's my fellow colleagues who don't want to try new things. I think it's being an untenured teacher who has to be evaluated on certain things. None of my individual learning goals for my professional development plan have to do with teaching controversial issues or building discussion skills. They have to do with managing student responses, engaging students, learning scales in those things, which I think are important. But I think if I was being evaluated on how to build positive civic discourse, I think that I'd be inclined to do it more.

An additional constraint was a school requirement for "common assessments." Unrelated assignments would count only as a formative assessment rather than a summative assessment. He had a pragmatic view of his current situation that differed from how ideally he would like to teach. He looked forward to expanding his practice over time:

> I do worry that I'm falling into the trap that we read about in our teacher education program, where we fall as teachers back on to the ways we were taught. So when I feel myself getting in those ruts, I want to change things up, and I want to challenge myself. But then I just am so overwhelmed with having to get the next day . . . figured out that I put on the back burner some of the . . . best practices that we talked about. Do I lose sleep over it? No because I'm always tired [laughs]. . . . I can live with it for the time being because I recognize my limits, but I know that it has to be something that I change.

Nick felt both encouraged and constrained by his students. He appreciated their interest in particular issues, but wanted to inject more "academically structured" reading and writing into teaching controversial issues. He wanted them to "produce something . . . more substantial" than just a conversation at the end of the lesson. Nick reflected that he had planned a "certain amount of content for a quarter" and then learned that "they moved at about a 50 percent pace of what I expected." He said part of that was the "student body" and another part was his "newness to the profession."

Eli benefited from his school's progressive culture and pedagogical tools he borrowed from a colleague. However, the world history curriculum was not conducive for teaching controversies. He also felt cautious about teaching issues that would be particularly charged for his students.

Eli said, "So, yeah, I think that's why I kind of went with college tuition for the second one, too. It's because it's not as—I would say it's not as controversial as maybe some other topics like immigration or like abortion or like gun control right now, and I would love to talk about those things. I just feel like it's—I would need some more support." Support meant pedagogical "guidance" from "experts or teachers who have been doing it for a while or administrators or just like a coach." Eli said that specifically, he needed guidance with framing "more contentious issues" that hit close to home. Paula Barstow from Northern Ireland would certainly have advice for him.

REMAINING QUESTIONS AND ADVICE
TO TEACHER EDUCATORS

From Liz's course, the preservice teachers gained robust tools for facilitating different types of discussion and valuable practice with participating in discussions as well as preparing and leading discussion-based lessons. They said they had learned ways of handling negative reactions from parents, but wanted to know more about how to deal with school administrators who did not support teaching controversial issues. They had also learned ways of handling difficult reactions from students, but still had some concerns. The anxiety reported by many of my informants suggests that although teacher education courses can help prepare for these challenges (Washington & Humphries, 2011), more is needed.

Nick wanted to know how to make sure no one left a controversial issues discussion feeling "undervalued because of a disagreement" and that positive peer relationships were preserved. Eli wished there were time in the course to discuss religion and how teacher and student religious identities might affect classroom teaching and dynamics.

Kenny wanted to know more about dealing with student resistance to exploring systemic injustice: "I don't think that in two months, by the end of this program, I'm going to feel well equipped enough to have those conversations productively, effectively." Concerns about handling difficult dynamics among students and resistance to having perspectives challenged echoed what I heard from the preservice teachers in the U.K.

Nick wished Liz's class had spent more time reflecting on the pedagogical choices they made while teaching their lessons in class. A particular question he had was about teacher disclosure. He felt it was potentially valuable, but somehow had interpreted McAvoy and Hess's (2013) treatment of the issue to mean that it was not justifiable. He understood that Liz "wanted to treat it like an open question," but he said that as a beginning teacher, "I need an answer on the self-disclosure end, and I can add nuance and change my answer as I get more and more experienced." He wished his instructors had disclosed their own views in class and believed that would make graduate students with different views feel more comfortable speaking up.

In our final interview, Nick spoke about wanting more emphasis on the "logistics" of teaching rather than the "philosophical angle." He explained:

> I think if I were Dr. [Nick], and I was teaching controversial issues at the graduate level, I personally would focus a lot more on the tactics, the logistics of doing it, because I think for me as a new teacher, that's what is needed. . . . I think her point . . . was we need to teach kids how to hold civic discourse, right? I need more ways of doing that. Make me run through more lesson plans. Make me teach more controversial issues or whatever. Read more of my lesson plans. Let's really get down to the nitty gritty of those technical things.

Nick suggested having preservice teachers write a lesson plan on a controversial issue and giving feedback: "[H]ow is this discussion going to go? What prep for the students did you miss? What assessment don't you have or do you have?" Both Eli and Kenny were also interested in learning more about how to assess discussions effectively.

Eli advised that teacher educators should, like Liz, show a variety of ways to teach controversial issues and get their students to think about them from different perspectives. He thought they should teach preservice teachers how to account for their own biases, for example, in selecting resources. Eli thought it was important to model discussion facilitation in the beginning, as Liz had done, but to leave plenty of time for preservice teachers to take turns preparing for and leading discussions.

Liz was the only teacher educator in my study to have students plan for and lead discussion. All her students did so at least twice. Nick was greatly appreciative and suggested that having students lead even more would prepare them even better. Eli agreed that, while the professor's modeling was important in the beginning of the course, taking charge of discussions was an effective way to prepare teachers. Important to remember is that their social studies program included more methods courses than those in the U.K., which allowed for specialization. This has implications for the structure of teacher preparation programs.

KEY TAKEAWAYS

1. Liz's students learned about developing classroom communities, dealing with difficult classroom dynamics, and using different discussion models such as Structured Academic Controversy. They valued opportunities to practice discussion preparation and facilitation.
2. All three teachers taught a controversial issue during the first several months of inservice teaching: two taught issues in economics classes and one taught an issue in a human geography class.
3. Supports for teaching controversial issues during the first year of inservice teaching included receptive students, the economics curriculum, and school culture.
4. Constraints on teaching controversial issues included a professional learning community, first-year teacher evaluation, and school assessments.
5. Advice to teacher educators included giving preservice teachers even more opportunities to plan and teach controversial issues lessons, discuss their pedagogical choices, and get feedback from the instructor and the class.
6. Remaining questions included how to deal with unsupportive administrations and negative student reactions and how to assess student performance in discussion of controversial issues.

Conclusions, Hard Questions, and Recommendations

Education scholar James Banks wrote in 1996: "In a postmodern world characterized by competing interests, a lack of civility, and enormous diversity, democracy is an extraordinarily ambitious and difficult ideal" (p. xi). Today, with extreme political polarization, the proliferation of disinformation, and antidemocratic governments in the most powerful nations, Banks's statement hits close to home and underscores why teaching controversial issues is both critical and hard.

Despite ringing endorsements from such organizations as the Center for Information and Research on Civic Learning and the Council of Europe and an abundance of resources to support teaching controversial issues, many teachers avoid it. They have multiple reasons for doing so. They have not been prepared for this practice. They fear losing control of the classroom agenda. And they dread hostile reactions from students, administrators, and community members.

Teaching controversial issues involves especially great risks for beginning teachers. Bringing conflict into the classroom opens up powerful learning opportunities (Bickmore, 1993; Bickmore & Parker, 2014). But for novices who must work out fundamental challenges of classroom teaching such as the construction of authority, controversy poses a significant threat (Britzman, 2003; Pace & Hemmings, 2006, 2007).

The university-based teacher educators featured in this book did not sweep these problems under the rug. Instead, they directly confronted them as they prepared preservice teachers for ambitious practice. And they did so under inhospitable conditions. Neoliberal economic interests undermine the democratic purposes of education in the United States (Kumashiro, 2015) and the United Kingdom (Ball, 2013). Standards-based accountability and competition among schools sabotage history, citizenship, and social studies. At the same time, university-based teacher education is subverted by government-supported alternative pathways to teacher certification that dramatically reduce coursework (Furlong, 2012; Kumashiro, 2010).

In the face of these and other challenges, the four teacher educators in this book provided powerful conceptual and practical tools for teaching controversy and for containing the risks that accompany this endeavor. This book is a testament to the potential of university-based teacher education courses taught by experts who have so much knowledge and experience to offer students. And it is a demonstration of novice teachers' readiness to engage their students in the investigation of controversial issues under real constraints.

The enthusiastic, intelligent, and thoughtful preservice teachers described in the preceding chapters had different educational backgrounds and national, religious, political, socioeconomic, and cultural identities. A major finding of my study is that most felt ready to tackle issues, try out methods that promote democratic inquiry and discourse, and maintain a supportive environment. Although their lessons were sometimes bursting with multiple activities, and discussion among students was often limited, many novices seemed, at least to some extent, to break through the apprenticeships of observation they experienced as students in classrooms focused on content mastery and didactic teaching (Barton & Levstik, 2004; Lortie, 1975).

This final chapter presents a synthesis of research findings about how the four teacher educators prepared their graduate students to teach controversial issues, what graduate students learned from their courses, what their efforts at teaching controversy entailed, and how these efforts were mediated by school-based factors. It considers questions raised by the findings and makes recommendations for practice, policy, and research. It concludes with the study's contributions to the field. Most of all, it is an attempt to knit together and make sense of the experiences of four courageous educators and their equally brave students.

TEACHER EDUCATORS' APPROACHES

In her cross-national study of citizenship classes in five countries, Carole Hahn (1998) identified three dimensions of an open classroom environment in the teaching of social and political issues—(1) "issues content," (2) pedagogical methods that "model democratic inquiry and discourse," and (3) creation of a "supportive atmosphere" (p. 232). The teacher educators in my study, although working in different contexts and school subjects, prepared their preservice teachers to thoughtfully tend to these dimensions. The following sections tease out key similarities and differences in their preparation.

Issues Content

The teacher educators taught preservice teachers how to frame issues content, teach it through rich resources, and plan learning activities around it. They modeled how to approach content in ways that would disrupt preconceptions and conventional ways of thinking.

Framing

The teacher educators modeled how to approach issues content through the formulation of questions that (1) stimulate inquiry-based learning, (2) call for engagement with multiple perspectives, and (3) frame issues as public versus private. Framing content with key questions was crucial for turning topics into issues (Ho et al., 2017, p. 322). For example, Ian framed his lesson on Police Battalion 101 around the question, Why did they shoot? Mark's simulation in his Citizenship course revolved around the question, Can you arrive at a compromise for a parading dispute that satisfies both parties?

Resources

The four teacher educators brought rich curricular-instructional resources to their class sessions. Ian taught his preservice teachers the power of using photographs, historical sources, and museum exhibits to confront student misconceptions, prompt them to examine evidence, and immerse them in historical narratives. Mark brought film clips, digital technology, fictional characters, and teacher-made packets that encouraged students to take up conflicting perspectives, link the past to the present, and reflect on their emotional attachments to certain viewpoints. Paula introduced preservice teachers to lesson planning tools, cards with community symbols, evocative picture books, and a teaching kit for human rights. Liz used programs such as the *National Issues Forums*, Brown University's *Choices* program, and a variety of texts including podcasts.

Activities

Most class sessions at all four sites were devoted to immersing preservice teachers in activities that got students to think critically about content. Practice with developing curricular plans for teaching controversial issues occurred in three courses. Using assigned texts, Liz's students developed discussion-based lessons they taught to their peers. Paula's students brainstormed ideas for teaching controversial issues that started with a specific case and later involved medium-term planning on a theme. Ian's assignment was the most ambitious. His students were to develop and teach a scheme of work revolving around a sensitive and controversial issue.

Pedagogical Methods

All four teacher educators taught pedagogical methods for democratic inquiry and discussion that varied depending on the discipline and individual. In the History courses, Mark and Ian taught preservice teachers how to work with source material in creative ways. In their Citizenship and Discussion in Social Studies courses, Paula and Liz modeled Structured Academic Controversies (also called deliberations). In Citizenship, Mark and Paula used the walking debate. Mark conducted a simulation. Paula taught other methods such as carousel conversation, silent conversation, and speed debate. Liz used case studies and Socratic Seminar.

Teacher education scholars have noted: "A truism in teacher education and teacher development concerns the need for teachers to experience a pedagogical approach from the standpoint of a learner before they are able to implement this approach" (Grossman et al., 1999, p. 20). All four teacher educators modeled how to use dialogic approaches for exploring controversial issues by immersing their students in them. They all conducted debriefs in which preservice teachers responded to the activities. Teacher educators accompanied modeled activities with conceptual tools such as principles of practice.

Supportive Atmosphere

To prepare preservice teachers to create a supportive atmosphere, teacher educators modeled how to build community in every session. They made their classrooms welcoming, encouraged humor, and were receptive to student ideas and concerns. In the Citizenship and Social Studies courses, they talked with their classes about creating classroom norms, using tools like Paula's FRED (Freedom of expression within a Respectful environment where everyone is seen as Equal and Diversity is celebrated).

Proactive Strategies

Hess and McAvoy (2015) suggest various proactive strategies to curb threats to a supportive atmosphere, such as offensive discourse. These include assessing the range of disagreement before discussion; establishing, teaching, and enforcing strong norms; scheduling more sensitive discussions only after developing classroom community; and knowing content sufficiently to correct misinformation. The four teacher educators in my study implicitly modeled and explicitly taught strategies that overlap with and extend Hess and McAvoy's suggestions. These strategies constituted a contained risk-taking approach.

Teacher Role and Stance

A crucial aspect of creating a supportive atmosphere is the teacher's role and stance. The teacher educators prompted preservice teachers to consider ethical issues when teaching sensitive and controversial issues (Hess & McAvoy, 2015). Ian highlighted the teacher's role in making curricular and pedagogical decisions. Mark, Paula, and Liz addressed positionality, stance, and disclosure through assigned readings and conversations in class, focusing on the teacher's role in creating an open and respectful classroom ethos. Paula's graduate students wrote an end-of-year essay on the role of the teacher when handling sensitive and controversial issues that drew on scholarship and their student teaching experience.

Social Aims

An additional dimension of preparing preservice teachers for teaching controversial issues was purposeful attention to social aims (Barton & Levstik, 2004; Husbands et al., 2003; Thornton, 2005). The teacher educators promoted the social aims of teaching controversial issues—and of citizenship, history, and social studies more generally—through their words, activities, and assigned texts.

Liz was emphatic about stressing the link between classroom discussion and democracy, particularly in a polarized society. Mark and Paula stressed building democracy and human rights in a post-conflict society. Paula focused on developing politically literate citizens prepared to press for collective responsibility and social justice. Mark worked for greater social cohesion in Northern Ireland. Ian raised moral questions as a way of encouraging social responsibility.

Contained Risk-taking

Collectively, the four teacher educators taught eight strategies to prepare novices to select and frame issues content, use democratic pedagogies, and build a supportive atmosphere. These strategies also serve to protect students against harm and safeguard the teacher from potential threats such as classroom management problems and hostile reactions from administrators or parents. The eight strategies, listed below, compose an approach to teaching controversial issues that I call *contained risk-taking* (Pace, 2019).

Contained risk-taking is especially helpful for teaching controversial issues in polarized societies and is developmentally appropriate for novice teachers, who are typically challenged by the twin tasks of establishing order while eliciting student engagement (Metz, 1978). It can adapt to different cultural contexts. And it mixes pragmatism with ambitious, reflective practice. Contained risk-taking consists of the following elements:

Cultivation of Warm, Supportive Classroom Environments

Teachers affirm students' ideas, build group cohesion, and engage students in collaborative learning. Their classes establish norms such as respectful listening. Humor contributes to bonding and trust building.

Thorough Preparation and Planning

Teachers continually expand their content knowledge. They develop a robust purpose, rationale, and goals for lessons and units. They create developmentally appropriate curriculum that fosters conceptual understanding, revolves around key questions, and utilizes rich resources and democratic pedagogies. And they incorporate in their planning knowledge of their students, school communities, and other contextual factors.

Reflection on Teacher Identity and Roles

Teachers are facilitators of inquiry, and they must not impose their views on students, but instead, let them reach their own conclusions. Teachers must reflect on their positionality, the stances they adopt (e.g., advocate or devil's advocate), and whether to disclose their views.

Proactive Communication with Parents, Other Teachers, and Administrators

Student teachers should let mentor teachers and department heads know when they are planning to teach controversial issues. All teachers must be ready to communicate their rationale to parents. They should let students know in advance the controversial issues they will be studying.

Careful Selection, Timing, and Framing of Issues

Teachers should start with less contentious issues in the curriculum that do not hit close to home and build to those more deeply felt. Issues are framed in public versus personal terms to promote understanding of different perspectives instead of debating personal opinions.

Emphasis on Creative Resources and Group Activities

Teachers introduce issues through creative resources to stimulate thinking and provide entry points to discussion. They use structured small group discussions to reduce threats to classroom management, decrease the demands of whole class discussion facilitation, and allow more opportunities for all voices to be heard.

Steering of Discussion

Teachers pose questions to guide students' thinking. Questioning, discussion formats, and protocols provide structure to discussion, which typically starts in small groups and may move to whole class plenaries.

Dealing with Emotional Conflicts

Teachers either avoid provoking emotions or balance affective and intellectual engagement. They use de-escalation techniques when things get heated. They get students to think metacognitively about emotionally entrenched perspectives and social divisions.

The teacher educators practiced contained risk-taking in their own teaching, modeling a cautious, structured, thoughtful approach to controversial issues. While they explored issues through evocative resources, democratic pedagogies, and conversations in their classes, they rarely engaged students in full-on deliberations of highly controversial questions, particularly those that provoked significant dissent or emotional reactions. Liz's course devoted the most time to discussion, yet the issues she taught were not notably divisive in her class.

DIVERSITY OF APPROACHES

Carole Hahn (1998) showed that teachers in different countries use a wide variety of approaches to teach social and political issues. She explained that "the forms education takes reflect the distinct set of values of a particular culture and for that reason 'what works' in one cultural context cannot be simply adopted in another setting with differing traditions, values, and meanings" (p. viii). This section examines two important differences among the four teacher educators in preparing for teaching controversial issues.

Classroom Discussion

I observed a marked difference between Mark's, Paula's, and Ian's courses in Northern Ireland and England and Liz's in the United States regarding class discussion. Importantly, Liz's course was explicitly focused on *teaching with and for discussion* (Parker & Hess, 2001). She made discussion an object of study as well as the primary method. Discussions in her course were often lengthy, some lasting an hour, and often steered by students. She was the only one to use whole class discussion formats such as Town Hall and Socratic Seminar.

By contrast, the U.K. courses emphasized *teaching with small group discussion activities*, but did not involve preservice teachers in the study of discussion's purposes, value, and challenges. While democratic inquiry and discourse played a central role in teaching controversial issues, whole class discussion was mainly reserved for walking debates, debriefs, and reflective conversations, and was steered by teacher questions and comments. And in Northern Ireland, students were not necessarily expected to verbally participate in open discussions, particularly if these could expose their personal identities and views.

The prominence of student-centered discourse in the United States versus teacher-directed discourse and classroom activities in England and Northern Ireland was shaped both by teacher educators' individual practices, pedagogical traditions, and perhaps by other contextual factors. One was simply that Liz had greater time and flexibility; program structure in England and Northern Ireland gave teacher educators more material to cover.

Another factor was the more relaxed classroom culture in the United States, where students felt entitled to airtime. The small size of Liz's class probably encouraged that. Mark and Paula explained that discussion in Northern Ireland was influenced by a protective and sensitive cultural climate reflecting past and present sociopolitical conflict. England too has a more reserved culture than the United States. Mark and Ian explained that in history classes, teacher questioning steered most discussion.

Additionally, an emphasis on Key Stage 3 (11- to 14-year-olds) in courses located in England and Northern Ireland versus high school (14- to 18-year-olds) in the U.S. course may have contributed to the difference. The comparison raises questions that we will consider later in this chapter.

Practice Teaching

Liz was the only teacher educator who had her students prepare and lead discussion-based lessons. She did not identify her approach as an example of practice-based teacher education, but it was a major attempt to bridge university course work and classroom teaching (Zeichner, 2012). It did not focus on a specific core practice such as discussion of historical texts (Reisman et al., 2018), nor did it include the decomposition of discussion facilitation into specific moves or provide explicit coaching aligned with those moves (Grossman et al., 2009). But it let preservice teachers rehearse teaching with discussion in a supportive setting. Once again, the flexibility and time afforded by teaching an advanced methods course in a 13-month program allowed for this approach.

NOVICE TEACHERS' LEARNING

What did novices learn about teaching controversial issues? This section provides an overview of what novices learned from the methods courses observed in this study and from their experiences in student teaching placements and first-year positions. It also presents a synthesis of conceptions of "controversial issues."

Learning from Coursework

Preservice teachers' reports on what they learned from course work aligned with generally accepted views of what teaching controversial issues involves. Their visions of teaching issues included getting students to work with resources that arouse their interest and challenge their preconceptions, explore issues from multiple perspectives with new evidence, engage in discussion activities with peers, and arrive at their own conclusions. They also aligned with the strategies of contained risk-taking.

To approach controversial issues, preservice teachers stressed that careful preparation of lessons is critical, which includes expanding one's own knowledge, selecting resources, formulating open-ended questions, and designing activities. They said that knowing students and anticipating and managing student reactions were also crucial. And they noted that creating a supportive classroom atmosphere, open to different viewpoints while fostering respectful interactions, was fundamental.

The novices said the teacher's main role is to model curiosity, open-mindedness, willingness to probe entrenched positions and conventional views, and tolerance. Although there was some variation in the preservice teachers' thinking about teacher stance, it seemed that most wanted to strike a balance between advocating social justice and being impartial. They would not tolerate hateful speech, and they would challenge bigoted views. However, nearly all felt strongly about not indoctrinating young people to their way of thinking. Only Sean and Nick expressed a keen desire to disclose their views on issues. Will said he would consider it when appropriate.

The preservice teachers said that teaching controversial issues was important for a variety of reasons similar to those reported in other studies (Ho et al., 2017). These reasons were more concerned with social aims than with learning subject matter for its own sake: Students would encounter these issues as adults, and they should examine multiple perspectives in an educational setting before heading off to university or the workforce. This learning experience could help students develop the capacity for good decision-making, having civil discussions, understanding social and political issues, and participating as democratic citizens.

Additionally, addressing controversial issues in class could counteract prejudiced and narrow-minded messages young people might learn at home and in their communities. In Northern Ireland, preservice teachers said that teaching controversial issues could make a real difference in moving society past its divisions.

The pedagogical method that Northern Irish and English teachers valued most was modeling by the teacher educator, particularly when it got them to explore issues using practical tools (Lunenberg et al., 2007). The vehicle that U.S. teachers valued most was rehearsing the planning and teaching of discussion-based lessons and participating in discussions.

Learning from Classroom Practice

In our initial interviews, many preservice teachers in England and Northern Ireland said they felt ready to try teaching controversial issues after a few weeks of concentrated course work. Through their student teaching experiences they learned what was actually involved in adopting tools within the real contexts of students, schools, and communities. In our subsequent interviews they spoke about their successes as well as challenges. Their stories revealed areas of accomplishment and their desire for more pedagogical knowledge.

Final interviews were conducted with Northern Irish and English teachers after they completed student teaching, except for Emma and Margaret who were available only for the first two interviews. Because of the timing of their Discussion in Social Studies course, final interviews with U.S. students occurred several months into their first year of inservice teaching. Like the preservice teachers in Dahlgren et al.'s (2014) study, enthusiasm for teaching controversial issues persisted across interviews, although a few expressed ambivalence after confronting challenges.

Nearly all of my interviewees taught at least one controversial issue, defined as a significant social, political, or historical question on which there is substantial public disagreement. By this standard, significant questions should have bearing on people today. They may be context-specific or universal. For example, Oliver Cromwell's legacy may not have significance in the United States, but it is meaningful in England and Northern Ireland.

The approaches novice teachers took to teach these issues varied based on their individual proclivities, subject, assigned curriculum, and constraints and supports in the school setting. Importantly, they all utilized conceptual and practical tools learned from the teacher educators, some more than others. The study underscores the key role curricular and pedagogical tools play in learning to teach.

Novices overall learned to approach controversial issues with a combination of containment and risk-taking, based on Kitson and McCully's (2005) continuum. On the risk-taking side, they often framed content with inquiry questions and resources such as film clips, primary sources, and provocative images to spur critical thought. They enacted pedagogies for democratic inquiry and discourse such as deliberation, source analysis, and walking debate to promote critical thinking about different perspectives and exchanges of ideas.

At the same time, examination of controversial issues was contained by curtailing elements of risk-taking, such as open discussion, probing analysis of resources, and connections between past and present. Immersive methods such as role-play or simulation were rarely used. Clear relevance to students' lives was sometimes tenuous or nonexistent. At times lessons were aimed toward arriving at particular understandings instead of investigating genuinely open questions.

The history lessons English teachers Ben and Kathy taught for their schemes of work on the execution of Charles I and D-Day, respectively, fit the Container category: Issues were "contained through the historical process," students were "not encouraged actively to engage in the root of the controversy," and topics were "not too close to home" (Kitson & McCully, 2005). Emma too, in her first placement, contained the study of Ireland's Partition. She had her students interpret propaganda posters, but did not frame her lesson as a controversy or make links to more recent history.

Generally speaking, the lessons taught by my interviewees that were most focused on a controversial issue embodied *contained risk-taking.* These lessons considered important questions about historical, social, or political issues. They were thoughtfully designed and engaged students with rich resources and democratic methods. The preservice and first-year teachers felt comfortable teaching issues lessons with structured student talk that occurred mostly in pairs and small groups, with short plenaries at the end if time allowed. Both Margaret in Northern Ireland and Eli in the United States had great success with Structured Academic Controversies.

Like the lessons taught by Dahlgren, Humphries, and Washington's (2014) preservice teachers, those described by my informants were highly structured and rarely included "free-ranging student discussions" (p. 219). Few organized sustained whole class discussion, except Nick who taught small classes at an alternative school and William who held a mock trial of Charles I. Alex, Will, and Sean used walking debates, but these were not lengthy.

Most novice teachers took an understandably cautious approach, given their status and lack of experience. Contained risk-taking helped them navigate the friction between bringing conflict into the classroom and maintaining control. Containment of controversy was reinforced by constraints and challenges, as we will see later in this chapter.

Conflated Conceptions of Controversial Issues

Ho et al. (2017) state, "One challenge of studying 'controversial issues' is that the meaning of the term is seldom examined" (p. 322). Preservice teachers held varied definitions of controversial issues, even after hearing and/or reading definitions provided by teacher educators. Many drew on common sense understandings. They often conflated sensitive issues, controversial topics, and controversial issues.

According to Ho et al. (2017), sensitive issues are questions or topics that are difficult to discuss and/or might trigger a strong emotional reaction, such as genocide. Controversial topics are ones that some stakeholders oppose being taught in school, such as sexual orientation. Controversial issues are questions that call for examination of competing views as well as deliberation, such as, "Why did the United States use atomic bombs to end the war with Japan" and "Should the minimum wage . . . be increased?" (p. 322).

When asked if they had taught controversial issues during school placements, the English and Northern Irish preservice teachers in particular cited examples from all three categories. They also offered examples of teaching content related to social justice, such as human rights abuses. Probing questions about the actual controversy in these examples and the content and pedagogy of lessons helped distinguish which ones actually addressed a controversial issue, be it a historical, political, social, and/or moral question. U.S. teachers cited examples of controversial issues, albeit Nick's plans for teaching cryptocurrency merged a public issue with questions of personal financial decision-making.

CONSTRAINTS, CHALLENGES, AND SUPPORTS

Identifying factors that constrained, challenged, or supported practice are key to understanding how learning to teach controversial issues was mediated by important influences located in different settings. Many of the factors the novices spoke about overlap with previous research findings based on interviews with inservice teachers (Ho et al., 2017; Kitson, 2007). But student teaching and first-year teaching brought unique influences into the mix.

Time

The most obvious influence on teaching controversial issues was time. Nearly everyone expressed frustration about insufficient classroom time. In Northern Ireland and England in particular, school timetables squeezed citizenship as well as history. Time for controversial issues was also constrained by pressures for curriculum coverage, exam preparation, and other mandates. Except for Margaret's and Eli's Structured Academic Controversies and William's mock trial, time devoted to discussion in lesson plans was limited. While content tended to dominate lesson plans (Simon, 2005), teachers reported that productive exchanges often had to be cut short.

Clearly, teaching controversial issues was supported when preservice and novice teachers had adequate instructional time. Schedules that afforded more time for citizenship, history, and other social studies subjects, specifically, having class periods of 70, rather than 35, minutes made a major difference.

Student Engagement

Teachers are dependent on student engagement to accomplish lessons. With struggling students, novices had to work hard to make lessons accessible. Meeting the needs of students in heterogeneous classes was demanding, but not as difficult as teaching lower-track classes, where students could be apathetic and disruptive. Importantly, some teachers—at all four research sites—said they needed additional help making resources and subject matter accessible to all students.

In the United States at an alternative high school, Nick felt free to openly discuss issues with his students. But he was hesitant to incorporate reading and writing into his lessons, fearing that would cause students to disengage. Aoife said that at her first placement she had to reconsider her expectations of students who struggled academically and had serious problems at home.

Student teachers in Northern Ireland said that in more diverse classrooms, with Catholics, Protestants, and ethnic minorities, they were challenged to be more sensitive to classroom discourse that could target particular groups. In less diverse classrooms, they needed to be conscious of their stance to avoid reinforcing existing biases or allowing intolerance to pass unchallenged.

A theme that surfaced in the teachers' accounts of controversial issues lessons was the importance of students' positive responses. Student participation was vital for successful lessons and their expression of different viewpoints made discussions interesting. Evidence of understanding bolstered teachers' confidence. Enthusiasm among students was most gratifying.

School Culture

Harrison, Ben, and Emma taught in locations they perceived as challenging—an economically depressed former mining town and a hot spot during the Troubles. Ben and Harrison experienced one of their placements as constraining, if not actually censoring, of controversy (Cornbleth, 2001). At that school, they felt the community's suspicion of outsiders and the oppressive demands of a traditional pedagogical culture. However, Harrison, who completed his second placement there, pushed back and was proud of his creative lessons.

As a first-year teacher, Kenny taught under different, yet notable, constraints situated in the school setting—his evaluation and professional learning community. These factors limited his autonomy. Although placements were concluding as Liz's course was starting, her preservice teachers' reports about student teaching in conservative suburban schools that stifled controversy are important to note.

Student teachers in Northern Ireland typically had one placement in a secondary (non-selective) school and a second placement in a grammar (selective) school. Most reported having an easier time teaching controversial issues in the grammar schools. Students at grammar schools were more affluent and performed at higher academic levels. The culture of these schools tended to be more liberal.

Will reported that teaching controversy was easier at his second placement, a prestigious grammar school with an unusually diverse intake for a state-controlled (Protestant) school, than at his first placement, a secondary school. Students were more open to different views, at least in part because the school culture encouraged it. Margaret felt well supported by a very strong mentor teacher at a Catholic grammar school with an excellent reputation.

Teachers and Departments

Another constraint was the relationship between student teachers and full-time teachers. In a couple of cases, student teachers reported they felt full-time teachers intervened in their teaching and in one case made them feel unwelcome. A few said that requirements to use curriculum developed by the department was a constraint.

On the other hand, sources of support included helpful mentor teachers and department heads. Not surprisingly, most interviewees said that working with supportive mentors who granted them autonomy was especially valuable. The ability to extend lessons beyond initial time constraints was particularly helpful. Some teachers spoke about using valuable curricular-instructional resources and schemes of work from their departments.

Curriculum

The press to cover curriculum, especially in history, was a significant constraint for many novices. In a few cases, a portion of class time had to be reserved for silent reading or writing.

Some teachers benefited from finding controversies in the official curriculum. Andrew said the religious education and citizenship curricula at his school placements were full of controversial questions. Harrison found the William Farr cowardice or casualty case in the history textbook. As stated previously, history teachers in Northern Ireland were assigned to teach contentious subject matter, but could choose to embrace, contain, or avoid exploration of conflict.

Cohort and University Faculty

Importantly, preservice teachers in England derived support from their history cohort, particularly with selecting age-appropriate resources that would stimulate discussion and frame controversial issues in ways that engaged students. They often texted each other with questions and suggestions, and a group of them met occasionally at a pub or for dinner.

Student teachers who had contact with university faculty while teaching controversial issues appreciated the moral support and/or helpful feedback they provided.

Anxiety

Most of the novice teachers expressed anxiety about student reactions to sensitive or controversial issues. Emma and Aoife were especially open about how it affected them. Emma identified as a "mother hen," and tried to avoid evoking difficult emotions in her students. And Aoife felt torn between her family and community's history of suffering discrimination on one hand and her teacher role of encouraging students to consider new perspectives on the other. Individual anxiety was intensified by wider factors. The history of conflict and division in Northern Ireland was close to the surface in the "hot spot" communities (Kitson, 2007) where they student taught. Those divisions were reflected in student discourse, increasing their anxiety.

Although they did not often confront this problem, most teachers worried about what to do if a student expressed intolerant views or was triggered by sensitive subject matter. One can infer that this concern influenced teaching, but other constraints, such as insufficient time, foreclosed the possibility of risk-taking in more obvious ways. The institutional pressures of covering curriculum and maintaining classroom control affected everyone's practice (Barton & Levstik, 2004), although these pressures were manifested in different ways.

ADVICE TO TEACHER EDUCATORS

The novice teachers had terrific advice for teacher educators on preparing students to teach controversial issues:

1. Follow the examples of the teacher educators in this book, particularly their modeling of approaches to teaching controversial issues.
2. Have preservice teachers develop curriculum and give them feedback.
3. Give preservice teachers opportunities to teach controversial issues lessons and give feedback.
4. Have classes dive into discussions of current, close-to-home controversial issues.
5. Schedule classes to convene during and after student teaching so students can discuss their experiences and get support.
6. Provide more explicit modeling and definition to clear up ambiguities regarding the meaning of controversial issues and the best ways to teach them, while addressing developmental and academic differences as well as students' emotional reactions.

QUESTIONS AND RECOMMENDATIONS FOR PRACTICE, POLICY, AND RESEARCH

The cross-national sample in this study offers diverse ways of thinking about teaching controversial issues and preparing new teachers to take up this work. Although we need to remember the small sample size, its findings raise important questions about practice, policy, and program structure. And while we know how difficult it is to change educational institutions, they lead to recommendations for reform.

Classroom Discussion

Classroom discussion was approached differently in England and Northern Ireland compared to the United States. Teaching approaches cannot be merely imported from one cultural context to another (Barton & McCully, 2007; Hahn, 1998). But asking hard questions about discussion encourages productive examination of the relative merits of different approaches.

Should educators in divided societies like Northern Ireland push for greater dialogue, as Sean suggested, or respect teachers' pedagogical tradition and students' right to remain silent, as Mark suggested? Is the array of discussion methods taught at the Northern Irish and English sites sufficient for teaching the skills of civic discourse, or are more sustained discussions needed, with explicit attention to their quality? Does the kind of questioning taught by Ian and Mark in history sufficiently orient students to one another (Reisman et al., 2018) so they engage in genuine dialogue? And, acknowledging the constraints described by preservice teachers in the U.K., is ten or 15 minutes enough time for discussion in a controversial issues lesson?

At the same time, we must also consider what is gained from a more cautious approach to discussion. As Paula explained, it offers more protection for students and teachers, which is particularly salient in a highly polarized context. And it makes the teaching of controversial issues accessible to a larger number of teachers. Highly structured or nonverbal methods that do not take up a lot of time may limit genuine dialogue. But in many circumstances, they are more feasible and may work well with particular groups of students. It is critical that educators from different cultural contexts discuss the trade-offs.

Emotion

What is the place of emotion in the classroom, especially when fundamental questions of identity, community, and ideology are raised? Barton and McCully (2012) suggest that to have an impact on Northern Irish students' perspectives on history, teachers need to engage their emotions as well as their intellect. Mark and Ian used narratives to involve students affectively and intellectually. Ian's student Harrison spoke about doing this as well. Mark encouraged preservice teachers to understand emotive responses and help students understand where they come from. His strategies could help educators deal with a major obstacle to critical thinking—motivated reasoning, in which affective factors such as emotion, social identity, and prior beliefs drive thinking (Clark & Avery, 2016).

On the other hand, Paula's model for teaching controversial issues pragmatically and protectively helps teachers keep emotions at bay. Its usefulness is apparent in this era of stark polarization and in schools with structural constraints on teaching such as insufficient time. It allays many teachers' fears about student reactions to controversy. Should teachers try to tap into emotional responses to controversy and help students understand them? Or are they better off avoiding the potential powder keg that emotions represent?

Teacher Education Pedagogy

Liz's use of practice teaching raises the question of what kind of teacher education pedagogy is most effective, especially for bridging the divide between university courses and schools. The teacher educators in my study were not familiar with the core practice model (Grossman, 2018). Peercy and Troyan (2017), teacher educators who conducted a self-study on their efforts at practice-based teacher education, explain that providing opportunities for systematic examination and rehearsal of core teaching practices in teacher education courses requires "massive epistemological and pedagogical shifts" (p. 27).

Is it possible to substantially nudge teacher education in this direction? What constraints would get in the way and how could they be addressed?

Teacher educators in England and Northern Ireland were already pressed for time. What changes are possible in university courses, given government regulations and intense competition from alternative pathways to certification? What supports would teacher educators need?

Clarifying What Are Controversial Issues

How much time should be spent clarifying conceptions of controversial issues, and whose definitions should be taught? Novices in England and Northern Ireland conflated controversial topics, controversial issues, sensitive questions, and social justice content, in some cases even after being provided definitions.

Spending more time conceptualizing controversial issues and identifying different types, especially open versus settled issues and public versus private issues, could improve lesson and unit design, particularly around framing issues. Also being able to identify the perennial issue (Hess, 2009) underlying a specific controversy would foster teaching for deep understanding. It would help teachers connect the past to the present. For example, teaching the case of a shell-shocked soldier executed for cowardice provides opportunities to ask larger questions about military justice and national values.

Another helpful scheme is the categorization of three types of issues offered by Zimmerman and Robertson (2017, pp. 49–50). "Maximally controversial issues" are issues of public concern about which knowledgeable people disagree and are emotionally invested. An example is whether the electoral college should be abolished. "Expert-Public disagreements" are issues on which knowledgeable people agree but a "significant portion of the public" strongly disagrees. The authors give the example of whether childhood vaccines cause autism. Finally, "disagreements among experts" involve disputes among knowledgeable people about questions, such as interpretations of literary classics, that do not concern the general public.

Conceptualizing controversial issues in post-conflict societies is more complex. Often sensitive questions, controversial topics, and controversial issues actually are conflated in real life. And while controversial issues call for "strategies designed to help students investigate, evaluate, or deliberate . . . multiple and competing views," it may not be wise to require that they "make a judgment about what should be done or which interpretation . . . is correct" (Ho et al., 2017, p. 322). Different conceptions and purposes are appropriate for different contexts.

Findings suggest that explicit discussion of the relationship between social justice and controversial issues also would be helpful. McAvoy (2016, p. 42) clarifies that teachers should teach that structural inequalities in society are demonstrable facts. The controversy lies in *what to do* about these inequalities, and this is an open question that should be discussed from different perspectives.

In Washington and Humphries's (2011) case study, the teacher spelled out for students the difference between open issues they would discuss from different angles and closed issues related to race. This distinction served to "foreclose the possibility that students might articulate perspectives that are viewed as racist in the larger society and could alienate their classmates and corrode the classroom environment" (p. 111). All of these ideas would help novice teachers make important distinctions and resolve perceived tensions between teaching for social justice and teaching controversial issues.

Academic Tracking and Selection

The challenges of teaching controversial issues in lower-track classes and non-selective schools point to serious problems. Tracking and selection work against the demographic diversity that is so important for high-quality discussion, which depends on exchanges of diverse viewpoints (Parker, 2010). These structures contribute to a "democracy divide" in which young people who lack racial or socioeconomic privilege are not educated to participate in politics the way racially or socioeconomically privileged students often are (Hess, 2008).

How can this problem be tackled? Greater attention to working with struggling students in teacher education should include knowledge that comes from practitioners and communities, so that preservice teachers gain practical tools as well as deeper understanding of students' assets and funds of knowledge (Zeichner, 2010). Stressing the social aim of expanding democratic learning opportunities to all students is key. But structural changes in schools, which are highly controversial, must be seriously considered to achieve that aim.

School Structures and Leadership

Prior research and my interviews with the novice teachers and their teacher educators indicate that school sites play a large role in supporting or constraining teaching controversial issues. Changing school structures and systems to create more diversity poses a serious, but important, challenge. Hess and McAvoy (2015) found that de facto segregation of students along racial and socioeconomic lines impeded successful teaching of controversial issues because students did not hear diverse perspectives, experiences, and ideas.

Most of Northern Ireland's schools are segregated along religious lines. How much does this interfere with learning opportunities across the divide? Shared Education, a program that promotes collaboration between Catholic and Protestant schools, is intended to advance social cohesion. Research on the program finds that regular, sustained contact among students from different schools is key (Gallagher, 2016). Can Shared Education create a significant number of classes in which students from different communities consistently engage in dialogue about issues that affect their society?

The majority of constraints on teaching controversial issues are located in the school setting. Should educators work around them or push for reform?

The "Human Rights and Democracy in Action" project, sponsored by the European Union and Council of Europe, generated the development of two remarkable tools. The first, *Living with Controversy: Teaching Controversial Issues through Education for Democratic Citizenship* (Kerr & Huddleston, 2015), is a training pack for teachers. The second, which builds on the first, is for school leaders and senior school managers to support teaching of controversial issues. In the introduction to the second pack, *Managing Controversy*, editors Huddleston and Kerr (2017) state, "The involvement and commitment of school leaders and senior management is the main factor affecting how controversial issues are approached in schools" (p. 15).

Both resources were piloted in several countries, including Austria, Cyprus, Ireland, Montenegro, and the United Kingdom. The one for school leaders and senior managers addresses school leadership, school ethos and culture, teaching and learning, the curriculum, student voice, guidance and support, parental engagement, risk management, and staff development and training. It makes it clear that teaching controversial issues should be supported by a whole school effort.

Interestingly, Huddleston and Kerr do not challenge school curriculum or timetabling for different subjects. They advocate taking up controversial issues in all subjects. The biggest constraint novice teachers in my study experienced was insufficient time for citizenship and history. What would it take to elevate the status of these subjects? Paula's international citizenship network tried that to no avail. Yet, in Northern Ireland and England, expanding time for citizenship and history as well as relieving pressures for coverage and exam prep are absolutely crucial to create room for teaching issues through democratic inquiry in a supportive atmosphere.

Program Structure, Policy, and Placements

Teacher preparation program structures and school placements can support or constrain teaching controversial issues. The following questions and recommendations are offered knowing that neoliberal policies have undermined university-based teacher education. Although a full discussion lies outside the scope of this book, it is critical to recognize that for many years, the British government has tried to move responsibility for teacher preparation from universities to schools (Furlong, 2012). The government regulates various

elements of PGCE programs, which have to compete with alternative pathways such as TeachFirst and Schools Direct.

Given these outside forces, are there program policies and structures that
can be improved? One issue regards supervision of student teaching. Ian's
scheme of work (SoW) assignment had the potential to advance the teaching of controversial questions in history. He acknowledged that the quality
of SoWs largely depended on the mentor teachers. Interviews with student
teachers indicated that many would have benefited from greater support from
both university and school personnel. This raises the question of how teacher
preparation should be shared between those two groups.

How involved in student teaching should university faculty be, and how
many visits with each student teacher should university-employed supervisors make? How much responsibility should mentor teachers in the schools
be given and how can they be prepared to support student teachers?

Most student teaching in England and Northern Ireland occurred in two
blocks of time that alternated with blocks devoted to courses, but there was
not much opportunity at the end of the year to debrief the second placement.
Student teachers did not attend a weekly seminar on student teaching to
debrief their experiences. Ian indicated that he planned to have student teachers return to the university once a week the following year, but also planned
to reduce university supervision to three visits a year due to a larger cohort
and a limited number of clinical supervisors.

My research indicates that more structured university involvement during student teaching could be a vital source of support. Obviously faculty
would have to be relieved of other responsibilities or clinical supervisors
who worked closely with faculty would need to be hired. Such involvement
could be particularly helpful when student teachers address the needs of
academically diverse students and manage difficult student reactions to new
perspectives. University personnel could also offer guidance in dealing with
time constraints as well as pressures to cover curriculum and prepare for
exams. Emotional support for student teachers tackling hard questions with
their students also would be of great help.

The quality of student teaching placements also matters. Finding good
placements can be difficult. Sometimes university staff or part-time faculty
take on this vital task. Partnerships are often built based on prior relationships. The question of how to find the best possible placements is critical.

Members of the U.S. cohort completed one of their placements in a conservative suburban district that restrained teaching controversy. The English
preservice teachers had one or both placements in schools where the vast
majority of students were white. In Northern Ireland, the preservice teachers interviewed taught in schools that represented their religious background
with the exception of two who taught in an integrated school. It seemed that,
exceptions notwithstanding, many preservice teachers got limited preparation

to teach controversial issues with students from diverse racial, cultural, and religious backgrounds (Montgomery & McGlynn, 2009).

The questions of who should be responsible for building partnerships with school sites and how faculty can support them are massively important. Although all parties are stretched in many directions, ideally, teacher educators would be working with mentor teachers in the schools to jointly support novices.

Future Research

Like my recommendations for policy, those for future research bump up against real-world constraints. The first recommendation is to recruit a more racially and culturally diverse sample of teacher educators and preservice teachers as well as to expand the national contexts of the research sites. Finding a strong sample of diverse educators doing this work in more varied national contexts is challenging but necessary.

Researchers should observe student teachers in their placements and follow them into their first few years as inservice teachers. The problem of gaining access to the schools where novice teachers are working, given increased concerns about security, is a serious obstacle but merits investigation. Perhaps a collaboration among researchers located in different countries is the way forward.

This study used a grounded theory approach to data analysis. Future studies can build on this research by drawing on Crocco and Livingston's (2017) recommendations for building a stronger base in social studies teacher education research. They could utilize particular conceptual frameworks, such as Shulman's (1987) concept of pedagogical content knowledge, to identify more precisely the knowledge and skills required for skillful teaching of controversial issues in different disciplines and how novices develop them. The current focus on core practices in practice-based teacher education holds great promise for building knowledge about how novices learn to facilitate discussion of historical texts (Reisman et al., 2018). But finding a sample of teacher educators using this model to prepare for teaching controversial issues impedes the goal of studying more diverse research participants in a wider variety of settings.

KEY CONTRIBUTIONS

This book breaks new ground by offering an in-depth account of how four accomplished teacher educators prepared preserve teachers for the difficult and risky practice of teaching controversial issues. In doing so, it responds to the rising call to make democratic teacher education a priority in these contentious times (Andrews et al., 2018). It presents the first empirical study to describe different approaches to this preparation through intimate views of practice. A significant part of the study's contribution is its detailed conversations with 15 preservice teachers about the lessons they learned from these experts and their real-world experiences in schools.

One of the major themes is the critical influence of education policy, school contexts, and sociopolitical and cultural climates. Comparisons across the cross-national sample illuminate how these influences shape teacher preparation and classroom teaching. In these ways, the book is a pathbreaking addition to what Crocco and Livingston (2017) called the "thin research base" in teacher education and, more specifically, in social studies teacher education.

The book's most significant contribution is its answer to the question posed at the beginning: How can new teachers learn to teach controversy in the realities of the charged classroom? The research presented here points to an approach adopted across these culturally and nationally distinct settings, which I have described as contained risk-taking.

This concept is based on a grounded theory of contained, constrained, and supported risk-taking. According to this theory, teacher educators show novices strategies for teaching controversial issues that contain the concomitant risks. Novice teachers creatively adopt these strategies to fit their own proclivities, the subjects they teach, their students, and school demands. Their efforts are shaped by constraints, such as short class periods, and by supports, such as encouraging mentors.

Through examining teacher educators at the university and their influence on novice teachers in classrooms and schools, the book highlights the irreplaceable role of university-based teacher education. It shows that teacher education courses can prepare preservice teachers by giving them practical and conceptual tools for ambitious practice. In these courses, theory was not divorced from, nor was it privileged over, practice.

The study demonstrates preservice and first-year teachers' enthusiasm for designing curriculum and trying new pedagogical methods. It shows that school sites can support or constrain novices' efforts. The findings make an argument for structures that foster greater involvement of university faculty during student teaching and that afford more instructional time for citizenship and history. Importantly, this study sheds light on critical challenges novice teachers confront in the charged classroom. Our understanding of these should inform school and university policies.

My hope is that rich and varied representations of teaching underpinned by principles of practice may contribute to educational developments in post-conflict societies. A visit to Bosnia and Herzegovina in September 2019 offered me the opportunity to meet inspirational educators who are collaborating across divisions to teach current issues as well as contested history that is still raw from the legacy of war, genocide, and ethnic cleansing. Educators in the region are working hard to reform primary and secondary education as well as teacher education. Examples of preparing teachers for democratic inquiry and discourse on controversial issues may be a great help in former Yugoslavia and elsewhere.

Fitting for a work on controversial issues, this book raises provocative questions about classroom practice, teacher education approaches, program structures, and school reform. It encourages teacher educators, classroom teachers, school and university leaders, researchers, and policymakers to forge ahead in advancing democratic education. At a time when we fear for the survival of democracy, these teacher educators and novice teachers give us hope that a new generation of teachers will contribute to the development of the informed critical thinkers, democratic decision-makers, and inspired activists we desperately need.

References

Andrews, D. C., Richmond, G., Warren, C. A., Petchauer, E., & Floden, R. (2018). A call to action for teacher preparation programs: Supporting critical conversations and democratic action in safe learning environments. *Journal of Teacher Education, 69*(3), 205–208. doi:10.1177/0022487118766510

Avery, P. G. (2002). Teaching tolerance: What research tells us. *Social Education, 66*(5), 270–276.

Avery, P. G., Levy, S. A., & Simmons, A. M. (2013). Deliberating controversial public issues as part of civic education. *The Social Studies, 104*, 105–114. doi:10.1080/00377996.2012.691571

Ball, S. J. (2013). *The education debate* (2nd ed.). Bristol: The Policy Press.

Banks, J. A. (1996). Foreword. In W. D. Parker (Ed.), *Educating the democratic mind* (pp. xi–xiii). New York: SUNY Press.

Barton, K. C., & Avery, P. G. (2016). Research on social studies education: Diverse students, settings, and methods. In C. A. Bell & D. Gitomer (Eds.), *Handbook of research on teaching* (5th ed., pp. 985–1038). Washington, DC: American Educational Research Association.

Barton, K. C., & Levstik, L. S. (2004). *Teaching history for the common good.* New York, NY: Routledge.

Barton, K. C., & McCully, A. (2007). Teaching controversial issues... where controversial issues really matter. *Teaching History, 127*, 13–19.

Barton, K. C., & McCully, A. W. (2010). "You can form your own point of view": Internally persuasive discourse in Northern Ireland students' encounters with history. *Teachers College Record, 112*(1), 142–181.

Barton, K. C., & McCully, A. W. (2012). Trying to "see things differently": Northern Ireland students' struggle to understand alternative historical perspectives. *Theory & Research in Social Education, 40*(4), 371–408.

Beck, T. A. (2013). Identity, discourse, and safety in a high school discussion of same-sex marriage. *Theory & Research in Social Education, 41*, 1–32. doi:10.1080/00933104.2013.757759

Bekerman, Z., & Zembylas, M. (2011). The emotional complexities of teaching conflictual historical narratives: The case of integrated Palestinian-Jewish schools in Israel. *Teachers College Record, 113*(5), 1004–1030.

Bickmore, K. (1993). Learning inclusion/inclusion in learning: Citizenship education for a pluralistic society. *Theory & Research in Social Education, 21*(4), 341–384.

Bickmore, K., & Parker, C. (2014). Constructive conflict talk in classrooms: Divergent approaches to addressing divergent perspectives. *Theory and Research in Social Education, 42*, 291–335. doi:10.1080/00933104.2014.901199

Blake, J. S. (2017, July 11). What a Protestant parade reveals about Theresa May's new partners. *The Atlantic.* Retrieved from http://www.theatlantic.com

Booth, M. B. (1969). *History betrayed?* London, UK: Longmans.

Britzman, D. P. (2003). *Practice makes practice: A critical study of learning to teach.* New York: SUNY Press.

Browning, C. (1992). *Ordinary men: Reserve police battalion 101 and the final solution in Poland.* New York: HarperCollins.

Calleja, S., & Kokenis, T. (2017). *Walling off or welcoming in? The challenge of creating inclusive spaces in diverse contexts.* Retrieved from http://www.justicein schools.org/files/playpen/files/walling_off_or_welcoming_in.pdf

Choices Program. (n.d.). *The struggle to define free speech: From Skokie to Paris.* Retrieved from https://www.choices.edu/teaching-news-lesson/struggle-define -free-speech-skokie-paris/

Clark, C. H., & Avery, P. G. (2016). The psychology of controversial issues discussions. In W. Journell (Ed.), *Reassessing the social studies curriculum: Promoting critical civic engagement in a politically polarized, post-9/11 world* (pp. 109–120). Lanham, MD: Rowman & Littlefield.

Cole, M. (1998). *Cultural psychology: A once and future discipline.* Cambridge, MA: Harvard University Press.

Corbin, J., & Strauss, A. (1990). Grounded theory research: Procedures, canon, and evaluative criteria. *Qualitative Sociology, 13*, 3–21. doi:10.1007/BF00988593

Cornbleth, C. (2001). Climates of constraint/restraint of teachers and of teaching. In W. Stanley (Ed.), *Critical issues in social studies research for the 21st century.* Greenwich, CT: Information Age Publishing.

Crocco, M. S., & Livingston, E. (2017). Becoming an "expert" social studies teacher: What we know about teacher education and professional development. In M. M. Manfra & C. M. Bolick (Eds.), *The Wiley handbook of social studies research* (pp. 360–384). West Sussex, UK: Wiley & Sons.

Dahlgren, R. L., Humphries, E., & Washington, E. Y. (2014). Preservice teachers and teaching controversial issues in New York and Florida. In T. Misco & J. De Groof (Eds.), *Cross-cultural case studies of teaching controversial issues* (pp. 201–219). Oisterwijk, The Netherlands: Wolf Legal Publishers.

Davies, I. (Ed.). (2000). *Teaching the Holocaust: Educational dimensions, principles and practice.* London, UK: Continuum.

Dearden, R. F. (1981). Controversial issues and the curriculum. *Journal of Curriculum Studies, 13*(1), 37–44.

Dow, P. (1991). *Schoolhouse politics: Lessons from the Sputnik era*. Cambridge, MA: Harvard University Press.

DuVernay, A., Averick, S., & Barish, H. (Producers), & DuVernay, A. (Director). (2016). *13th* [Film]. United States: Kandoo Films.

Engle, S. H. (2003). Decision making: The heart of social studies instruction. *The Social Studies, 94*(1), 7–10.

Erickson, F., & Shultz, J. J. (1982). *The counselor as gatekeeper: Social interaction in interviews*. New York: Academic Press.

Ersoy, A. F. (2010). Social studies teacher candidates' views on the controversial issues incorporated into their courses in Turkey. *Teaching and Teacher Education, 26*, 323–334. doi:10.1016/j.tate.2009.09.015

Foster, S. (2014). Teaching controversial issues in the classroom: The exciting potential of disciplinary history. In M. Baildon, L. K. Seng, I. M. Lim, G. Inanc, & J. Jaffar (Eds.), *Controversial history education in Asian contexts*. London, UK: Routledge.

Furlong, J. (2012). Globalisation, neoliberalism, and the reform of teacher education in England. *The Educational Forum, 77*(1), 28–50.

Gallagher, T. (2004). *Education in divided societies*. London, UK: Palgrave Macmillan.

Gallagher, T. (2016). Shared education in Northern Ireland: School collaboration in divided societies. *Oxford Review of Education, 42*(3), 362–375.

Goldhagen, D. J. (1997). *Hitler's willing executioners: Ordinary Germans and the Holocaust*. New York: Vintage Books.

Gregory, I. (2000). Teaching about the Holocaust: Perplexities, issues, and perspectives. In I. Davies (Ed.), *Teaching the Holocaust: Educational dimensions, principles and practice* (pp. 49–60). London, UK: Continuum.

Gross, M. H., & Terra, L. (2018). What makes difficult history difficult? *Phi Delta Kappan, 99*(8), 51–56.

Grossman, P. (Ed.). (2018). *Teaching core practices in teacher education*. Cambridge, MA: Harvard Education Press.

Grossman, P., Hammerness, K., & McDonald, M. (2008). Redefining teaching, reimagining teacher education. *Teachers and Teaching: Theory and Practice, 15*, 273–289. doi:10.1080/13540600902875340

Grossman, P., Smagorinsky, P., & Valencia, S. (1999). Appropriating tools for teaching English: A theoretical framework for research on learning to teach. *American Journal of Education, 108*, 1–29. doi:10.1086/444230

Grossman, P. L., Valencia, S. W., Evans, K., Thompson, C., Martin, S., & Place, N. (2000). Transitions into teaching: Learning to teach writing in teacher education and beyond. *Journal of Literacy Research, 32*(4), 631–662.

Gutmann, A. (2000). Why should schools care about civic education? In L. M. McDonnell, P. M. Timpane, & R. Benjamin (Eds.), *Rediscovering the democratic purposes of education: Studies in government and public policy* (pp. 73–90). Lawrence, KS: University Press of Kansas.

Gutmann, A. (2004). Unity and diversity in democratic multicultural education: Creative and destructive tensions. In J. A. Banks (Ed.), *Diversity and citizenship education: Global perspectives* (pp. 71–98). San Francisco: Jossey Bass.

Hahn, C. L. (1998). *Becoming political: Comparative perspectives on citizenship education*. Albany, NY: SUNY Press.

Hahn, C. L. (2006). Comparative and international social studies research. In K. C. Barton (Ed.), *Research methods in social studies education: Contemporary issues and perspectives* (pp. 139–158). Greenwich, CT: Information Age Publishing.

Hahn, C. L. (2011). Issues-centered pedagogy and classroom climate for discussion: A view from the United States. In K. J. Kennedy, W. O. Lee, & D. L. Grossman (Eds.), *Citizenship pedagogies in Asia and the Pacific* (pp. 315–331). Dordrecht, Netherlands: Springer.

Hand, M. (2008). What should we teach as controversial? A defense of the epistemic criterion. *Educational Theory, 58*(2), 213–228.

Hand, M., & Levinson, R. (2012). Discussing controversial issues in the classroom. *Educational Philosophy and Theory, 44*(6), 614–629.

Hess, D. E. (2001). Teaching to public controversy in a democracy. In J. J. Patrick & R. S. Leming (Eds.), *Principles and practices of democracy in the education of social studies teachers* (pp. 87–109). Bloomington, IN: Educational Resources Information Center.

Hess, D. E. (2002). Discussing controversial public issues in secondary social studies classrooms: Learning from skilled teachers. *Theory & Research in Social Education, 30*(1), 10–41.

Hess, D. E. (2003). Using video to create a vision for powerful discussion teaching in secondary social studies. In J. Brophy (Ed.), *Using video in teacher education* (pp. 53–72). Bingley, UK: Emerald Group Publishing.

Hess, D. E. (2005). How do teachers' political views influence teaching about issues? *Social Education, 69*(1), 47–49.

Hess, D. E. (2008). Controversial issues and democratic discourse. In L. Levstik & C. Tyson (Eds.), *Handbook of research in social studies education* (pp. 124–136). New York: Routledge.

Hess, D. E. (2009). *Controversy in the classroom: The democratic power of discussion*. New York, NY: Routledge.

Hess, D. E., & McAvoy, P. (2009). To disclose or not to disclose: A controversial choice for teachers. In D. E. Hess (Ed.), *Controversy in the classroom: The democratic power of discussion* (pp. 97–110). New York, NY: Routledge.

Hess, D. E., & McAvoy, P. (2015). *The political classroom: Evidence and ethics in democratic education*. New York, NY: Routledge.

Hess, D. E., Stone, S., & Kahne, J. (2015). Should high school students be required to pass a citizenship test? *Social Education, 79*(4), 173–176.

Ho, L., McAvoy, P., Hess, D., & Gibbs, B. (2017). Teaching and learning about controversial issues and topics in the social studies. In M. Manfra & C. M. Bolick (Eds.), *The Wiley handbook of social studies research* (pp. 319–335). Hoboken, NJ: Wiley-Blackwell.

Huddleston, E., & Kerr, D. (2017). *Managing controversy: Developing a strategy for handling controversy and teaching controversial issues in schools*. Council of Europe. Retrieved from https://rm.coe.int/16806ecd25

Husbands, C., Kitson, A., & Pendry, A. (2003). *Understanding history teaching: Teaching and learning about the past in secondary schools.* Maidenhead, UK: Open University Press.

Jackson, P. W. (1968). *Life in classrooms.* New York, NY: Holt, Rinehart and Winston.

Jerome, L., & Elwick, A. (2019). Identifying an educational response to the prevent policy: Student perspectives on learning about terrorism, extremism and radicalisation. *British Journal of Educational Studies, 67*(1), 97–114.

Johnson, D. W., & Johnson, R. T. (1979). Conflict in the classroom: Controversy and learning. *Review of Educational Research, 49*(1), 51–69.

Journell, W. (2016). Introduction: Teaching social issues in the social studies classroom. In W. Journell (Ed.), *Teaching social studies in an era of divisiveness: The challenges of discussing social issues in a non-partisan way* (pp. 1–12). Lanham, MD: Rowman & Littlefield.

Kahne, J., & Middaugh, E. (2008). Democracy for some: The civic opportunity gap in high school. CIRCLE Working paper #59. Retrieved from http://www.civicyout h.org/PopUps/WorkingPapers/WP59Kahne.pdf

Keefe, P. R. (2019). *Say nothing: A true story of murder and memory in Northern Ireland.* New York, NY: Doubleday.

Kello, K. (2016). Sensitive and controversial issues in the classroom: Teaching history in a divided society. *Teachers and Teaching, 22*(1), 35–53.

Kelly, D. M., & Brandes, G. M. (2001). Shifting out of "neutral": Beginning teachers' struggles with teaching for social justice. *Canadian Journal of Education, 26,* 437–454.

Kerr, D., & Huddleston, E. (2015). *Living with controversy: Teaching controversial issues through education for democratic citizenship and human rights.* Council of Europe. Retrieved from https://rm.coe.int/16806948b6

King, J. T. (2009). Teaching and learning about controversial issues: Lessons from Northern Ireland. *Theory & Research in Social Education, 37*(2), 215–246. doi:10 .1080/00933104.2009.10473395

Kitson, A. (2007). History teaching and reconciliation in Northern Ireland. In E. A. Cole (Ed.), *Teaching the violent past: Reconciliation and history education* (pp. 123–154). Lanham, MD: Rowman & Littlefield.

Kitson, A., & McCully, A. (2005). 'You hear about it for real in school.' Avoiding, containing and risk-taking in the history classroom. *Teaching History, 120,* 32–37.

Kühl, S. (2017). *Ordinary organisations: Why normal men carried out the Holocaust.* Hoboken, NJ: John Wiley & Sons.

Kumashiro, K. K. (2010). Seeing the bigger picture: Troubling movements to end teacher education. *Journal of Teacher Education, 61*(1–2), 56–65.

Kumashiro, K. K. (2015). *Against common sense: Teaching and learning toward social justice.* New York: Routledge.

Lampert, M. (2009). Learning teaching in, from, and for practice: What do we mean? *Journal of Teacher Education, 61*(1–2), 21–34.

Lampert, M., & Graziani, F. (2009). Instructional activities as a tool for teachers' and educators' learning. *The Elementary School Journal, 109*(5), 491–509.

Levinson, M. (2012). *No citizen left behind.* Cambridge, MA: Harvard University Press.

Libresco, A., & Balantic, J. (2016). Every issue is a social studies issue: Strategies for rich discussion in the upper elementary classroom. In W. Journell (Ed.), *Teaching social studies in an era of divisiveness: Challenges of discussing social issues in a non-partisan way* (pp. 13–30). Lanham, MD: Rowman & Littlefield.

Lightfoot, S. L. (1983). *The good high school: Portraits of character and culture.* New York: Basic Books.

Lortie, D. C. (1975). *Schoolteacher: A sociological study.* Chicago, IL: University of Chicago Press.

Lunenberg, M., Korthagen, F., & Swennen, A. (2007). The teacher educator as a role model. *Teaching and Teacher Education, 23*(5), 586–601. doi:10.1016/j.tate 2006.11.001

McAvoy, P. (2016). Preparing young adults for polarized America. In W. Journell (Ed.), *Teaching social studies in an era of divisiveness: The challenges of discussing social issues in a non-partisan way* (pp. 31–46). Lanham, MD: Rowman & Littlefield.

McAvoy, P., & Hess, D. E. (2013). Classroom deliberation in an era of political polarization. *Curriculum Inquiry, 43*(1), 14–47.

McCully, A. (2006). Practitioner perceptions of their role in facilitating the handling of controversial issues in contested societies: A Northern Irish experience. *Educational Review, 58*(1), 51–65.

McCully, A., & Emerson, L. (2014). Teaching controversial issues in Northern Ireland. In T. Misco & J. De Groof (Eds.), *Cross-cultural case studies of teaching controversial issues* (pp. 143–165). Oisterwijk, The Netherlands: Wolf Legal Publishers.

McCully, A., & Reilly, J. (2017). History teaching to promote positive community relations in Northern Ireland: Tensions between pedagogy, social psychological theory and professional practice in two recent projects. In C. Psaltis, M. Carretero, & S. Cehajic-Clancy (Eds.), *History education and conflict transformation* (pp. 301–320). Cham, Switzerland: Palgrave Macmillan.

McNeil, L. M. (1986). *Contradictions of control: School structure and school knowledge.* New York: Routledge.

Metz, M. H. (1978). *Classrooms and corridors: The crisis of authority in desegregated secondary schools.* Berkeley, CA: University of California Press.

Miller-Lane, J., Denton, E., & May, A. (2006). Social studies teachers' views on committed impartiality and discussion. *Social Studies Research and Practice, 1*(1), 30–44.

Misco, T., & Patterson, N. C. (2007). A study of preservice teachers' conceptualizations of academic freedom and controversial issues. *Theory & Research in Social Education, 35*(4), 520–550.

Montgomery, A., & McGlynn, C. (2009). New peace, new teachers: Student teachers' perspectives of diversity and community relations in Northern Ireland. *Teaching and Teacher Education, 25*(3), 391–399. doi:10.1016/j.tate.2008.11.002

National Issues Forums. (n.d.). *End of life: What should we do for those who are dying?* Retrieved from https://www.nifi.org/es/issue-guide/end-life

Nerve Center. (n.d.). *Teaching divided histories.* Retrieved from https://www.ner vecentre.org/teachingdividedhistories

Pace, J. L. (2006). Saving (and losing) face, race, and authority: Strategies of action in a ninth-grade English class. In J. L. Pace & A. Hemmings (Eds.), *Classroom authority: Theory, research, and practice* (pp. 103–128). New York: Routledge.

Pace, J. L. (2008). Teaching for citizenship in 12th grade government classes. In J. Bixby & J. L. Pace (Eds.), *Educating democratic citizens in troubled times: Qualitative studies of current efforts* (pp. 25–57). Albany, NY: SUNY Press.

Pace, J. L. (2011). The complex and unequal impact of high stakes accountability on untested social studies. *Theory & Research in Social Education, 39*(1), 32–60.

Pace, J. L. (2015). *The charged classroom: Predicaments and possibilities for democratic teaching.* New York, NY: Routledge.

Pace, J. L. (2017). Preparing teachers in a divided society: Lessons from Northern Ireland. *Phi Delta Kappan, 99*(4), 26–32. doi:10.1177/0031721717745552

Pace, J. L. (2019). Contained risk-taking: Preparing preservice teachers to teach controversial issues in three countries. *Theory & Research in Social Education, 47*(2), 228–260.

Pace, J. L., & Hemmings, A. (2006). Understanding classroom authority as a social construction. In J. L. Pace & A. Hemmings (Eds.), *Classroom authority: Theory, research, and practice* (pp. 1–31). New York: Routledge.

Pace, J. L., & Hemmings, A. (2007). Understanding authority in classrooms: A review of theory, ideology, and research. *Review of Educational Research, 77*(1), 4–27.

Page, R. N. (1991). *Lower-track classrooms: A curricular and cultural perspective.* New York: Teachers College Press.

Palmer, P. J. (2010). *To know as we are known: Education as a spiritual journey.* San Francisco: Harper Collins.

Parker, W. C. (2003). *Teaching democracy: Unity and diversity in public life.* New York, NY: Teachers College Press.

Parker, W. C. (2006). Public discourses in schools: Purposes, problems, possibilities. *Educational Researcher, 35*(8), 11–18.

Parker, W. C. (2010). Listening to strangers: Classroom discussion in democratic education. *Teachers College Press, 112*(11), 2815–2832.

Parker, W. C., & Hess, D. (2001). Teaching with and for discussion. *Teaching and Teacher Education, 17,* 273–289. doi:10.1016/S0742-051X(00)00057-3

Parker, W. C., & Lo, J. C. (2016). Reinventing the high school government course: Rigor, simulations, and learning from text. *Democracy & Education, 24*(1), 1–10.

Peercy, M. M., & Troyan, F. J. (2017). Making transparent the challenges of developing a practice-based pedagogy of teacher education. *Teaching and Teacher Education, 61*(1), 26–36.

Reisman, A., Cipparone, P., Lightning, J., Monte-Sano, C., Kavanagh, S. S., McGrew, S., & Fogo, B. (2018). Facilitating whole-class discussions in history: A framework for preparing teacher candidates. *Journal of Teacher Education, 69*(3), 278–293.

Shackle. (2017, September 1). Trojan horse: The real story behind the 'Islamic plot' to take over the schools. *The Guardian.* Retrieved from https://www.theguardian.c

om/world/2017/sep/01/trojan-horse-the-real-story-behind-the-fake-islamic-plot-to
-take-over-schools

Shulman, L. (1987). Knowledge and teaching: Foundations of the new reform. *Harvard Educational Review, 57*(1), 1–22.

Simon, K. G. (2005). Classroom deliberations. In S. Fuhrman & M. Lazerson (Eds.), *The public schools* (107–129). New York: Oxford University Press.

Stradling, R., Noctor, M., & Baines, B. (1984). *Teaching controversial issues.* London, UK: Edward Arnold.

Terra, L. (2014). New histories for a new state: A study of history textbook content in Northern Ireland. *Journal of Curriculum Studies, 46*(2), 225–248.

Thornton, S. J. (2005). *Teaching social studies that matters: Curriculum for active learning.* New York: Teachers College.

Walzer, M. (1997). *On toleration.* New Haven, CT: Yale University Press.

Washington, E. Y., & Humphries, E. K. (2011). A social studies teacher's sense making of controversial issues discussions of race in a predominantly white, rural high school classroom. *Theory & Research in Social Education, 39*(1), 92–114.

Wasserman, J. (2011). Learning about controversial issues in school history: The experiences of learners in KwaZulu-Natal schools. *Journal of Natal and Zulu History, 29*, 131–157. doi:10.1080/02590123.2011.11964167

Wertsch, J. V. (Ed.). (1981). *The concept of activity in soviet psychology.* Armonk, NY: Sharpe.

Wideen, N. M., Mayer-Smith, J., & Moon, B. (1998). A critical analysis of the research on learning to teach: Making the case for an ecological perspective on inquiry. *Review of Educational Research, 68*(2), 130–178.

Woolley, R. (2011). Controversial issues: Identifying the concerns and priorities of student teachers. *Policy Futures in Education, 9*(2). doi:10.2304/pfie.2011.9.2.280

Worden, E. A., & Smith, A. (2017). Teaching for democracy in the absence of transitional justice: The case of Northern Ireland. *Comparative Education, 53*(3), 379–395.

Wright-Maley, C. (2015). On "stepping back and letting go": The role of control in the success or failure of social studies simulations. *Theory & Research in Social Education, 43*(2), 206–243.

Zeichner, K. (2010). Rethinking the connections between campus courses and field experiences in college- and university-based teacher education. *Journal of Teacher Education, 61*(1–2), 89–99.

Zeichner, K. (2012). The turn once again toward practice-based teacher education. *Journal of Teacher Education, 63*(5), 376–382.

Zembylas, M., & Bekerman, Z. (2008). Education and the dangerous memories of historical trauma: Narratives of pain, narratives of hope. *Curriculum Inquiry, 38*(2), 125–154.

Zembylas, M., & Kambani, F. (2012). The teaching of controversial issues during elementary level history instruction: Greek-Cypriot teachers' perceptions and emotions. *Theory & Research in Social Education, 40*(2), 107–133. doi:10.1080/0093 3104.2012.670591

Zimmerman, J., & Robertson, E. (2017). *The case for contention: Teaching controversial issues in American schools.* Chicago, IL: University of Chicago Press.

Index

Note: Page numbers in *italics* refers to table.

Abu Ghraib, 91
academic tracking and selection, 175
advice to teacher educators: Ian's
    students, 115–16; Liz's students,
    154–56; Mark's students, 37–39;
    Paula's students, 76–77
American Civil Liberties Union, 128
anxiety, 171
The Atlantic, 10
avoiders, 26

Balantic, J., 80
Banks, James, 157
Barstow, Paula, xxvi, 41–59; approach,
    42, 48, 58–59; biographical
    influences, 42; citizenship course,
    43–59; human rights, 42, 54–55;
    PowerPoint presentation, 50, 51;
    teaching model, 45–48; university
    program, 43–44; workshop, 49–53.
    See also preservice teachers (Paula's
    students)
Barton, K. C., 173
Battle of the Boyne, 10
Bauby, Jean-Dominique, 74
Bekerman, Z., 38–39
Bloody Sunday, 2

bonfires, 13
Booth, Martin, 85–86
Bosnia and Herzegovina, 179–80
Brexit, xxv
Brown University, 128
Bruner, Jerome, xviii

careful preparation, 66
Catholic Christian Brothers school, 42
The Charged Classroom (Pace), xx,
    xxiii, 114
Charles I, King of England, 107
Charlie Hebdo, 128–30
The Choices Program, 128
citizenship education: designing
    curriculum, 55–58; Mark's course,
    4, 7–13, 43; Paula's course, 43–59;
    school policy for, 44–45; workshops,
    42, 49–53
citizenship test, 125–28
classroom community, 142–43
classroom discussion, 163–64, 172–73
collective memories, 36, 38
conceptions of controversial issues,
    xvii–xviii; clarifying, 174–75;
    conflated, 160; Ian's students, 102–4;
    Liz's students, 141–42; Mark's

students, 21–22; Paula's students, 63–64

"Conflict in the Classroom: Controversy and Learning" (Johnson and Johnson), 126

Congo, 81

contained risk-taking, xvi, 161–63; collaborative learning, 162; creative resources and group activities, 162; dealing with emotional conflicts, 163; elements, 161–63; framing of issues, 162; Paula's approach, 48; proactive communication, 162; reflection on teacher identity and roles, 162; strategies for, 5–7; thorough preparation and planning, 162

containers, 26

contemporary public issues (CPI), xxii

"Contrasting Views on Human Rights," 128

controversial issues: clarifying conceptions of, 174–75; conceptions, xvii–xviii, 174–75

critical pedagogy, 41

Crocco, M. S., 178, 179

Cromwell, Oliver, 103, 108–9, 112, 166

Cromwell in Ireland, 108

cross-national research, xxiii–xxvii; data collection and analysis, xxvi–xxvii; teacher education contexts, xxvi

cryptocurrency, 150–51

curriculum, 170–71

Curriculum, Examinations and Assessment (CCEA), 44, 45

Dahlgren, R. L., xxii, 166, 167

Daily Express, 86–87

dangerous memories, 38–39

data collection and analysis, xxvi–xxvii

Davison, Emily Wilding, 84

D-Day, 110–11

dealing with emotional conflicts, 163

Dearden, R. F., xviii

decision-making in alternative school, 149–51

de-escalation techniques, 133

democratic discussion, 123–36; deliberation, 167; diverse classrooms, 133–34; rigorous and warm climate, 124–25; SAC model, 125–28; Socratic seminar, 131–33

democratic inquiry and discourse, 164

Democratic Unionist Party (DUP), 70–71

departments, teachers and, 170

Derby Day, 84

designing curriculum, 55–58

dialogic pedagogies, 25–26

discussions. *See* classroom discussion

Drummond, Mark, 1–18; approach to teaching preparation, 4–7; biographical influences, 1–2; citizenship course, 4, 7–13, 43; contained risk-taking strategies, 5–7; dialogic pedagogies, 25–26; history course, 3, 13–17; university program, 3–4. *See also* preservice teachers (Mark's students)

Duvernay, Ava, 148

Easter Rising, 15

emotion, 173–74; dealing with, 163

engagement with discussion models, 143–44

England: Brexit, xxv; history curriculum in, 3, 79–95. *See also* Shepherd, Ian

English Civil War, 107, 109, 111, 112

"Every Issue Is a Social Studies Issue" (Libresco and Balantic), 80

FRED, 52

"Freedom of Expression in Skokie: A Case Study on Human Rights," 128

freedom of speech, 128–31

genetically modified organisms (GMO), 149

genocide, 81
Good Friday Agreement, 71–72
Gove, Michael, 86
Great Education Reform Bill of 1988, 86
Grossman, P., xxix, 124

Hahn, Carole, 158, 163
Hawking, Stephen, 73
Hess, Diana, xxii, 6, 120, 124, 126, 141, 155, 160, 175
Hill, C. P., 86
History Betrayed (Booth), 85–86
history curricular/course: Mark's course, 3, 13–17; Shepherd's course, 82–95
Hitler, 85
Ho, L., xviii, xix, xxi, 168
Holocaust, 87–91
Huddleston, T., 176
human rights, 42, 54–55
"Human Rights and Democracy in Action" project, 176
Humphries, E., 167, 175
Hunger Strikers, 15

imaginative structured inquiry, 100–101
immigration, xxv, 57, 71
inquiry-based approach to teaching history, 13
issues content, 159

James II, 10
Johnson, Boris, xxv
Johnson, David, 126
Johnson, Roger, 126
Journell, W., xxi
July 12th marching. *See* "the Twelfth" marching

Kello, K., 72
KEQ (Key Enquiry Question), 108
Kerr, D., 176
Kitson, A., xxviii, 3, 26, 36, 67, 108, 115, 166–67

learning, 164–68; classroom practice, 166; coursework, 165–66; Ian's students, 99–102; Liz's students, 142–46; Mark's students, 22–26; Paula's students, 64–67
"Learning for Life and Work," 73
Learning for Life and Work (LLW), 44
Libresco, A., 80
linguistically diverse students, 151–53
Livingston, E., 178, 179
Living with Controversy: Teaching Controversial Issues through Education for Democratic Citizenship, 176
Local and Global Citizenship (LGC), 4, 42, 45

Major, John, 86
Managing Controversy: A Whole-School Training Tool, 176
marching disputes, 10–13
McAvoy, P., 77, 141, 155, 160, 174–75
McCully, A. W., xxviii, 26, 67, 108, 115, 166–67, 173
Me Before You, 73
moral complexity, 104–7
Muhammad (Prophet), 128
museum visit, 101–2
Muslims, 128

National Issues Forum, 125, 150
National Socialist Party of America, 128
Northern Ireland: Local and Global Citizen Curriculum, 4; same-sex marriage, 13. *See also* Barstow, Paula; citizenship education; Drummond, Mark

On Tolerance (Walzer), 131
Orange Order, 10

Parker, Walter, xxii, 6, 66
pedagogical content knowledge, 178
pedagogical methods, 160

pedagogical risk assessment, 47
pedagogical strategies, 47
Peercy, M. M., 173
policy and program structure, 176–78
Post Graduate Certification in Education
    (PGCE), 2
PowerPoint presentation, 50, 51, 108
practice-based teaching, 144–45, 164
preservice teachers (Ian's students),
    97–116; advice to teacher educators,
    115–16; conceptions of controversial
    issues, 102–4; learning from history
    course, 99–102; profiles of, 98–99;
    supports and constraints, 113–15;
    teaching experiences, 104–13
preservice teachers (Liz's students),
    139–56; advice to teacher educators,
    154–56; conceptions of controversial
    issues, 141–42; learning from social
    studies course, 142–46; profiles of,
    140–41; supports and constraints,
    153–54; teaching experiences,
    146–53
preservice teachers (Mark's students),
    19–39; advice to teacher educators,
    37–39; conceptions of controversial
    issues, 21–22; learning from courses,
    22–26; profiles of, 20–21; supports
    and constraints, 36–37; teaching
    experiences, 26–36, 27
preservice teachers (Paula's students),
    61–77; advice to teacher educators,
    76–77; conceptions of controversial
    issues, 63–64; learning from
    citizenship course, 64–67; profiles
    of, 61–63; supports and constraints,
    74–76; teaching experiences, 67–74
proactive strategies, 160
Professional Learning Community
    (PLC), 148
profiles of preservice teachers: Ian's
    students, 98–99; Liz's students, 140–
    41; Mark's students, 20–21; Paula's
    students, 61–63

racially diverse students, 151–53
racism, xviii
realistic goal, 45
religious education, 67, 68
risk-takers, 26
Robertson, E., 174
Rwanda, 81

same-sex marriage, 13
scheme of work (SoW), 92–93, 97–98,
    102, 177
school culture, 169–70
school policy for citizenship, 44–45
Schools History Project (SHP), 85, 86,
    99
school structures and leadership, 175–76
sectarian violence, 69
Shared Education, 175–76
Shepherd, Ian, 79–95; approach,
    79; education background and
    philosophy, 79–81; history course,
    82–95; scheme of work (SoW)
    assignment, 92–93; university
    program, 82–83. *See also* preservice
    teachers (Ian's students)
Simmons, Liz, xxvi, 119–36; biography
    and philosophy, 119–22; democratic
    discussion, 123–36. *See also*
    preservice teachers (Liz's students)
Sinn Fein, 70
Smith, A., 44
social aims, 161
social justice, 41
social justice issues, 147–48
social studies course, 142–53
Socratic seminars, xxii, 124, 131–33
Structured Academic Controversy
    (SAC), xxii, 70, 124–28, 131, 132,
    143–44, 147, 152–53
student-centered discourse, 164
student engagement, 169
supportive atmosphere, 160–61

teacher-directed discourse, 164

teacher education pedagogy, 173–74
teacher educators: approaches, 158–64; classroom discussion, 163–64; contained risk-taking, 161–63; issues content, 159; pedagogical methods, 160; practice-based teaching, 164; social aims, 161; supportive atmosphere, 160–61
teachers and departments, 170
teacher stance, 66–67
Teaching Divided Histories, 17
teaching experiences: Ian's students, 104–13; Liz's students, 146–53; Mark's students, 26–36, *27*; Paula's students, 67–74
Thatcher, Margaret, 86
13th (documentary), 148
Thirteenth Amendment to U.S. Constitution, 148
time for controversial issues, 168–69
tolerance, 131–33
Troyan, F. J., 173
Trump, Donald, xxv, 133

"the Twelfth" marching, 10–12

Ulster Plantation, 21, 27, 34
Understanding History Teaching (Husbands), 80, 94
United States, 119–36. *See also* democratic discussion; Simmons, Liz
Universal Declaration of Human Rights (UDHR), 54, 68, 74
university faculty, 171

Walzer, Michael, 131
Washington, E. Y., 167, 175
William of Orange, 10
Worden, E., 44
workshops, 42, 49–53
World War I, 80–81
World War II, 109

"Young Ned of the Hill," 108

Zembylas, M., 38–39
Zimmerman, J., 174

About the Author

Judith L. Pace is a professor of teacher education in the School of Education at the University of San Francisco. Before moving to California, she taught English-language arts and social studies in the Boston area and worked on school reform projects at Harvard Project Zero. Her research investigates the social, cultural, and political dynamics of curriculum and teaching. She has studied the social construction of classroom authority and academic engagement, teaching of government classes in diverse school contexts, social studies teaching under high-stakes accountability, and preparing preservice teachers to teach controversial issues. Her articles appear in leading journals such as *Teachers College Record, Theory & Research in Social Education, Sociology of Education,* and *Review of Educational Research.* She is co-editor, with Janet Bixby, of *Educating Democratic Citizens in Troubled Times: Qualitative Studies of Current Efforts* (2008) and co-editor, with Annette Hemmings, of *Classroom Authority: Theory, Research, and Practice* (2006). She is also the author of *The Charged Classroom: Predicaments and Possibilities for Democratic Teaching* (2015).